Figurations of Modernity

Eigene und fremde Welten
Representations of Patterns of Social Order

The series »Eigene und fremde Welten« is edited by Jörg Baberowski, Vincent Houben, Hartmut Kaelble and Jürgen Schriewer, in connection with the Collaborative Research Center no. 640 (SFB 640) »Changing Representations of Patterns of Social Order. Cross-Cultural and Cross-Temporal Comparisons« based at Humboldt-Universität, Berlin (Germany)

Volume 12

Vincent Houben is professor of the history and societies of Southeast Asia at Humboldt University, Berlin. *Mona Schrempf* is a research fellow at the Central Asian Seminar at Humboldt University, Berlin.

Vincent Houben, Mona Schrempf (eds.)

Figurations of Modernity

Global and Local Representations in
Comparative Perspective

Campus Verlag
Frankfurt/New York

Bibliographic Information published by the Deutsche Nationalbibliothek.
Die Deutsche Nationalbibliothek lists this publication in the Deutsche Nationalbibliografie;
detailed bibliographic data are available in the Internet at http://dnb.d-nb.de.
ISBN 978-3-593-38682-9

All rights reserved. No part of this book may be reproduced or transmitted in any form or by any means, electronic or mechanical, including photocopying, recording, or by any information storage and retrieval system, without permission in writing from the publishers.
Copyright © 2008 Campus Verlag GmbH, Frankfurt/Main
Cover illustration: Family in Tibet/Private Photo Archive
Printed on acid free paper.
Printed in Germany

For further information:
www.campus.de
www.press.uchicago.edu

Contents

Introduction: Figurations and Representations of Modernity 7
Vincent Houben and Mona Schrempf

Colonial and Modern Spaces

Representations of Modernity in Colonial Indonesia 23
Vincent Houben

Performing the Metropolitan *habitus*: Images of European
modernity in cross-cultural encounters in nineteenth
century Eastern Africa 41
Michael Pesek

Becoming Modern through Education

Modern Indians: the Training of Indigenous Teachers
in Post-Revolutionary Mexico 67
Eugenia Roldán Vera

Representations of Modernisation and Vocational Education
in Argentina at the Beginning of the 20th Century 85
Verónica Oelsner

Ethic and Ethnic Identities

Modernity and the Problem of Secular Morality in Tibet 105
Vincanne Adams

Planning the Modern Tibetan Family in China 121
Mona Schrempf

Of Heritage and Heroes

The Modernity of Heritage: Visualizing the Past in a
Nigerian City Kingdom 155
Peter Probst

Heroes in the Museum: Soviet Hero Constructions and
Multiple Meanings of Modernity on the Soviet Periphery 179
Olaf Guenther

List of Figures.. 195
Notes on the Contributors 197

Introduction: Figurations and Representations of Modernity

Vincent Houben and Mona Schrempf

This collection of essays arose out of an interdisciplinary workshop on *Figurations of Modernity* (07–08.04.2006), organised by the working group ›Modernity‹ at the collaborative research centre *Representations of Social Order and Change* at Humboldt University Berlin. The regions and topics covered in this book concern colonialism and multiple figurations of modernity in Africa and Southeast Asia; education in Latin America; ethnicity and morality in post-Mao China; and hero construction and heritage in soviet Central Asia and Africa. The essays offer a fresh theoretical and empirical perspective on the multiple and complex dimensions of non-European figurations of modernity.[1]

To understand our world as ›modern‹ has become something taken for granted, yet ›modernity‹ remains a vexed issue. Modernity encompasses all spheres of human life and, in recent centuries, has unfolded as a matrix for national and global histories, framing our understandings of past, present and future, and of centres and peripheries. Many social scientists have tried to make sense of it, moving more recently from a homogenous concept to one of multiple or alternative modernities. To grasp the phenomenon of modernity, new meanings and adjectives have been attached to it, in an attempt to tackle accelerated change occurring in space, place and time. At the same time, grasping modernity's complex figurations as well as explaining their multiple causes and effects, has helped to situate modernity in different contexts and has added the understanding that it is closely connected with power, subjectivity and insecurity. Although the modernity debate of the 1970s lost some of its dynamics in the 1980s, it has since re-emerged with full vigour under conditions of increasing globalisation, facilitated by the ending of the Cold War. Also, it has acquired important political dimensions in the face of current global socio-cultural and environmental crises.

Modernity is usually understood as a program for socio-cultural change and transformation, originating in the Western world. Standard definitions of modernisation are strongly imbued with the idea of linear change in a particular

---

[1] The editors wish to acknowledge the indispensable help of Deborah Johnson and Toni Huber, as well as Anja Gottschalk, Nike-Ann Schröder, and Felix Herrmann.

direction, involving an ever-increasing degree of functional and structural differentiation on the level of institutions, social groupings and even the individual. Modernisation has thus been grasped as something real, a self-sustaining process that has permeated human existence and becoming manifest in the rise of industrialised economies; horizontally and vertically mobile societies; and, in centralised bureaucratic, socialist, as well as democratic polities.

Modernity presupposes, as is implied by standard historical theory, a particular, rational view of the world that has its roots in Europe, where it can be traced back to ancient Greece and Rome, re-emerging in Renaissance Italy and coming to full bloom during the Age of Enlightenment of the eighteenth century. This meta-narrative has then been extended to include nineteenth century European imperialism in other parts of the world, reaching its culmination in the present condition of globalisation, in which modernity has become a universal phenomenon. Social theorists have focused less on the historical diffusion of modernity instead concentrating on explaining its dominant characteristics in its transformation of human societies. Anthony Giddens has analysed the consequences of modernity, arguing that the separation or ›distanciation‹ of time and space has infused social systems with new forms of control over human activities.[2] Ulrich Beck argued that modernisation has now deepened to the point that it has turned back onto itself and has become ›reflexive‹ in nature, leading to a second modernity that is, for instance, no longer directed at taking control over nature, but redefines the way in which human agency shapes it.[3]

Leaving European grounds and departing from a homogenising, universal view, in this introductory essay we argue that modernity can be meaningfully considered as a distinct practice of representation, one resulting from *multiple* figurations that are negotiated though various spaces and in fragmented and potentially conflicting ways by a range of different modernising actors endowed with non-European agency. More than anything, the notion of ›figurations of modernity‹ necessitates a refined reflection on, and comparison of, what it is that links together all of the diverse developments covered by this term. First, we would like to show how in recent scholarly debates the meta-narrative of a singular ›real‹ modernity emanating from the West has increasingly been questioned and what kind of suggestions have been made to overcome the still prevalent bias in the common Eurocentric understanding of it. Secondly, we have to clarify what we mean by representations and figurations of modernity and what are

---

2 Anthony Giddens, *The Consequences of Modernity* (Stanford Calif.: Stanford University Press 1990), and Giddens cited in Roger Friedland and Deirdre Boden (eds.), *Now Here. Space, Time and Modernity* (Berkeley/Los Angeles/London: University of California Press, 1992), pp. 28–29.

3 Ulrich Beck, Anthony Giddens and Scott Lash (eds.), *Reflexive Modernization. Politics, Tradition and Aesthetics in the Modern Social Order* (Cambridge: Polity Press, 1994).

the benefits of using these terms. Thirdly, we would like to explain what the contributions of the collected essays in this volume add to the ongoing debate.

Critiques of, and new approaches to, modernity

Recent contributions to the modernity debate have moved beyond old structural notions of a single homogeneous (Western) modernity. The bifurcated view of binary oppositions that also underlies the division of the world into the ›West‹ and the ›rest‹, the thinking about what existed before and after modernity, as well as its one-directional impact on particular societies have been challenged. Shmuel Eisenstadt was among the first to question the single nature of modernity. He proposed instead to talk of multiple modernities, and argued:

> The idea of multiple modernities presumes that the best way to understand the contemporary world – indeed to explain the history of modernity – is to see it as a story of continual constitution and reconstitution of a multiplicity of cultural programs [...] Western patterns of modernity are not the only authentic modernities, though they enjoy historical precedence and continue to be a basic reference point for others.[4]

Although Eisenstadt departed from a standard interpretation of modernity by stressing its multiplicity and its ideational dimensions, his interpretation still presupposes a singular origin and a distinct point of origin of the many modernities that exist side-by-side. On the other hand, leaving an exclusivist preoccupation with Western modernity behind, he opened up the possibility for its conceptualisation in new dimensions. Critiques of Eurocentrism and Orientalism that prevail in anthropology, non-Western history and so-called Area Studies have in the meanwhile added new understandings of regions and cultures that lie beyond the West, endowing these with agency and different forms of modernity.[5] Thus, the modernity paradigm has shifted from what Eisenstadt critiqued as the totalising, hegemonic Western-based concept to a plurality of modernities. However, the debate about multiple modernities has barely touched upon the particularities of non-Western societies.[6]

---

4 Shmuel N. Eisenstadt (ed.), *Multiple Modernities* (New Brunswick and London: Transaction, 2002), pp.2–3.
5 Cf. Marshall Sahlins, »What is Anthropological Enlightenment? Some Lessons of the Twentieth Century«, in: Marshall Sahlins (ed.), *Culture in Practice. Selected Essays* (New York: Zone Books, 2000), pp. 501–526.
6 Cf. Charles Taylor, *Modern Social Imaginaries* (Durham: Duke University Press, 2004). Taylor's philosophical analysis understands western modernity as both a ›moral order‹ and as en-

Another strand in the critique against mainstream modernisation theory looks at what it excludes and therefore cannot explain. Eisenstein and many others argue that the classical notion of a Westernised modernity does not provide an explanation for counter-tendencies, such as anti-Western and anti-capitalist movements. Neither does it explain the particular appropriation of modernity by socialist states, such as the former Soviet Union and present-day China that do not fit the classic characteristics of Western modernity, such as capitalism, democracy and individualism. Their common frame of reference, nevertheless, always gravitates towards (Western) modernity.

A further critique of modernity as a universal Western model tries to show that non-European societies also possessed modern characteristics at an early stage in their history. In this vein, Alexander Woodside has recently submitted an intriguing portrait of the Chinese, Vietnamese and Korean bureaucracies, based on merit and being the product of ›rational thought‹ on politics and economics.[7] Although it is unlikely that a transfer of East Asian bureaucratic models towards Europe ever took place, at least non-Western ›modernities‹ could prefigure Western ones, and have occurred simultaneous with, or possess structural similarities with, Western modernities. This is exactly what Joel Kahn illustrated in his study of the relationship between modernity and exclusionary practices, which developed in a parallel fashion in the three different ›social spaces‹ of Great Britain, the United States and Malaya.[8]

Timothy Mitchell has put the notion of a plurality of modernities itself into question, since the modification by local circumstance still presupposes a singular generic to start with. Also it ignores the ›power of replication and expansion‹ imperialising modernity unfolded, subordinating and excluding elements that appeared incompatible with it. He calls this very process ›representation‹:

Representation does not refer here to the making of images or meanings but to forms of social practice that set up in the social architecture of the world what seems an absolute distinction between image (or meaning, or plan, or structure) and reality, and thus a distinctive apprehension of the real. This effect of the real has been generalized in modern social engineering and the management of nature, in organized schooling and entertainment, in the military, legal, and administrative disciplines of colonialism and nation-making [...] In sphere after sphere of social life, an immediacy of the really real is promised by what appears in contrast to be the mere abstractions of structure, subjectivity, text, plan, or idea.[9]

---

dowed with multiple ›social imaginaries‹, among them the economy, public sphere and popular governance.

7 Alexander Woodside, *Lost Modernities. China, Vietnam, Korea, and the Hazards of World History* (Cambridge, Mass./London: Harvard University Press, 2006) passim, in particular pp. 4–6.
8 Joel S. Kahn, *Modernity and Exclusion* (London: Sage, 2001).
9 Timothy Mitchell (ed.), *Questions of Modernity* (Minneapolis: University of Minnesota Press, 2000), pp. xii – xiv.

Modernity itself therefore becomes something staged, a representation, which necessarily incorporates the production of difference and displacement.

Eisenstadt's ›multiple modernities‹ concept has been extended by notions of particular qualitative features, that have been associated with it. One such quality is ›alternative‹ modernity. Dilip Gaonkar has argued that each transition to modernity has had a different starting-point, which has therefore led to a different outcome.[10] According to him, modernity cannot be escaped but it takes on different forms than in the West and develops differently at every national or cultural site. Thus, modernity is reborn through creative adaptation by postcolonial subjects who are not simply recipients, but agents, of many alternative modernities.

In the critiques of older conceptions of modernity, thinking in terms of binary oppositions had to be overcome. A very dominant way of interpretation, perpetuating colonial projections, was to see the world beyond modern Europe as that governed by ›tradition‹ or as the site of interaction between a rising modernity against that of tradition in decline. However, as the idea of ›modernity‹ has been subjected to further scrutiny, likewise the notion of ›tradition‹ has been substantially modified. As Arjun Appadurai has pointed out, traditional practices are both defended and transformed in the process of becoming modern.[11] Furthermore, to be a ›traditionalist‹ is in any case a modern phenomenon. According to Hobsbawm's definition of ›invented traditions‹, modernity is an invented tradition and social process: it symbolically offers social cohesion and collective identity, establishes and legitimises social hierarchies and institutions, and has the ability to socialise people into particular social contexts.[12] Similarly, Jonathan Friedman has described modernity as another ›tradition‹ in terms of its ideological value, as a »charter of a social order rather than an aid to its understanding«.[13] Modernity is social order *per se*. Its own discourse and logic is a social construct based on binary oppositions of (progressive) modernity versus (backward or lost) tradition, and thus needs to be revealed as such. Any analytic understanding needs to take this opposition into account without being trapped by it, asserts Friedman.

---

10 Dilip P. Gaonkar, »On Alternative Modernities«, in: Dilip P. Gaonkar (ed.), *Alternative Modernities* (Durham: Duke University Press, 2001), pp. 1–23.
11 Arjun Appadurai, *Modernity At Large. Cultural Dimensions of Globalization* (Minneapolis: University of Minnesota Press, 1996).
12 Eric Hobsbawm, »Introduction: Inventing Tradition«, in: E. Hobsbawm and T. Ranger (eds.), *The Invention of Tradition* (Cambridge: Cambridge University Press, 1983), pp. 1–14, in particular p. 9.
13 Jonathan Friedman, »Modernity and Other Traditions«, in: Bruce M. Knauft (ed.), *Critically Modern. Alternatives, Alterities, Anthroplogies* (Bloomington: Indiana University Press), pp. 287–314, in particular p. 287.

Similarly, Prasenjit Duara has rightly highlighted that the depiction of tradition and modernity is a *discursive* representation, i.e. *a way of* thinking about the past, present and future that is crucial for individual identity and state building.[14] Therefore, some figurations of modernity remain something to be sought after, something to be achieved; something that is difficult or impossible to gain access to or engage with as ethnic ›others‹.[15] Thus, Andreas Wimmer maintains that policies that lead to nationalist exclusion and ethnic conflict are no by-products of modern state-formation, but are rooted in modernity itself. Modernity leads to the politicisation of ethnicity as state elites adopt political closure along ethnic and national lines in conjunction with the establishment of modern institutions of inclusion and institutions for the distribution of collective goods.[16]

A further binary opposition underlying the construction of modernity has been that of homogeneity versus heterogeneity, which is also connected with identity issues and ethnic conflicts as part of nation building processes. Zygmunt Baumann has characterized modernity as the most ideologically and normatively homogenising production of the nation state. Since national unity connected with state territory is the absolute *conditio sine qua non*, disloyalties and divisions among the population are to be eliminated. Cultural, ethnic, linguistic and ideological homogeneity are subject to the state's social engineering of its own past, present and future, including its power to define and classify its ›natives‹.[17] Modernity is a future oriented project, and thus one that requires constant effort and progress towards its completion. However, its constructed-ness does not depend upon a uniform (Western) model of modernity and its diffusion into, or adaptation in, different parts of the world, but it depends on each particular nation-state and its own ›cultural production‹ of modernity, as well as various internal collective figurations of modernity. Therefore, modernity requires performative acts »that are elaborated and codified in the course of various moments of sociality«.[18]

---

14 Prasenjit Duara, *Rescuing History from the Nation* (Chicago: The University of Chicago Press, 1995), p. 90.
15 Cf. Louisa Schein, *Minority Rules. The Miao and the Feminine in China's Cultural Politics* (Durham & London: Duke University Press, 2000).
16 Andreas Wimmer, *Nationalist Exclusion and Ethnic Conflict. Shadows of Modernity* (Cambridge: Cambridge University Press), pp. 1–12.
17 »National states promote ›nativism‹ and construe their subjects as ›natives‹. (...) They construct joint historical memories and do their best to discredit or suppress such stubborn memories as cannot be squeezed into shared tradition. (...) The state enforced homogeneity is the practice of nationalist ideology«. Zygmunt Baumann, »Modernity and Ambivalence«, in: *Theory, Culture & Society* 7 (1990), pp. 143–169, in particular p. 154.
18 Louisa Schein, *Minority Rules,* op. cit. (note 15), p. 25.

Similarly, the binary oppositions of centre and periphery have been revealed as hegemonic power structures for constructing and reiterating modernity. Urban public spaces and the ›public sphere‹ (media, Internet, etc.) have become national and global centres of modernity, whereas rural peripheries have been constructed as less modern or more ›traditional‹. Friedman extends this model to the global arena by distinguishing central and peripheral societies.

> It may be useful to refer to alternative modernities, or whatever term might seem appropriate, to characterize a particular form of articulation between peripheral societies in the world system and centrally initiated capitalist processes. These vary along two axes: one, the degree of transformative integration into the global system, and the other, the representations of the center as future, wealth, well-being, as well as strategies related to such representations.[19]

Another qualitative feature of modernity that seems, however, to be rather dominated by the modern – post-modern divide is Bauman's approach based on the idea of two modernities: a ›heavy‹ or ›solid‹ modernity as characterised by Karl Marx and Max Weber with fixed territorial power structures, work places and instrumental rationality; and a ›light‹ or ›liquid‹ modernity of insecurity, risk, mobility and flexibility of organisational forms, de-territorialised transnational politics, economics, as well as a de-socialised individuality and a loss of a sense of community.[20] However, his differentiation seems to be implicitly trapped by the divide between an empowered post-modern elite of an intellectual and economically privileged class and the factory workers and rural poor being still stuck in modernity's fixed structures. Transferred to the global arena, we are facing once more a centre and a periphery of modernity and power, although in a de-territorialised form. Thinking in binary oppositions seems to be implicit here, rather than transcending them by shifting to more complex webs of meaning-making by different cultures, societies and social classes.

By emphasising the cultural dimensions of modernity, possibilities for the appreciation of dramatic differences among modernities, that older either Western-based or institutionally focused theories of modernity could not appreciate, have been created and their contingent, situated and relational traits made discernible. Joel Kahn noticed that the recent ›discovery‹ of culture by theorists of modernity allowed for the introduction of subjectivity, for the notion of modernity as a state of mind. Also, by taking up culture as a constituent part of modernisation, contradictory or conflicting dimensions of modernity came into focus.[21]

---

19 Cited in Friedman, Jonathan, »Modernity and Other Traditions«, op. cit. (note 13), in particular p. 308.
20 Zygmunt Bauman, *Liquid Modernity* (Cambridge: Polity Press, 2000).
21 Joel S. Kahn, *Modernity and Exclusion* (London: Sage, 2001), in particular p. 11.

Taken together these new theories make figurations of modernity a fruitful approach for acquiring a deeper understanding of the general as well as the unique in each path of modernisation. As Appadurai notes: »Genealogy of cultural forms is about their circulation across region, the history of these forms is about their ongoing domestication into local practice«.[22] Circulation as a consequence of media development and migration has been studied by Appadurai in order to show how historical, uneven and localised the process of modernisation has been. Kahn takes modern social movements and the media as the arena of »middle level discursive formations« in which »popular meanings and performances of the modern condition« are being (re)constructed.[23]

Representations and Figurations of Modernity

Human beings are representers. People make representations.[24]

Representations are even more vexed than modernity, eluding a general definition. Yet they are part of the human condition. They also affect human social life. Are they the real thing – reality – or just an appearance, an image created of it? Ian Hacking understands representations as external and as ›public likenesses‹ creating their own reality. Since he defines human beings as primary representers, the question of reality only appears as a secondary after-effect, as an attribute arising out of multiple systems of representations. One particular complex system of representations is modernity. Hacking claims that, contrary to Locke's approach,

we [first] make public representations, form the concept of reality, and, as systems of representation multiply, we become skeptics and form the idea of mere appearance.[25]

According to Rabinow, representations have taken on a different value in the age of modernity, contrasting them further with the post-modern ›self-conscious‹, self-reflexive representations. Thus, whatever ›we‹ talk about has to be first read through this lens of modernity as an underlying matrix. Rabinow speaks of »discourses and practices of modern representation«.[26] Consequently, one has

---

22 Arjun Appadurai, *Modernity at Large,* op. cit. (note 11), p. 17.
23 Joel S. Kahn, *Modernity and Exclusion,* op. cit. (note 21), in particular. p. 19.
24 Ian Hacking, *Representing and Intervening. Introductory Topics in the Philosophy of Natural Science.* (Cambridge: Cambridge University Press, 1983), in particular p. 132.
25 Ibid., in particular pp. 141–142.
26 Paul Rabinow, »Representations are Social Facts. Modernity and Post-Modernity in Anthropology«, in: J. Clifford and G. Marcus (eds.), *Writing Culture. The Poetics and Politics of Ethnography* (Berkeley: University of California Press, 1986), in particular p. 261.

to take into account one's own modern presumptions when it comes to understanding processes of multiple figurations of modernity. »Representations are social facts« concludes Rabinow, by linking the problem of representation to Foucault's emphasis on social and political practices in and of the modern world, with its distinctive concerns with order, truth and the subject.²⁷

We conclude from the above that it is within the relational processes between representational forms and social practices that one has to situate and analyse modernity's multiple figurations. Modernity is both a representation of, and a strategy for, social order. ›Figurations of modernity‹ leaves aside outdated social-evolutionary and functionalist assumptions, which regard modernity as a universal and uniform force of social change, and replaces them with the understanding of the importance of contingency, complexity, timing and context. The case studies in this book demonstrate the particular non-European, historical and socio-cultural situated-ness of diverse modern projects, as well as their constructed-ness, and highlight autochthonous strategies that are traceable through time and space and to different agents.

All the contributions in this book feature non-Western figurations of modernity and have been subsumed under four thematic headings. Part 1 comprises contributions by Vincent Houben and Michael Pesek that deal with the spatial and bodily dimensions of colonial modernity in Indonesia and East Africa. In Part 2 Eugenia Roldán Vera writing on Mexico and Verónica Oelsner on Argentina highlight the transfer of modern ideas by indigenous agents of modernity through formal educational practices. In Part 3, Mona Schrempf and Vincanne Adams discuss ethnic and ethical problems affecting Tibetans in relation to Chinese modernity. Part 4 deals with phenomena of heritage and memorialising the past in Nigeria (Peter Probst), and of Soviet hero construction as means of modernising collective memory in Uzbekistan (Olaf Günther).

In the first chapter dealing with colonial Indonesia, Vincent Houben reviews different indigenous responses to ›colonial modernity‹ in terms of a particular figuration of modernity – that of modern transport and communications technology. With reference to Frederick Cooper, Houben argues that it is most important to show »how the concept [of modernity] is *used* in the making of claims«. Based on our understanding of representation in this introduction, he interprets the relationship between representations and social order as follows:

Representations are culturally bound forms of knowledge that position people as well as objects within a spatially and temporally embedded social order [...] representations also enable people to establish their own views of the world and to change the existing social order.

---

27 Ibid., p. 240.

Four dimensions of modernity in colonial Indonesia are highlighted: vehicles, advertisements, contestations and the transcending of borders. Using the literary testimonies of local advocates of modernity as well as the comments of critics of the new ›Western‹ modernity, he shows how ›colonial modernity‹ comes to be appropriated and fixed into a more indigenous mould by means of the modern infrastructure of trains and communication technology. Peasants as well as factory unionists and intellectuals reclaim their territory through a re-appropriation of space and, thus, become agents of a new figuration of modernity.

Michael Pesek looks at Eastern Africa in the 1880s where German travellers acted as agents of modernity. Acting out their ›metropolitan habitus‹ during encounters in particular contact zones through their bodily presence, these men were, on the African side, constructed as part of a distinct culture yet at the same time embedded in a variety of representations. For their part, as a result of their obsession with hygiene and discipline, they tried to keep a distance with the ›natives‹, but failed to succeed. With their ›metropolitan habitus‹ in a state of crisis, they were forced to adopt strategies of mimicry, learning from the Africans and adopting their foods and culinary practices. Thus, German colonialism had to base itself on a bricolage of practices, after the ›metropolitan habitus‹ as a marker of difference had failed in the African context. The dependence on the local environment was to lessen with the emergence of a colonial infrastructure, but this offered only temporary relief as Germany was forced to retreat after World War One.

Eugenia Roldán Vera studies the training of indigenous teachers in the postrevolutionary Mexican context of the 1920s and 1930s. The *Casa del Estudiante Indígena* in Mexico City was a site for the promulgation of modernity, where the state pursued a pedagogical program with elements of both homogenisation and individualisation aimed at turning young Indians into healthy, productive and rational human beings, as well as model citizens. After completing their studies, they were supposed to return to their local rural communities in order to modernise the indigenous rural population. The strategies of control applied in teacher training were firmly set within the modernity narrative of Westernisation and nationalism, but also contained ambiguities since Indio folklore was idealised as something pure. On their part, the students of the college modified and adapted the school program by means of selective appropriation and empowerment through resistance and by incorporating dominant representations of modernity while also developing a new consciousness of their own ›traditional‹ values. Although the *Casa* was intended as a model of Mexican modernity, the way in which the school program and its recipients turned out proved to be highly ambiguous.

In her contribution, Verónica Oelsner discusses the growth of vocational education that accompanied the modernisation of independent Argentina. She focuses on differing representations of progress that were formulated by three of the main actors involved: the national ministry of education, the Society for Industrial Education and the Engine Drivers Union. The ministry promulgated various proposals for legislation aimed at the creation of an industrious people – pitting itself in vain against the prevalent orientation of the educational system towards the humanities. The Society for Industrial Education wanted to promote industrialisation, whereas the union saw vocational training as a means to defend the engine drivers' position against the impact of rapid technological change. Thus, within one national context, various actors competed by formulating different representations of modernity, all taking vocational education as the main avenue to promote it, but differing in how it should be realised.

Mona Schrempf deals with Chinese state family planning policies since the 1980s in the Sino-Tibetan border region of Qinghai province. She focuses on the experiences of Tibetan women and their families and their representations of the impact of the state's modernity project. At one level, as Mona Schrempf argues, there exists a clear contrast between the official representations of family planning programs and the local representations of the consequences of its implementation for Tibetan families. There is a juxtaposition of two different worlds – one of Chinese modernity on the one hand and, on the other, a self-reflexive ethnic identity as part of a Tibetan figuration of modernity. This contrast is judged from the Tibetan side as that between the ›authentic‹ or ›true‹ as against that which is ›false‹; and as ›insiders‹ standing against the forces that come from the ›outside‹. However, Chinese and Tibetan figurations of modernity are not only juxtaposed, but are interconnected and negotiated in daily life. Different intermediaries operate on the fault line between both worlds: local Tibetan cadres, village heads, barefoot doctors and family planning personnel whose personal families are scrutinized even more than ordinary families.

Adams, drawing upon Foucault and Rabinow, points to the »interstitial spaces between the ›modern‹ Tibetan and his or her (often rural) counterpart who is represented as ›not yet‹ modern« in China. In this modern subjectivity she finds exemplified »a ›figurative‹ approach to modernity more generally«.[28] The gap is characterised by different beliefs in the connection between truth and morality: the rationality of the modern state is based on a secular morality in connection with modern science that refers back to itself rather than to a socially established and moral ›way of knowing the world‹. However, Tibetans' foundational beliefs in karma and morality are based on a particular world-view that is not accepted as ›truth‹ by secular state morality. »In this gap we find clues as to what it really means to be modern and what might be entailed in sustaining

---

28 See this volume, p.111.

it«.²⁹ Tibetans feel this gap as a loss of ›knowing truth‹ and of trust, a feeling that touches upon the more general issue of loss of values as a consequence of modernity, provoking the rekindling of, or search for, new religious meanings, for example. Yet, »what the Tibetan case suggests is the need to read through the back and forth of processes of modernisation that force persons to reflect critically on their ways of knowing and being in the world«.³⁰

Peter Probst examines the global phenomenon of museums and the making of visual heritage as a figuration of modernity. Starting with a »history of visual heritage politics in Europe«,³¹ he takes the case study of a heritage site in southwest Nigeria to exemplify the particular figuration of modernity that it entails. He explains it as being closely connected with representing and implementing both national history and a globalised spacialisation of heritage. »Global organisations like UNESCO ›reconfigure‹ national objects of memory into a universal global heritage«,³² appropriating them as global ›properties‹. This appropriation, however, reveals both the cultural politics of authentication by producing world heritage sites and the conflicted national and local interests in representing ›correctly‹ their own past. Thereby, the role of the media, Probst claims alongside James Clifford, has altered not only visual representations of the past but also the practices and meaning of memory. Representations of the past become the arena for different understandings of modernity with the aim of defining the ›correct‹ way of representation.

The last chapter of this volume by Olaf Günther continues the focus on the connection between representing the past and memory making. His theme concerns the construction of a Soviet hero in Kokand, a city in the Ferghana Valley of Uzbekistan. On the basis of two contrasting examples, he shows how modernity became enshrined within the local collective memory. On the one hand, the life history of the young communist Abdulla Nabiev was gradually turned into that of a modern Soviet hero, whereas the famous nineteenth century local Muslim poet Muqimi was represented as modern in order to preserve an Islamic religious school (*madrasa*). The modernising of Nabiev exemplified a top down state project; the case of Muqimi was a bottom up local project to preserve and get official recognition for a local Muslim hero. This double ›museumisation‹ of modernity was realised by the installation of sites of memory, using objects, rituals and histories as tools.

During discussion at the conference, three ways of understanding modernity or modernisation were brought forward. In the first, modernisation is understood as a program of socio-cultural transformation within colonial as well as

---

29 Ibid.
30 See this volume, p.119.
31 See this volume, p.157.
32 Ibid.

postcolonial nation-state settings. A second, more subtle view defines modernity as a metaphor with several possible readings, something that is future-oriented and constitutes a break with the past, but also includes the need for the continuous recreation of itself. A third understanding of modernity is that of a practice of representation, which produces meaning for a broad range of phenomena. Its features are at the same time multiple, plural, fragmented and contradictory. In this sense modernity is produced through narratives and also needs to be mediated through books, newspaper articles, images, material objects, oral testimonies and performances.

Three essential figurations of modernity were arrived at as a result of our intellectual exchanges, first its embedded-ness and situated-ness, secondly its processual character and thirdly its agency. Embedded-ness was shown to have at least five dimensions: contexts, levels, thematic fields, places and temporal scopes. Our case studies deal with colonial, post-colonial and post-revolutionary contexts as well as that of the intertwined dynamics of globalisation and localisation. A whole range of levels comes into play, ranging from the self, the individual body and mind, to the private and public spheres. Our thematic fields include politics, economics, education, religion, history, literature, medicine and identity. Our places are non-European, situated in Asia, Africa and Latin America. They involve imperial states, nation-states, colonial states, urban and rural sites, sea- and landscapes. In our case studies, particular sites for negotiating the modern are schools, clinics, public places, museums and modern means of transport. Temporal scopes cover the aftermath of turning points, caused by regime change, revolution, violence, civil wars, situations of occupation or changes as a consequence of global power shifts.

Modernity is an ongoing process and not a fixed state of development. This process is fuelled by representations, conditions, perceptions and experiences. Local perceptions of modernity may produce discomfort, contestation and a sense of loss, but also may lead to empowerment. Experiences are of a doxic (or self-evident) nature, such that, as Bourdieu has argued, the processes of modernisation challenge the conservation of the social order through the tendency to see it as natural and self-evident. Socio-economic transformation promotes reconfigurations of the modern condition. Finally, the different ways in which modernity takes shape are influenced by modernising agents, both institutions and human beings, who take an active role in its processes, and include government agencies, civil servants, doctors, missionaries, intellectuals, activists and civilians.

What do the essays in this book reveal? As long as the history of modernity remains largely unwritten, it is hard to decide whether the plurality of figurations of modernity is the outcome of a diffusion of something particular into different settings; or whether separate ›peculiar‹ modernities, be they Islamic, Chinese or Western, developed out of their own contexts. Probably, it is both. The transfers implied in the existence of multiple figurations of modernity entail both a multiplication of a modern core and, at the same time, lead to differences and disjuncture. Modernities are also not neutral, they involve norm-setting as well as loss of a morality that is perceived to be ›false‹ or ›failed‹. Modernity has a strong epistemological side to it, a particular way of being in and understanding the world, as these essays demonstrate.

Furthermore, certain qualities of non-Western modernities stand out when reading the contributions to this volume. They include figurations of modernity which are deeply ambiguous, since they are the result of negotiation, selective adaptation, rejection and alteration at the local level. This seems to imply that modernity is an external force that needs to be adapted in order to be able to become internalised. Once it is internalised or stabilised in a particular context, it becomes an internal process. Secondly, and connected to the previous observation, modernities are based on hierarchical power arrangements, with mostly the state, be it colonial or postcolonial, as the initiator of programs of modernity and the population as its recipients. Thirdly, modernities are strongly set within a moral universe. Depending on the perspective of its human or institutional agent, modernity can be something good that contributes, enlarges, empowers; or, on the contrary, it can be something bad that creates havoc and brings about a decline of autonomy. In most of our cases, however, it is both at the same time: a power that transforms the individual and the society, creating loss on one hand, but opportunity on the other.

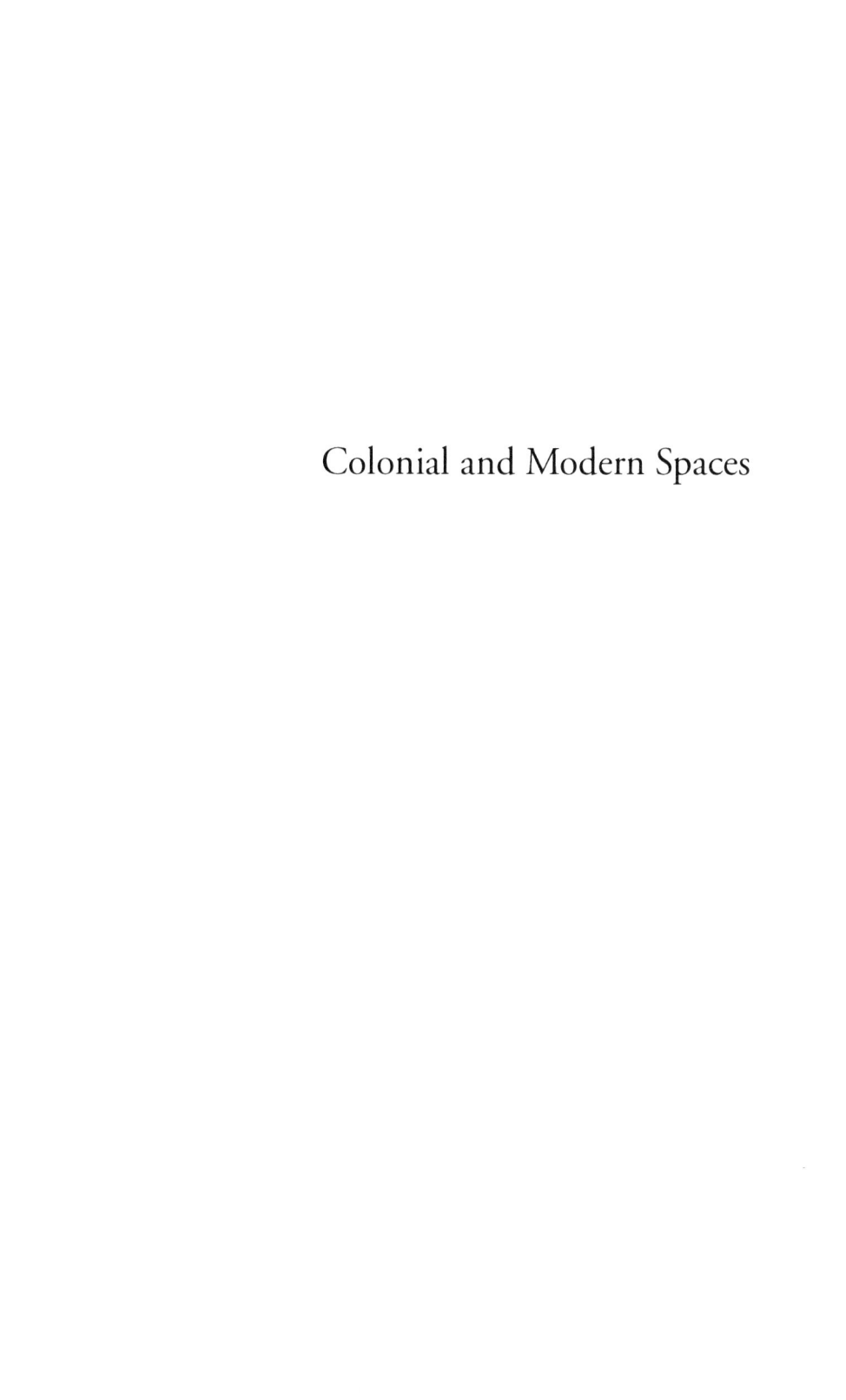

Colonial and Modern Spaces

Representations of Modernity in Colonial Indonesia

Vincent Houben

Modernity and the theory of colonialism

In the histories of non-western societies, the period of colonisation is often connected with the introduction of modernity. Although modernity had different configurations in different contexts, its origin is supposed to lie in the European Enlightenment and Industrial Revolution. Legal-rational forms of rule, the capitalist economy and the nation-state are said to be phenomena of modernity, which in the wake of colonisation were transferred from Europe to other parts of the world. Neo-institutionalists such as John Meyer argue that, in spite of their cultural embedded-ness, modern societies within the current global order are structurally similar since they are characterised by the extension of the single formal structure of the nation-state.[1] Other social theorists have begun to break up the universality of modernity of western provenance by talking of ›alternative‹ or ›multiple‹ modernities, arguing that the contexts within which modernity unfolded and its subsequent trajectories were subject to great variation.[2]

Colonial situations produced a distinct kind of modernity. Colonial modernity was never a simple copy of the western model, its externalities being remodelled and transformed as agency turned it inwards. More importantly, however, the asymmetrical power relationship that was imported with colonial rule caused western modernity to be introduced only in part and to be maintained from the outside. Colonialism in Southeast Asia not only meant the introduction of western systems of rule and the maintenance of social order by military control; it also entailed the creation of a modern infrastructure, economic system and bureaucracy along with a racist ideology of western superiority. All this was aimed at maximising the exploitation of human and natural resources to the benefit of the coloniser. Classic histories of colonialism deal with the triumph of west-

---

1 John W. Meyer, John Boli, George M. Thomas & Francisco O. Ramirez, »Die Weltgesellschaft und der Nationalstaat«, in: *Weltkultur. Wie die westlichen Prinzipien die Welt durchdringen*, ed. by John W. Meyer (Frankfurt am Main: Suhrkamp, 2005), pp. 85–132.
2 Dilip Parameshwar Gaonkar (ed.), *Alternative Modernities* (Durham, NC: Duke University Press 2001); Shmuel N. Eisenstadt (ed.), *Multiple Modernities* (New Brunswick and London: Transaction Publ., 2002).

ern modernity and the processes of subjugation of indigenous people implicated in its ascendancy. Other kinds of mainstream history writing on colonialism deal with how subjugated peoples contested their marginalisation; or how non-western societies were transformed by colonialism, eventually demanding political emancipation through struggle for independent nationhood.

The connection between colonialism and modernity has been part of global history itself, but can also be linked to a number of specific thematic issues such as race, gender, culture and ethics.[3] Frederick Cooper goes beyond this and discusses the value and limits of thinking about modernity in colonial situations. In his view, the issue is not whether ›modernity *is* singular or plural, but how the concept is *used* in the making of claims‹.[4] He argues against essentialising modernity as the core of colonial rule in the ›modern‹ era, simply because many of the arguments and counterarguments within colonialism rested on this concept. Instead, he calls not for the abolition of the word ›modernity‹, but for its ›unpackaging‹ through historical practice that is sensitive to the many possibilities and openings it offered.[5]

Modernity can only be studied fruitfully as part of locality, set within a particular space and a singular timeframe. As Sorokin observed, the concept of space itself is transformed when applied to socio-cultural phenomena. Socio-cultural space expresses positional relationships and is composed of three main ›planes‹: the system of meanings, vehicles and human agents. The socio-cultural universe, according to Sorokin, is simultaneously ideational (as derived from the system of meanings) and sensate (as represented by manifestations of physical space i.e. vehicles and human agents that ›objectify‹ meanings by turning them into socio-cultural reality).[6]

Space cannot be thought of without its temporal dimension. Sorokin argued that time does not flow evenly in the same group and in different societies, having a strong qualitative dimension. Changes in the understanding of time were a factor in the rise of modernity and also were implicated in colonisation. Modern time was linear and objective since it was measurable. It was also subjective since it pointed towards progress. Through modern technology and the capitalist

---

3 Paul Gillen & Devleena Ghosh, *Colonialism and Modernity* (Sydney: University of New South Wales Press, 2007).
4 Frederick Cooper, *Colonialism in Question. Theory, Knowledge, History* (Berkeley and Los Angeles: University of California Press, 2005), p. 131.
5 Ibid., pp. 142–149.
6 Pitirim A. Sorokin, *Sociocultural Causality, Space, Time. A Study of Referential Principles of Sociology and Social Science* (New York: Russell & Russell, 1964), pp. 108–139. The original book was written in 1943.

organization of labour, time was felt to be accelerating. Linear time laid the groundwork for the historical and national consciousness of modernity.[7]

The foregoing discussion suggests that it may be rewarding to try to understand colonial modernity as ›representation‹, as something which links the real and the imagined in a specifically ›modern‹ way. Colonialism refers to a very distinct temporal-spatial setting for modernity. Colonialism can be conceived as a modernizing project, which was wilfully hegemonic in nature. According to Van Doorn, the Dutch East Indies after the middle of the nineteenth century possessed a project-like character, exemplified by instrumental rationality, interventionism and technocratic planning, having the gradual transformation of colonial society as its aim. The triumph of Dutch technology was embodied in the typical Delft Technical University engineering graduate, who went on to build the railroads and irrigation systems in the colonial setting.[8]

This essay explores some instances of the staging of modernity in colonial Indonesia, focusing on the qualitative dimensions of modern colonial space and time. It suggests that modernity not only transformed as well as increased the modes of control, it at the same time entailed the potential for, what I call, the ›reversion of modernity‹. Instead of being merely an instrument of rule, it is argued that modernity was a ›discursive space‹ or a form of representation which was both unsettling for colonial subjects and at the same time reversible in that it had the potential to empower them. My analysis will deal with four dimensions of modernity: its vehicles, advocates, contestations and its transcending of borders.

The Colonial Vehicles of Modernity

The Indonesian Archipelago was a massive expanse, within which the Dutch tried to realise their colonial dreams and thereby enhance their status from being a small state in western Europe to being a middle-sized power in the Asian region. They arrived there early in the seventeenth century and established a trading empire with Batavia (currently Jakarta) as a centrally located port. Starting from the early nineteenth century, a shift occurred away from maritime trade towards an attempt to mobilise the agricultural resources of the main islands of Indonesia. In order to be able to establish territorial control, a concerted effort was needed

---

7 Ibid., pp. 171–172; Gillen & Ghosh, *Colonialism and Modernity*, op. cit. (note 3), pp. 199, 204–206 and 214.
8 J.A.A. van Doorn, *De laatste eeuw van Indië. Ontwikkeling en ondergang van een koloniaal project* (Amsterdam: Bakker, 1994), pp. 83–87, 95–96 and 112.

to overcome the distances between the many islands; and, also on the islands by connecting coasts with hinterlands. Controlling space was both a political and an economic priority, a matter for public as well as private endeavour.

Whereas the north coast of Java, the island at the heart of the Dutch colonial possessions, had been given a west-east postal service road as a result of a state-led compulsory labour project that was concluded in 1810, the connections between the interior and the coast remained difficult for a long time. It was only after private planters had established huge plantations in South Central Java, in an area that was still nominally ruled by indigenous princes, that they started to lobby for the construction of a railway between the port-city of Semarang and the interior towns of Surakarta and Yogyakarta. In 1860, a transport committee led by engineer T.J. Stieltjes was established, which initiated a flurry of land surveying and mapping activities in an area that had hitherto been largely inhabited by Javanese peasants. Ten years later, in 1870, after a massive enterprise financed from the public purse and involving thousands of mainly Javanese wage labourers, the first trains started rolling between the heartland of Java (*kejawèn*) and the coast.[9]

The completion of the first Dutch railway in Asia was hailed as a triumph of modern progress. The trading community of Java had earlier already submitted several formal petitions to the government expressing gratitude for the granting of the concession to allow the construction of the railway.[10] It clearly had been in the interests of the planters to have a fast and regular vehicle for transporting plantation products to ships waiting in Semarang harbour, and to no longer be dependent on uncertain road conditions during the monsoon season and the on availability of Javanese cart-drivers. For the colonial government, the establishment of a fast connection to the interior of Java was also reassuring, since this area had seen a widespread revolt against Dutch authority between 1825 and 1830, and the system of indirect rule established afterwards was still felt to be a potential risk to the colonial peace.

How critical the railway construction was from the Javanese viewpoint became evident several years before its completion. In 1867 a middle ranking member of the Surakarta court offered to the Dutch Resident a letter that had been sent from Semarang by mail to him and other senior courtiers. It had put him into, what he himself described as, a state of ›bewilderment‹. Copies had also been sent to the leader of the local Muslim community, Kyai Tapsir Anom, and to Radèn Ngabehi Ranggawarsita, a famous court poet and teacher of the

---

9 Vincent J.H. Houben, *Kraton and Kumpeni. Surakarta and Yogyakarta 1830–1870* (Leiden: KITLV Press, 1994), pp. 288–289; regarding the importance of railways in the context of empire building, see: Clarence B. Davis and Kenneth E. Wilburn (eds.), *Railway Imperialism* (New York: Greenwood, 1991).

10 National Dutch Archive The Hague, Colonies 5964, File 24 June 1863 F6 kabinet

young princes. The Dutch translator H.K.H. Wilkens rendered the text of the message as follows:

This letter comes from Medina. [...] After this salutation I wish to report to you, that there is a prophet, dressed up as a begging pupil of religion (santri). He is now residing in Semarang. If the train reaches Surakarta Adiningrat the Javanese empire will succumb. The final hour of the Dutch has come. I am the one who proclaims the true teaching.[11]

The report attracted the interest of the colonial authorities but we are not informed about the follow-up. It shows, however, that the symbol of modernity, in the form of the train was expected, as soon as it reached the Javanese capital, to trigger a dramatic political turnaround, destroying the Javanese realm and its present foreign power holders with it. The introduction of modernity, reaching its culmination at the moment that the first train entered the centre of the Javanese world, was connected with old messianic beliefs about crisis occurring at a turning point in time, provoking rural revolt. The approaching end of the world was announced in terms of »the winding of bands of iron around Java«.[12] Therefore, the Javanese elite was thrown into deep sorrow and passed on the letter to the Dutch authorities.

The completion of the railway went on largely undisturbed, however, and once in operation train travel was adopted astonishingly rapidly by large parts of the Javanese population. Besides being an instrument facilitating economic exploitation by reducing the cost of transportation of plantation produce, the train literally mobilised rural Javanese society. The number of ordinary Javanese using the line between Semarang and Surakarta, that is those who travelled third class special tariff, totalled 374,427 in 1874 and rose to 509,218 in 1883. These figures were considerably higher and rose more rapidly than the numbers for people travelling as first, second and third class passengers. Not all Javanese train passengers were peaceful petty traders, enjoying the advantage of bringing their goods to new, up-level markets. In the 1870s train traffic was also connected with the spreading phenomenon of criminals (*kècu*), who robbed the houses of Europeans living close to train stops and who then were able to disappear quickly.[13]

A second vehicle of modern communication was the telegraph. Contrary

---

11 National Dutch Archive The Hague, Colonies 5991, File 28 March 1867 S3 kabinet
12 Houben, *Kraton and Kumpen,* op. cit. (note 9), p. 233; on messianism in Java, see: Sartono Kartodirdjo, *Protest Movements in Rural Java. A Study of Agrarian Unrest in the Nineteenth and Early Twentieth Centuries* (London/New York/Melbourne: Oxford University Press, 1973), chapter 3.
13 Irawan, »Het vervoer via de spoorlijn Semarang-Vorstenlanden als welvaartsindicator voor de bevolking in Java's Vorstenlanden (1874–1883)«, in: *Between People and Statistics. Essays on Modern Indonesian History,* ed. by F. van Anrooij, D.H.A. Kolff, T.J.M. van Laanen & G.J. Telkamp (The Hague: Martinus Nijhoff, 1979), p. 61; Djoko Suryo, *Social and Economic Life*

to the situation with the public transport system, it remained exclusively in the hands of westerners, being an instrument to enhance colonial control enabling the colonial authorities to react rapidly when a crisis occurred, irrespective of its location. Messages could be exchanged across the Indies within several minutes. In telegram no.125 of 8 July 1865 11:25 a.m. addressed to the Governor-General in Bogor, the Resident of Surakarta reported the apprehensions of a certain Mangkuwijaya, who had publicly announced that the princely states of Surakarta and Yogyakarta would be destroyed; a new royal palace (*kraton*) would be established at Prambanan; and, the new king should carry the name of Sunan Adil (the righteous king).[14] On 10 June 1867, Yogyakarta was hit by a severe earthquake and in telegram no. 284 the local Resident reported: »The catastrophe is large, almost no house is inhabitable anymore, until now in [the] town [there are] 81 confirmed dead, my house [is] uninhabitable, shall accommodate my family in [a] bamboo shed.«[15]

The telegraph connection also affected relations between the colony and the motherland. From the 1860s onwards a telegraph link came into existence between the Dutch East Indies and the Netherlands, although in the beginning the Suez was needed as a connection point. On 24 November 1864 telegram no. 746, reporting the demise of Prince Sasradiningrat of Yogyakarta, was presented in Suez and received in The Hague a mere two days later.[16] The shrinking of distance between the Ministry of Colonies in Holland and the colonial administration in the Indies meant a shift in authority away from the colony and back to Europe, where the guidelines for the realisation of colonial modernity were being developed. In general, the telegraph introduced modern time and space, allowing for immediate communication concerning critical events in distant locations. The infusion of present-time local information at the top of the colonial hierarchy fundamentally transformed imperial knowledge and the potential to coordinate as well as to intervene.

Steam shipping was a third vehicle of colonial modernity, making it possible for the islands of Indonesia to become one interconnected space. An expanding shipping network was established by the *Koninklijke Paketvaart Maatschappij* (KPM), originally a branch of the colonial administration but later privatised, though a close connection with the colonial state continued to exist. A. Campo has observed that »spatially the Paketvaart network provided a maritime infrastructure which made the colonial state a geopolitical reality«.[17]

---

    in rural Samarang under colonial rue in the later 19th century (Ph.D. thesis, Monash University 1982).
14 National Dutch Archive The Hague, Colonies 1646, File 29 August 1865 no.2
15 National Dutch Archive The Hague, Colonies 5993, File 2 August 1867 C2 kabinet.
16 National Dutch Archive The Hague, Colonies 5971, File 28 November 1864 H12 kabinet.
17 J.N.F.M. A. Campo, *Koninklijke Paketvaart Maatschappij. Stoomvaart en staatsvorming in de*

After a period of experimentation, the 1850–1865 period was one of initiation, with the establishment of a radial pattern of connections. The network was subsequently rapidly extended, developing from a tree-like into a spider-web network. Whereas in 1866 a total of 44,346 miles was covered, in 1890 the mileage had tripled, expanding to 593,738 miles in 1913. Captains of KPM ships were involved in informal surveillance and occasionally intervened when local problems occurred. Early in June 1907 a revolt erupted in Endeh (Flores), but when a KPM ship appeared the ›unruly mountain dwellers‹ seemed to retreat. Thereupon the ship changed course towards Kupang, which enabled Dutch troops to land only two days later to break the siege of the Dutch post in this trouble-spot.[18]

The train, telegraph and steamship were western vehicles of modernity, adding a new immanency to colonial rule as distance could be overcome more quickly. Also the repetitive character of technologically sustained communication created the impression that the Dutch were much more present on a permanent basis. This had a reverse side, though. The number of critical incidents that could be reported and reacted to swiftly increased, producing a heightened sense of insecurity amongst colonial officials. For the Indonesian population, western technology made the colonial situation much more visible and therefore provoked contestation, but at the same time Indonesians could use modern transport to overcome distance and thus it created new opportunities for them, too.

The Advocates of the Modern Condition

In 1865, with the assistance of the Dutch, the Regent of Kudus, a region on the north coast of Java, published a book in Javanese entitled *Lampah-lampahipun Raden Mas Arya Purwa Lelana* (›the travels of an old noble roamer‹). Its author, Raden Mas Arya Candranegara, who lived between ca. 1836 and 1885, was a model intellectual and member of the indigenous elite, who had adopted a modern lifestyle and was even admitted as a member of the Batavian scientific academy. His book was in the style of a traditional didactical Javanese text (*piwu-*

Indonesische archipel 1888–1914 (Rotterdam: Verloren, 1992), p. 640; a summary of his findings can be found in: A. Campo, »Engines of Empire: the Role of Shipping Companies in British and Dutch Empire Building«, in: *Shipping, Technology and Imperialism,* ed. by Gordon Jackson & David M. Williams (Aldershot: Scholar Press, 1996), pp. 63–96.
18 A. Campo, *Koninklijke Paketvaart Maatschappij,* op. cit. (note 17), p.148.

lang), but its subject matter was utterly modern. Its contents can be summarised in the following manner.[19]

On his first trip Purwa Lelana travelled to Semarang, where he was impressed by the liveliness of the place. The habits of the Javanese, he noted positively, had changed because of its cosmopolitan character and the presence of so many strangers. There were only a few low-born people remaining who were still proficient in high Javanese (*krama*) and the locals were no longer prepared to pay him, a Javanese nobleman, due respect. People dressed in a way that was hard to define, since their *batik* dress was Javanese but they wore a head cloth just like the Malays and no longer carried a dagger (*keris*). The women followed Arab custom, having their hair cut, their eyelids painted black and they wore bracelets and pearl necklaces.

From Semarang he travelled by steamship to Batavia, the harbour of which resembled a forest of leafless trees, since so many ship masts were visible. The journey by sea had been unpleasant for the author, because, travelling at such high speed, he became sick (*mendem*) and had to stay in his cabin. In the second edition of Purwa Lelana's travels, a story describing his subsequent train ride from Batavia to Bogor was added. The locomotive was named using old Javanese as ›*lokam tar*‹, which literally means »the place where a cannon is fired«.[20]

Purwa Lelana made a second trip in the opposite direction, travelling eastwards from Semarang to Surabaya, where he marvelled at the uninterrupted flow of ships and the enormous mass of people. Whereas he described Batavia as a city with many government buildings, symbols of Dutch power, in the industrial city of Surabaya the Javanese nobleman was struck by the presence and signs of advanced technology. He was »amazed to the utmost« seeing smelting furnaces that were driven by steam. The floating dock resembled the uncovered box in which *wayang* puppets are kept. When he climbed on board and got a look at a ship that was being repaired, all of the sudden he almost fainted and nearly fell down.

Purwa Lelana, the first advocate in writing of the modern condition in Java, gave a splendid literary image of what the colonial world around 1860 had to offer. From the perspective of a Javanese official with high social status, modernity was connected to urban spaces, new cosmopolitan modes of social behaviour and the speed as well as the scale of modern technology. Being exposed to all this dynamism, the country gentleman experienced strong bodily sensations, being at the same time overwhelmed and positively impressed. As a Javanese didactical text printed by the government press (*landsdrukkerij*), the travel account

---

19 There is a recent French edition and commentary of his travel book. See: Marcel Bonneff, *Peregrinations Javanaises. Les voyages de R.M.A. Purwa Lelana: vision de Java au XIXeme siecle (c.1860–1875)* (Paris: Maison des sciences de l'homme, 1986).
20 Ibid., p. 117: footnote 51.

was clearly aimed at demonstrating the potential of western modernity that was already transforming Javanese society. It was therefore a subtext to western orientalist perspectives which meant to demonstrate that colonial rule produced progress.

More than seventy years later, in 1936, another ›enlightened‹ Regent, Pangeran Achmad Arya Djajadiningrat, put his experiences down on paper. His format was that of an autobiography, describing his career in the indigenous administration of west Java and making public specific details concerning his personal and family life. The first decades of the twentieth century were the years of the so-called Ethical Policy, in which the Dutch claimed a civilising mission. As a consequence, the author's administrative service work was much involved with matters of irrigation, public health, combating threats to the colonial peace and surveillance of the daily work of village heads[21] His activities in these fields are described extensively throughout the book. It is striking that this monograph, like Purwa Lelana's account, was not written in a local language (in this case it should have been Sundanese); it was written in Dutch.

Djajadiningrat was no longer exclusively Javanese, but, as someone with formal European education, he felt himself to be a broker between east and west. However, this left him feeling a certain uneasiness, as evidenced in his quoting of the Sundanese saying ›from above one fears the thunder, from below the worms‹ (*ti luhur siun guludug, ti handap siun ku cacing*). At the same time he criticised the increasing westernisation of the indigenous official elite (*priyayi*), who seemed to have lost contact with indigenous society. He commented: »it is regrettable also that indigenous officials nowadays seek their fortune more on the tennis courts and in the clubs rather than in the *desa* [village]«.[22]

Dajadiningrat's reminiscences, like Purwa Lelana's, were in the form of a didactic text on modernity, but there is a difference, reflecting the preoccupations of the late colonial period. No longer is there the awe for western modernity, as he had already become part of it. As a regent he was actively involved in the execution of the ›colonial project‹. The format of an autobiography written in Dutch under his own name is illustrative of another kind of self-awareness than that usually displayed by the nineteenth century Javanese gentleman. Modernity had appropriated the body and mind of this West Javanese regent, his main worry being losing his roots, his contact with the commoners and, thus, his embedded-ness in local society. Although being an advocate of modernity, its dangers had also become visible. Therefore this text in Dutch was, besides being intended as a proof of individual merit, was meant mainly to stimulate his fellow

---

21 Pangeran Aria Achmad Djajadiningrat, *Herinneringen* (Amsterdam/Batavia: Kolff, 1936).
22 Ibid., p. 212. A *desa* is a village.

administrators to be diligent in the pursuit of their modernising mission, while at the same time advising them to be wary of becoming too westernised.

Djajadiningrat's text was basically apolitical since it did not address the nationalist movement that had started in Indonesia in the 1910s, with the exception of one incident which is mentioned. In 1911 Djajadiningrat went by train to Surabaya and on board he ran into Eduard Douwes Dekker, a radical Eurasian nationalist. According to Djajadiningrat's account, Douwes Dekker immediately started to propagate his ideas about the foundation of a local Indisch party, directed towards achieving independent statehood for the Dutch East Indies. If we are to believe him, Djajadiningrat reacted in a rather restrained manner, but on one issue he professed to be in agreement with Douwes Dekker. This was his critique of legal dualism, which had created two separate judicial systems, one for the indigenous population and another for the Europeans. He agreed with Douwes Dekker that »dualism [had] resulted in a slowing down of the development of the Indies, in general, and that of the indigenous population, in particular«.[23]

Djajadiningrat's meeting with Douwes Dekker recorded in his 1936 memoirs was featured again more recently by the Indonesian author Pramoedya Ananta Toer (1925–2006) in his novel *Jejak Langkah* [Footsteps].[24] Pramoedya's account is loaded with representations of colonial modernity: the movement of the train through time and space in the direction of the modern city of Surabaya; the awareness that the pace of progress in the development of a colonised people is dependent on the level of enlightenment of colonial law; and, the encounter between a Javanese advocate of modernity who embodies colonialism and a person of mixed race who works hard to end it. Thus, in a portion of text supposed to advocate modernity under western leadership, Pramoedya highlights the inner contradictions of the colonial project and foreshadows its ending.

The Contests over Modern Space

Colonial modernity introduced novel and more permanent control over spaces that were once indigenous but had become increasingly westernised. Indigenous ritual spaces in Java – sacred sites connected to Javano-Islamic culture; and

---

23   Ibid., pp. 278–279; on legal dualism, see: Cees Fasseur, »Corner stone or stumbling block«, in: *The Late Colonial State in Indonesia. Political and Economic Foundations of the Netherlands East Indies, 1880–1942*, ed. by R. Cribb (Leiden: KITLV Press, 1994), pp. 31–56.
24   For details of the manner in which history has been literary represented in this novel: A. Teeuw, *Pramoedya Ananta Toer. De verbeelding van Indonesië* (Breda: De Geus, 1993), pp. 235–236.

large gatherings at religious festivals – were mostly left untouched by the Dutch, whereas ritual at the Javanese courts was remodelled and upgraded in an attempt to generate legitimacy for colonial rule through the invention of tradition. But as time went by the colonial state extended itself deeper into indigenous society, as it endeavoured to establish more control on the ground. From the beginning of the twentieth century, this provoked many instances of resistance and attempts to regain control over physical space either as part of, or as a rejection of, modernity. I will give two examples of this reversal.

The setting of the first incident was the *krapyak* territory, a princely domain in Central Java where an extensive agrarian reorganisation had just got underway, breaking up age-old rural relationships.[25] In 1915 Deputy Controller Westhues, a Dutch colonial official, was on a tour of inspection in the *krapyak* lands of Surakarta. When he reached the village Nglunggé, division Klaten, he got out of his car and started to inspect a number of yards and fences. His binoculars were on a strap around his neck but he had left his gun behind. He then continued on foot, crossing the Gandul stream (*kali*) and heading in the direction of a tobacco shed on the other side.

When a young Javanese man saw the Controller coming, he immediately got up and rushed off to the shed, shouting that a »Dutchman ... [was] coming to get you« (*welanda cekel*). This provoked an outbreak of panic in the shed, whereupon women and children started to cry and men grabbed their grass knives and bamboo sticks. Some women were beating the *tong tong* (wooden alarm bell), signalling what the Javanese call *titir angganter* (emergency, signifying a robbery or murder). The Dutchman stopped in his tracks, facing a crowd of around fifty Javanese, all armed with sticks, clubs, knives and lances. A deputy village head (*wakil bekel*) stepped forward and asked him in Javanese who he was. Westhues replied that he was a Deputy Controller on an inspection tour, but this explanation was not accepted by the crowd, who started crying out »don't believe him« (*aja percaya*).

Being under acute threat, the Dutch Controller decided to make a run for it and descended back into the bed of the stream. Shouting »we will kill you« (*pantèni hancur*), the Javanese villagers started throwing stones and beating up the Dutchman with their bamboo sticks. Only with the utmost difficulty, with both his arms gone limp, Westhues managed to escape. He then informed his superiors about what had happened over a phone in a nearby town.[26] A few years later Nglunggé again became the site of major peasant resistance in the form of strikes, organised by Insulinde, a radical association of mainly Eurasians.[27]

---

25 Takashi Shiraishi, *An Age in Motion. Popular Radicalism in Java 1912–1926* (Ithaca and London: Cornell University Press, 1990), pp. 18–23 and 153.
26 National Archive The Hague, Appendix B of Mailreport 1916 no. 1393.
27 Shiraishi, *An Age in Motion*, op. cit. (note 25), pp. 157–159.

Our second example is set in Surabaya, the harbour town that had developed into a fully-fledged industrial city during the closing decades of the nineteenth century.[28] Its industrial plants processed enormous amounts of sugar cane, harvested from the East Java hinterland. Besides that, metal processing, machine manufacturing and printing industries developed there, which led to the emergence of an Indonesian working class, ranging from the artisan (*bengkel*) to the manual labourer *(buruh)*. Social tensions acquired spatial dimensions, as indigenous environs were flattened to make way for expansive European neighbourhoods and for industrial production sites. Compared to the rural hinterland of Central Java, Surabaya was a wholly modern city.

At the end of 1920 major strikes suddenly broke out, after Javanese and Chinese labourers had begun setting up labour unions. The wheels of the colonial economy were brought to a halt. Crowds of people marched into the city centre, which was at that time considered to be a space under uncontested European control. A mass rally of around five thousand workers was held in a central park and watched with suspicion by police squads. The leader of the strikes, a man called Jahya, gave a public speech demanding further talks with employers.[29]

The Europeans were completely taken by surprise when the strikes broke out, as is evident in a commentary by the chief editor of the main Dutch daily, the *Soerabaiasch Nieuwsblad*. He wrote:

With the speed of an express train, Indies society, politics and economy is passing through the stages which took European countries many decades of slow and cautious steps. The labour movement, which developed slowly and painfully in Europe, has, by its sudden appearance and development, taken our society by surprise [...].[30]

The biography of the leader of the strikes, Jahya, shows him to be a man of modernity but someone who was a lot less elitist compared to Djajadiningrat, the regent in West Java. He seems to have been the son of a railway conductor from Jember. He was a graduate from the Hollandsch-Indische school and was literate in Dutch as well as Malay. After a short spell as an advocate for sugar factory workers, he advertised himself as an organiser of labour unions, whereupon he was commissioned by the Surabaya workers to head their workers' association (*Perserikatan Kaum Buruh*).[31] A vivid though highly mocking portrait of this ›king of the strike‹ (*raja mogok*) was published in another European newspaper:

---

28 Howard Dick, *Surabaya, City of Work: A Socioeconomic History, 1900–2000* (Athens: Ohio University Press, 2002).
29 A description of the strike events can be found in: John Ingleson, *In Search of Justice. Workers and Unions in Colonial Java, 1908–1926* (Singapore: Oxford University Press, 1986), pp. 135–146.
30 Commentary by B.B. Faber in: *Soerabaiasch Nieuwsblad* (11 December 1920).
31 Ingleson, *In Search of Justice*, op. cit. (note 29), pp. 135–136.

He is dressed in a brown *pakean* [suit] according to the latest fashion, with a shining green tie and a helmet-hat, in which his royal head sinks from view. To continue, he wears trousers with turn-ups, low-cut shoes and multi-coloured socks [and] turtle-rimmed goggles to bluff the bourgeois.[32]

Behind this mocking description of a Europeanised dandy, there was a lot of fear and contempt, showing how confused the European public had become as a result of the workers taking up their right to modernity.

Both cases – the violent reaction of Javanese villagers against a Dutch Controller and events surrounding the strike in the city of Surabaya – at first sight seem to have little in common since the peasants reacted against modernity whereas the workers were emancipating themselves within it. But there are important parallels as well. Both incidents, albeit in a countervailing manner, had to do with taking action against the imposition of change by colonial modernity, which had produced a heightened degree of social tension. The Javanese villagers felt threatened, because in the course of agrarian reform Dutch colonial officials started to show up inspecting princely lands, where they had not been present earlier. The Surabaya workers had already become part of economic modernity and had now embarked upon their struggle for better pay and labour conditions, whereas the Europeans still had the feeling they were dealing with 'backward natives'. Both the Javanese peasants and the urban labourers tried to reoccupy spaces (of land and power) that had been lost to them. In both the source documents there is mention of body language as well as a sense of immediacy and rapid speed – giving expression to sensations of the modern.

Transcending Borders

Using modern communications technology as a vehicle, the colonial presence became more omnipresent as distances shrank. At the same time, however, space expanded since borders could be transcended more easily. Because there was a dearth of labour in the new centres of colonial activity in the plantation and mining economies of Sumatra and Kalimantan and also beyond the Dutch East Indies, Javanese labourers were transported by the thousands to, what they called, ›the lands at the opposite side of the sea‹ (*tanah sabrang*). The alienation involved in being uprooted from their villages of origin and working in harsh environ-

---

32 *Nieuwe Soerabaiasche Courant* (29 November 1920); On the politics of dress, see: Henk Schulte Nordholt (ed.), *Outward Appearances. Dressing State and Society in Indonesia* (Leiden: KITLV Press, 1997).

ments were also important characteristics of colonial modernity. But even under these unfavourable conditions instances of reversal of modernity did occur.

Once having been a seafaring people, the Javanese of the late nineteenth and early twentieth centuries had become peasants bound to their rural villages. Rapid population growth during the nineteenth century had, particularly in the rural areas of Central Java, led to a decline in welfare and a willingness on the part of young males to look for work elsewhere. Like China and India, the interior of Java developed into a huge reservoir of labour that was tapped by plantation owners throughout the Asia Pacific region. Most of the officially assisted, Javanese labour migrants went to the plantations and mines in Sumatra and Borneo, but a minority were sent to foreign destinations, such as British Malaya, British North Borneo, French Indochina and French New Caledonia.[33]

Prior to his departure for work overseas, each Javanese was brought before the Dutch magistrate in the inland town where he was enlisted. The Dutch official was instructed to inform the prospective coolie labourer about what would await him in the near future, in an attempt to establish whether or not he was going ›voluntarily‹. One such encounter went as follows:

Do you know the meaning of *tanah sabrang*? I will explain this to you precisely and please don't always say *inggih* [›yes‹]. *Tanah sabrang* is far off and over the sea, outside of Java and you will go there by ship, which is a large *prau* [boat] that can go over the sea. That is why the land to which you are going is named *tanah sabrang*, because you cross the sea (*nyabrang*). For instance, Deli, Sarawak, Sawah Lunto are all places overseas whereas Semarang, Surabaya, Batavia are not. Please remember that your contract is for three years and that during this period your family can't come to visit you. [A digression on wages, working hours and other details of the working conditions follows here.] Please consider carefully whether you wish to continue with your plans. If you want to leave now, nobody will stop you and you will not have a *perkara* [legal suit, trouble].[34]

In an attempt to explain modern realities to an illiterate rural dweller, who had already received an advance on his first wage and therefore was in a situation of debt, a host of information on geography and labour conditions was transmitted, probably in vain. When the prospective labourer agreed to be sent overseas, he was transported by train to the coast, got a medical examination, signed a contract for the duration of three years and went as a deck passenger on a KPM steamer to his/her destination.

Labour conditions in the capitalist enterprise, involving a very strict time schedule and no freedom of movement, were utterly different from what the Ja-

---

33 On the intra-Indonesian labour migration, see; Vincent Houben and Thomas Lindblad, *Coolie Labour in Colonial Indonesia. A Study of Labour Realtions in the Outer Islands c.1900–1940* (Wiesbaden: Harrassowitz, 1999).
34 National Archive the Hague, Colonies 988, File 11 December 1912 no.41

vanese had previously experienced in the rural villages of Central Java. Transgression of the rules or trying to run off was punished severely. Western plantation overseers and managers feared instances of violent resistance or of coolie labourers running amok, since this constituted something beyond rationality, and was seen as unreasonable and disproportionate. In East Sumatra in the 1970s, Javanese villages still surrounded the plantations, being firmly Javanese on the one hand and a geared to an external reality on the other. Doing fieldwork in the village of Simpang Lima in the late 1970s, Ann Stoler noted the double orientation of social space and time:

> Although ceremonial events for childbirth, circumcision, marriage, and death closely adhere to a specifically Javanese pattern, in practice the temporal rhythms of work and leisure are tuned to, and dominated by, the cadence of the estate industry.[35]

It would seem that nothing much had changed since the colonial days.

Neither were all coolies mere victims nor was their social position the same everywhere. In New Caledonia being a Javanese worker meant something different altogether when compared to Sumatra. New Caledonia was not so much engaged in plantation agriculture but in the mining of nickel and other minerals. Since 1910, every year on average between a hundred and two hundred Javanese labourers were transported there, most of them not working as miners but as housekeepers. The treatment of the Javanese by the French was, according to a 1919 field visit report by a Dutch labour inspector, much more relaxed than in the Dutch East Indies. Communicating in French, a language that they mastered only a few months after arrival, they were considered more as equals than as native labourers. Every Sunday the Javanese men in New Caledonia put on European clothes in the form of a blue ›serge‹ suit with white [detachable] collar, tie and Panama hat.[36]

The transcending of boundaries of racial ascription did not lead to a loss of Javanese-ness, but local circumstances did lead to shifting socio-cultural configurations. The feeling of being Javanese was first and foremost connected to religion. In New Caledonia no mosques, religious leaders (*penghulu*) or returned pilgrims (*haji*) were available to perform the rituals of matrimony or burial, which was a matter of complaint amongst the Javanese working population on the island. According to the Dutch labour inspector, this led to marriage not being registered, giving the females the impression of not being married at all and therefore they were prone to engage in prostitution. An official of the labour office wrote:

---

35 Ann Stoler, *Capitalism and Confrontation in Sumatra's Plantation Belt, 1870–1979* (New Haven and London: Yale University Press, 1985), pp. 48 and 181.
36 National Archive The Hague, Colonies 2186, Openbaar Verbaal 22 October 1920 no. 13.

Because there are too few Javanese women in New Caledonia, polygamy hardly exists, whereas women arrogate to themselves many rights that are not in line with the dependent and humble position attributed to them by Islam.[37]

The advisor of indigenous affairs, E. Gobee, reacted rather soberly to these observations. He considered it to be unlikely that among the 5,000 Javanese in New Caledonia not one would be able to pronounce the very simple marriage formulas and offer rudimentary religious instruction. He also thought that the performance of an official marriage ceremony would not change much regarding the social position of women. The fact that the Javanese lived in very scattered localities affected Javanese family life much more. Despite this, the Dutch and French authorities agreed to ship one or two *modin* (someone who calls to prayer) from South Sumatra to New Caledonia.

Concluding Observations

Timothy Mitchell has defined the representation of modernity as a form of social practice that splits image or idea from reality.[38] The approach taken here is slightly different, arguing that representations connect to social order, being as much constituents of a particular order as reflecting it. Representations are culturally bound forms of knowledge that position people as well as objects within a spatially and temporally embedded social order. Representations also enable people to establish their own views of the world and to change the existing social order. The colonial order was no different, but had its own particular qualities. It was driven by a project of modernity that took place in a particular time period (roughly 1860–1930) in particular places (here mostly rural and urban Java). This modernising project changed indigenous society but colonial subjects were able to reverse this by creating their own realities and shaping their social practices in ways that had not been foreseen by the architects of western hegemony.

In this chapter, four dimensions of colonial modernity have been highlighted: the vehicles of modernity in the form of modern means of transportation and communication; testimonies by indigenous agents of colonial modernity, both

---

37 Letter of Labour Office to the deputy advisor for indigenous affairs 29 April 1930, in: National Dutch Archive The Hague, Colonies 344 Mail report 1930 nr. 1030; for a sociological-historical study on the Javanese in New Caledonia, see: Jean-Luc Maurer, *Les Javanais du Caillou. Des affres de l'exil aux aléas de l'intégration* (Paris: Association Archipel, 2006).
38 See Chapter 1 (Introduction) p. 12–13

advocates and opponents; contests over the control of rural and urban space; and border transgressions. Each of these dimensions merits a short discussion.

The introduction of trains, telegraph services and steamships changed the face of colonialism. Being a creation of modernity, technology itself was transported to new places and spaces. Technology is socially shaped, yet technologies shape their own social contexts, so both are entangled.[39] It is striking how quickly after their introduction in the west, the new technologies were transferred and implemented in the colonies. There was strong pressure to do so, since by more effectively connecting and controlling space and time, colonial rule could be stabilised and strengthened. At the same time, the mobility of indigenous subjects was enhanced too. Spatial divides between regions and islands were bridged, while opponents of the colonial order could extend the area in which they made an impact. Modern transport speeded up the sequence of events, giving rise to bodily sensations of bewilderment and surprise; and even the expectation of an apocalypse and end to the colonial era.

The indigenous advocates of modernity made use of modern transport. Over time a shift took place, with advocates moving from outside observation of urban modernity to becoming part of the project of rural modernisation as agents or brokers. Yet these advocates met with modern counterparts, who opposed the colonial order instead of defending it. Educated in modernity, Douwes Dekker and Jahya wanted to regain control over space, over the Indies as a whole or the city of Surabaya, in particular. In this they were so different from the villagers from Nglunggé who chased the Dutch Controller off their lands. Contest over rural as well as urban space was also a dimension of modernity, since it presupposed the awareness of territorial space as something that was worth controlling.

Finally, by means of the transgression of borders, involving the physical movement of great numbers of Javanese from their villages in Java to sites of capitalist production across the Asia-Pacific region, Javanese-ness was reproduced elsewhere, prefiguring current transnational networks. Migration beyond the physical borders of the known and over time periods which transcended several generations was also an important dimension of colonial modernity.

Modernity is movement, flux and change, transforming the connection between representation and social order. As this essay has attempted to demonstrate, colonial modernity in Indonesia was driven by both non-human vehicles and human agents of change. It was far from one-sided, the Dutch inscribed the Indonesian colonial ›Other‹, but were not able to deprive them of their own agency. Colonial modernity constituted a discursive space, which allowed for

---

39 Philip Brey, »Theorizing Modernity and Technology«, in: *Modernity and Technology*, ed. by Thomas J. Misa, Philip Brey & Andrew Feenberg (Cambridge Mass./London: MIT Press, 2003), pp. 33–71.

contestation and reversal, geared towards bringing the colonial part of the equation to an end.

Performing the Metropolitan *habitus*: Images of European modernity in cross-cultural encounters in nineteenth century Eastern Africa[1]

Michael Pesek

In nineteenth century East and Central Africa, Europe was mainly present through travellers whether they were travelling for the sake of exploration, bringing the gospel to Africans, or, with the beginning of colonialism, as conquerors and administrators. Half here, half there – European travellers in nineteenth century Eastern Africa were acting in situations of cultural differences and were moving through temporary spaces constituted by different cultures and their peoples. Leaving their societies of origin and encountering situations of cultural difference, they were in a Bourdieuan sense ›alone‹. I refer here to Pierre Bourdieu's notion of the *habitus* as a product of a continuous process of socialization, which enables individuals to act according to the rules and norms of their societies.[2] *Habitus* is a »sense of place«, as Jean Hillier and Emma Rooks have recently pointed out: a socialised, embodied and lived out familiarity with the social, cultural and economic relationship, that according to the French philosopher Henry Lefebvre, constitutes a certain space.[3]

The ›lonely traveller‹ brings us to the very heart of European discourses of modernity as they emerged at the end of the nineteenth century. The literary critic and archaeologist of nineteenth century discourses Walter Benjamin writes that, with the »*flâneur*« (somebody who is idling or loafing about), the French poet Charles Baudelaire had created a major figure in the pantheon of European modernity. In the anonymous and disturbing jungle of the modern metropolis, the *flâneur* is experiencing the modern condition as a difference between himself and the strange and exotic tableau made of shimmering spectacles of electricity, gas lamps, shop fronts and the waving faceless masses of peoples of different social and regional origin.[4] Moreover, with his peripatetic gazing he is typolo-

---

[1] Parts of this paper were published in Michael Pesek, *Koloniale Herrschaft in Deutsch-Ostafrika. Expeditionen, Militär und Verwaltung seit 1880* (Frankfurt a. M.: Campus, 2005). I am gratefull to Campus for allowing me to reproduce these sections here. I also wish to thank Anika Stegemann and Mona Schrempf for their very helpful comments on my paper.
[2] Pierre Bourdieu, *Entwurf einer Theorie der Praxis* (Frankfurt a. M.: Suhrkamp, 1979), p. 183; Pierre Bourdieu, *Sozialer Sinn. Kritik der theoretischen Vernunft* (Frankfurt a. M.: Suhrkamp, 1993), p. 101.
[3] Henri Lefebvre, *The Production of Space* (Oxford: Blackwell, 2004), p. 73.
[4] Walter Benjamin, »Charles Baudelaire. Ein Lyriker im Zeitalter des Hochkapitalismus«, in:

gising, objectifying and exoticising the urban environment; the *flâneur* himself embodies European modernity of the late nineteenth century as peculiar way of experiencing his world. What the *flâneur* is for the urban jungle, the traveller is for exoticised places (places in which the differences of the ›Other‹ arose in the traveller's discourse as awe and wonderment), whether they be situated just behind the town's gates or in faraway places. What makes both the traveller and the *flâneur* modern in a nineteenth century sense is ›loneliness‹, the inherent promise of an unlimited individuality that arises from the difference between his *habitus* and the other place. The traveller has become a prominent focus in debates about the emergence of European modernity.[5]

Nevertheless, modernity is not only a discourse or a concept of personality but also a social, political and economic condition that can be roughly described as being the product of processes of industrialisation, urbanisation, the emergence of modern states and civil societies.[6] Thus, when Eric J. Leed notes that travel is a history-making force, this is probably a very modern view of the role of travel in history.[7] In Europe, the history of travelling has been part of, and a particular dynamism in, the emergence of modernity. Since the early modern age, the movements of travellers have contributed to a refashioning of European space. The development of infrastructure, such as roads, bridges and canals contributed to a process that resulted in the radical development of a mass traffic of goods and human beings in the industrial age. Even before the epoch-making steam engine and railway (which were then about to become what are probably European modernity's most iconic imaginaries), improvements and innovations in technologies had been arising in the context of early modern travelling. New concepts of time first emerged with the timetables of coaches; the emergence of

---

    Walter Benjamin (ed.), *Gesammelte Schriften* (Frankfurt a. M.: Suhrkamp, 1991), pp. 509–706, in particular p. 541.

5 See for instance David Rollison, *The Local Origins of Modern Society. Gloucestershire 1500–1800* (London: Routledge, 1992); Judith Adler, »Origins of Sightseeing«, in: Carol T. Williams (ed.) *Travel Culture: Essays On What Makes Us Go* (Westport: Praeger, 1998), pp. 3–25.

6 This is of course only a rough summarisation of a highly complex and controversial issue under debate. I am referring here to Mike Featherstone, Scott Lash & Roland Robertson, *Global Modernities* (London; Thousand Oaks Calif.: Sage Publications, 1995); Arjun Appadurai, *Modernity at Large: Cultural Dimensions of Globalization* (New Delhi: Oxford University Press, 1997); Shmuel N. Eisenstadt, »Multiple Modernities«, in: *Dædalus* 129 (2000), 4, pp. 1–30; Dilip Parameshwar Gaonkar, *Alternative Modernities* (Durham: Duke University Press, 2001); Wolfgang Knöbl, »Modernization theory, modernization & African modernities«, in: Jan-Georg Deutsch, Peter Probst & Heike Schmidt (eds.), *African Modernities: Entangled Meanings in Current Debate* (Oxford: James Currey, 2002), pp. 158–178; Charles Taylor, »Modern Social Imaginaries«, in: *Public Culture* 14 (2002), 1, pp. 91–124; Frederick Cooper, *Colonialism in Question: Theory, Knowledge, History* (Berkeley: University of California Press, 2005). See also the introduction to this volume.

7 Eric J. Leed, *Die Erfahrung der Ferne. Reisen von Gilgamesch bis zum Tourismus unserer Tage* (Frankfurt a. M.: Campus, 1993), p. 29.

the nation state found its first visible expressions in border regimes and custom laws. Inns and roadside hotels became places for the transmission of news and political discussion – the nuclei for the emergence of a civil society, something that Jürgen Habermas has exclusively attributed to the bourgeois cafes of the eighteenth century.[8]

The traveller, therefore, is in many senses an agent of Europe's modernity, as he is a performer of a peculiar imaginary of that modernity. It is this latter aspect that will be the focus of the following pages. Writing about what he calls »colonial modernity«, the American historian Frederick Cooper understands modernity as a product of European history and he connects its dispersal around the globe to the historical processes of colonialism and imperialism of the nineteenth century. Modernity, he notes, has at once a »powerful claim of singularity« and a promise of plurality. It is, he writes, a »European project and a European accomplishment, to be defended against others, who may knock at the gate, but whose cultural baggage renders the mastery of modernity unattainable.«[9] However, especially in the process of their transfer towards non-Western societies, European concepts of modernity underwent significant changes when they were adapted or referred to by local populations, thus giving way to »multiple modernities« or »alternative modernities«.[10] Moreover, »colonial modernities«, if we see them as the schemes of colonial rulers to transform non-Western societies, were in a certain sense »alternative modernities« since their implementation was never a pure application of models designed in the metropolis. These schemes underwent many changes which the colonial rulers felt were necessary in order to adapt to the local situations.[11] One important characteristic of this colonial modernity is that it was thought to be an exclusive export product of Europe. Its adoption and circulation in the colonies was regarded as having to be controlled by Europeans.

Whereas Cooper discusses at length the plurality of colonial modernity as a condition arising from the fragmentary nature of Europe's colonial projects, the plurality of modernity as a representation somehow escapes his attention. It is at this point my own paper takes up the discussion, by referring to the traveller's *habitus* as something that incorporated the modern condition; and, also to performances in which the European body became an important media for a European modernity imaginary. What configured the peculiar modernity that

---

8 Holger Th. Gräf & Ralf Pröve, *Wege ins Ungewisse: Reisen in der frühen Neuzeit, 1500–1800* (Frankfurt/Main: S. Fischer, 1997), p. 12. For Habermas' theory of the emergence of civil societies in Europe as a cornerstone of modernity see his *Strukturwandel der Öffentlichkeit. Untersuchungen zu einer Kategorie der bürgerlichen Gesellschaft* (Neuwied: Luchterhand, 1962).
9 Cooper, *Colonialism in Question*, op. cit. (note 6), p. 113.
10 Ibid., p. 114.
11 This argument is basically made by me, see Pesek, *Koloniale Herrschaft*, op. cit. (note 1).

became visible in such performances is, I will argue, the dynamics of performative acts in cross-cultural encounters.

First of all, performance is all about acting in concrete situations. It is the way »in which the cultural content of a tradition is organized and transmitted on particular occasions through specific media.«[12] Performance as an event has both social and cultural dimensions, and most of all it is a public event that creates and displays meanings. It engages people who are acting either as actors or as audience, but who at the same time are involved in a web of various social relations. It is at the same time »make believe«, the evocation of an illusion,[13] and social practice with sometimes serious consequences for the social lives of people involved. Indeed, many of the performances I will discuss here were intended to to create social relationships between travellers and local communities, whether they were ceremonies of blood brotherhood or negotiations about food, water and the porters the travellers needed for their journey.

The travellers were not professional performers, but many believed that performance was an important part of their profession. This belief arose from an understanding that they acted in situations where communication was as important as it was demanding. Few of them spoke any of the local languages, but all were dependent on speaking with locals. Power, they believed, was the key to achieve status and prestige in these situations, but seldom did they have the wherewithal available to accumulate such resources. It was, thus, with the spectacularity of performances, that they hoped to create at least the illusion of such power, to make the Africans believe they were important. Tales about Europeans who had been welcomed by locals as gods or kings were still part of Europe's imaginary of encounters with non-Western people; James Cook and Hernán Cortés still haunted the minds of nineteenth century travellers, and still it was the splendour of Western technology that made the difference between ›us‹ and ›them‹.

Illusions, make-believe and performances belong to cross-cultural encounters. They are strategies to negotiate imaginaries of the ›Self‹ and the ›Other‹ as well as for mediating social relations. Writing about what he calls the »reflexivity« of performances, Victor Turner states that people in performances »are acting representatively, turn, bend or reflect back upon themselves, upon the relations, actions, symbols, meanings, codes, roles, statuses, social structures, ethical and legal rules, and other socio-cultural components which make up their public ›Selves.‹«[14] In cross-cultural encounters this ›public self‹ is much more open to illusions and elusions because of the ephemeral relationships between the traveller

---

12 Maurice Bloch, *Ritual, History and Power: Selected Papers in Anthropolgy* (London: Athlone Pr., 1989), p. 40.
13 Richard Schechner, *Performance Theory* (New York/London: Routledge, 1988), p. xiv.
14 Victor Turner, *The Anthropology of Performance* (New York: PAJ Publications, 1986), p. 24.

and local communities. Locals might present to the traveller what they think is an essential or useful image of their society that supports their individual position and strategies, or one which they think is understandable to the traveller. Performances in this regard are the means of translation and transfer of imaginaries. They are the currency by which people set each other into relationship. Performances provide people with a set of common practices to incorporate strangers as well as artefacts and concepts, which are not the product of local histories. Mary Douglas speaks about ritual performances as a venture into the unordered space of social orders, into the border zones of the society.[15] Travellers are people who, from the perspective of local communities, embody the border zone. To integrate them at least temporally into their social and cultural worlds they have to be dealt with in performances. For the traveller, performances serve to overcome his speechlessness and his ambiguous status. Artefacts, which symbolise the status and prestige of the arriving traveller, play an important role in this process of negotiating the relationship.[16] But the meanings of such artefacts are highly contested. Whatever meanings the traveller might connect to the use of such artefacts, this view is not necessarily that of local communities and peoples. Artefacts always have their own social history and cultural biography, which is dependant upon their circulation and use.[17]

But how we can grapple with all this, with the fluidity of cross-cultural encounters and the historicity of experiences and cultural practices that are accumulated and condensed into performative scripts and moral economies that order the behaviour of people acting in these contexts? I think one way to do this is with James Clifford's concept of contact zones. Contact zones, as Clifford notes, are made by movements of people and are constantly transformed by historical processes; they are constantly renegotiated by those who are interacting within such zones.[18] Despite this notion of ephemera, travelling cultures have their own history (or histories) containing the experiences of encounters in different contact zones, but they are also intersections of local and global histories. European exploration of Eastern Africa relied to a great extent upon the infrastructure of the interregional caravan trade. Most expeditions were organized

---

15 Mary Douglas, *Reinheit und Gefährdung: Eine Studie zu Vorstellungen von Verunreinigung und Tabu* (Frankfurt a. M.: Suhrkamp, 1988), p. 125.
16 Susann Baller, Michael Pesek, Ruth Schilling & Ines Stolpe, »Einleitung«, in: Susann Baller, Michael Pesek, Ruth Schilling & Ines Stolpe (eds.), *Die Ankunft des Anderen. Empfangszeremonien im Interkulturellen und Intertemporalen Vergleich* (Frankfurt a.M.: Campus, 2008), pp. 9–32, in particular p. 16.
17 Arjun Appadurai, »Introduction«, in: Arjun Appadurai (ed.), *The Social Life of Things: Commodities in Cultural Perspective* (Cambridge: Cambridge University Press, 1986), pp. 1–43, in particular p. 36.
18 James Clifford, *Routes: Travel and Translation in the Late Twentieth Century* (Cambridge: Harvard University Press, 1997).

by coastal traders and staffed by people who had previously served in the caravans. Expeditions followed almost the same routes that the coastal traders used for their trade with African societies in the interior. The caravan trade, itself an intersection of local histories and the history of the Indian Ocean and its bordering regions, produced its own contact zones, within which a particular symbolic language and moral economy evolved.[19]

In the historicizing of contact zones we have to reveal the processes of negotiation concerning the kinds of language to be used in these encounters. Such language concerns not only the spoken word but also the use of symbols, bodies and ceremonial choreographies. Components of this language are like traces of previous encounters – an archaeology of the contact zone. Previous experiences of encounters form something like a moral economy that is underlying the ceremonies, rituals and behaviour used by people. Often these experiences are embedded and negotiated by intermediaries, translators or diplomats. As Clifton Crais reminds us, European colonial rule in Africa involved »an astoundingly complex interplay of African and European modes and models of power and political practice«.[20] And as much as actual power relations structured the choreographies of encounters in contact zones, ceremonies and rituals were spaces in which these power relations were negotiated and monuments by which they were made visible. The economic, technological and political advances in Europe in the nineteenth century made, without doubt, European travellers into powerful actors on the African scene. European colonial powers had, even before the colonial conquest of Eastern Africa, more than once demonstrated their military and political will. Since the 1870s, the British had deployed gunboat politics to put pressure on the sultans of Zanzibar to abandon slavery and to protect European travellers and economic interests. Nevertheless, in encounters between Europeans and the local communities in the interior of Africa this asymmetry was often only of marginal importance. The role of Europe as a force for historical change in this region was first negotiated in the contact zones of European exploration and the interregional caravan trade. Thereby, Africans firstly accessed Europe through its consumer products and technology that was swept in through the caravan trade. While at the same time, Europe's presence in nineteenth century Eastern Africa can also be described as a process of adaptation by travellers to these contact zones.

The travellers' performance of an imaginary of modernity used several media. In encounters with Africans it was their bodies and the artefacts they carried with them that were used to mediate this imaginary. Their reports in the various books, journals and letters they wrote about their travels re-staged these perfor-

---

19 For further details, see Pesek, *Koloniale Herrschaft*, op. cit. (note 1).
20 Clifton C. Crais, *The Politics of Evil: Magic, State Power, and the Political Imagination in South Africa* (Cambridge: Cambridge University Press, 2002), p. 7.

mances for a European audience. It is here, where the travellers reflected upon their acting in these cross-cultural encounters, that they gave their performances the meanings that they thought to be essential. Johannes Fabian, whose book *Out of Our Minds* mentions some of the travellers discussed here, has pointed out that this re-presentation developed it own strategies.[21] There were the long-established European imaginaries of Africa that had to be at least referred to, there were the rules of the genre of travel-writing and scientific knowledge production that had to be followed, and of course, travellers had to reconfirm their self-image as bearers of progress and civilisation.

My focus is on German travellers, who travelled during the 1880s for various reasons throughout East and Central Africa. Hermann von Wissmann (on his first expedition of 1880–1883) and Paul Reichard, Paul Kaiser and Richard Böhm travelled mainly for the sake of exploration. They belonged to two separate expeditions of the German branch of the International African Association. At that time, the German Africa Association had been transformed from an academic circle into a colonial interest group. Yet, the project of Peters' expedition to Usagara in 1883 was much more clearly formulated as a colonial endeavour. He aspired to make history by founding a German colony in Eastern Africa by collecting protection treaties with local chiefs. On his second expedition to the Kassai River, von Wissmann acted on behalf of the Belgian king Leopold II, and his newly founded Congo Free State. It was here where he began a colonial career, which culminated in his inauguration as the first Governor of German East Africa.

Clearly these travellers belonged to a European project of bringing modernity to the ›dark continent«, although they interpreted it in rather different ways. For the members of the Eastern African Expeditions of the German African Association, this project was connected with the scientific exploration of the African interior and with the establishment of trading posts. Their stations were called centres of civilisation, being in part bases for their expeditions to collect botanical, zoological and geographical knowledge and also early attempts to influence local politics. Von Wissmann had both a scientific and a colonial interest, while Peters most clearly interpreted his role in Africa as a political endeavour. Nevertheless, what they shared was their social background. Most German travellers at that time came from the middle-classes, which were in 1880s the backbone of the colonial movement in Germany. To a certain extent, they shared a common understanding of what they performed in Africa as a European or German civilisation. For them such a civilisation was connected with achievements in science and technology, and with their mastery by way of a disciplined and edu-

---

21 Johannes Fabian, *Out of Our Minds. Reason and Madness in the Exploration of Central Africa* (Berkeley: University of California Press, 2000), pp. 244–253.

cated body. This very notion of body as an embodiment of Western modernity is what I call a metropolitan *habitus*. What the travellers understood as European culture was typical for the Europe of the metropoles, industrialization and modernity. The industrialization the travellers carried in their baggage was typified in their equipment including their tents and guns, their first aid kits, and their scientific instruments. Most travellers derived their intellectual frame from the natural sciences, which they used to make their experiences intelligible.[22]

Travelling bodies

Despite an extensive literature on European travellers and a widespread interest among historians, social and cultural scientists regarding the human body, we know little about the bodily dimensions of European explorations in Africa. In recent studies, European travellers mainly appear as agents of European discourses, who observed, described and constructed images of Africa that followed the coordinates and predispositions of these discourses. However, seldom is the practice of travelling taken into account as an important ground for their knowledge production. Although the bodily dimension is often neglected in academic analysis, the travellers were nevertheless taken by their contemporaries, as well as by later historians, as embodiments of European cultures or civilisations. In many historiographies, the arrival of travellers in Africa serve as the beginning of historical processes: Stanley's expedition of 1878 to the Congo Basin is connected to the establishment of the colonial rule in Central Africa; Peters' expedition of 1883 to Usagara has marked the beginning of German colonialism in many studies. What exactly these expeditions meant for local societies and what historical processes they provoked in the concrete contexts in which they were undertaken is seldom analyzed by this history.

Paradoxically, the notion of travellers as embodiments of Europe's arrival in Africa has contributed to a neglect of the bodily dimensions of European exploration. Nevertheless, the travellers' tales are full of narratives regarding their bodies. Often they describe the crises that the body endured due to topical illnesses, food shortages and attacks by local people. Moreover, in their thinking, the body of the European embodied the expedition. For most travellers, their willpower and personal abilities were the guarantee for the success of the expedition. The successful and famous travellers of the nineteenth century were not

---

22 Cornelia Essner, *Deutsche Afrikareisende im neunzehnten Jahrhundert: Zur Sozialgeschichte des Reisens* (Wiesbaden: Steiner, 1985), p. 62; Fabian, *Out of Our Minds*, op. cit. (note 21), p. 127.

so much the great scientists, but the survivors of expeditions. Only the person who kept his body in tact, only the person who survived, was able to glean the fruits of all the hardships he endured during his journey. A striking case was the expedition of the German African Society to Eastern Africa from 1880 to 1883. When the expedition reached Unyamwezi, it consisted of three Europeans. Two of them, Kaiser and Böhm, were renowned natural scientists both with a doctoral degree. The third was Reichard, a craftsman, who was only able to join the expedition because he paid all his expenses out of his own pocket. While Kaiser and Böhm dedicated themselves to their scientific studies, Reichard's tasks were of a more organisational nature. He managed the station and organised the expedition for his colleagues. But after three years Reichard was the only survivor. Following his return home, he published several accounts of his journey and was therefore regarded as one of the most experienced travellers concerning East Africa.[23]

The body of the traveller was much more than just a physical entity. It was full of meanings; it was a symbolic body that carried a variety of representations. In their thinking, the European traveller embodied the European culture or their particular nation, which was absent or only present through the travellers' presence. Their travels were much more than just exploration; they were also spectacles of Europe in African contexts. We find this notion in the writings of Oskar Baumann, an Austrian traveller, who, in the 1880s, undertook several expeditions to Mount Kilimanjaro:

A traveller, especially when he enters unknown regions, is never a private person, even if he likes to appear as such. He is, and remains for the Africans, a representative of his nation, or of European culture. Moreover, he has to act accordingly, if he does not want to bring shame to the flag under which he travels and if he does not want to cause damage to the great endeavour for which we all, whether we travel in the name of an institution or not, risk our lives.[24]

It was the *habitus* of the traveller – its performance and celebration – that served as a signifier of difference. Such thinking was rooted in the anthropological and ethnographic discourses of the nineteenth century, in which the body was taken as a marker of cultural and social characteristics. It found expression in innumerable attempts to catalogue the human body by the emerging disciplines of

---

23 See the reports of the expedition in: *Mitteilungen der Afrikanischen Gesellschaft in Deutschland* (henceforth MAGD) and his publications; Paul Reichard, »Die Wanjamuesi«, in: *Zeitschrift für Erdkunde* 24 (1889b); Paul Reichard, *Deutsch-Ostafrika. das Land und seine Bewohner, seine politische und wirtschaftliche Entwicklung* (Leipzig: Spamer, 1892); Paul Reichard, *Stanley und die deutsche Afrikaforschung* (Berlin: 1897).

24 Oscar Baumann, *Durch Massailand zur Nilquelle. Reisen und Forschungen der Massai-Expedition des Deutschen Antisklaverei-Komite in den Jahren 1891–1893* (Berlin: D. Reimer, 1894), p. 108 [my translation].

anthropology and ethnology. Measurements and descriptions of human bodies served to prove the thesis of racial difference. Ethnological museums collected not only artefacts but also human bones and skulls. For the contemporary ethnologists and anthropologists, bodies were evidence of a particular culture as much as they were artifacts.[25] Ethnographic showcases – embedded in popular beliefs in fairies as well as in academic discourses – exhibited artefacts arranged into sceneries of native villages, as well as human beings.[26] The European construction of non-European bodies as cultural ›others‹ has been discussed at length.[27] However, this thinking also had its consequences for the construction of European bodies as embodiments of a distinct European culture at the times when they travelled through the African continent. When, in European discourses of those times, African bodies were taken as embodiments of difference, the European traveller, one can argue, performed with his body in Africa the embodiment of Europe.

---

25 An example of such cataloging is to be found in Felix von Luschan, »Instruktion für ethnographische Beobachtungen und Sammlungen in Deutsch-Ostafrika. Zusammengestellt im Auftrage der Direktion des Königlichen Museums für Völkerkunde in Berlin«, in: *Mitteilungen von Forschungsreisenden und Gelehrten aus den deutschen Schutzgebieten* (1896), 2, pp. 89–99. For the history of European perceptions of African bodies see John L. Comaroff & Jean Comaroff, *Ethnography and the Historical Imagination* (Boulder: Westview Press, 1992); Gail Ching-Liang Low, *White Skins/Black Masks*. *Representation and Colonialism* (London: Routledge, 1996); Alexander Butchart, *The Anatomy of Power. European Constructions of the African Body* (New York: Zed Books, 1998); Catherine Hall, *Cultures of Empire: Colonizers in Britain and the Empire in the Nineteenth and Twentieth Centuries: a Reader* (New York: Routledge, 2000); Andrew Zimmermann, *Anthropolgy and Antihumanism in Imperial Germany* (Chicago: Chicago University Press, 2001).
26 Raymond Corbey, »Ethnographic showcases, 1870–1930«, in: Jan Nederveen Pieterse & Bhikhu C. Parekh (eds.), *The Decolonization of Imagination: Culture, Knowledge and Power*, ed. by (London: Zed Books, 1995), pp. 57–80, in particular p. 195; Zimmermann, *Anthropolgy*, op. cit. (note 25), p. 19.
27 E. M. Collingham, *Imperial Bodies. The Physical Experience of the Raj, c. 1800–1947* (Cambridge: Polity, 2001), p. 122. For the history of the European notion of civilization see Raymond Williams, *Gesellschaftsgeschichte als Begriffsgeschichte. Studien zur Historischen Semantik von Kultur* (München: 1972). For European discourses on races in the 19th century see Robert Young, *Colonial Desire: Hybridity in Theory, Culture and Race* (London: Routledge, 1995) and for the circulation of certain arguments regarding superiority in European discourses see Valentin Y. Mudimbe, *The Invention of Africa. Gnosis, Philosophy, and the Order of Knowledge* (Bloomington: Indiana University Press, 1988); David Spurr, *The Rhetoric of Empire. Colonial Discourse in Journalism, Travel Writing, and Imperial Administration* (Durham: Duke Univ. Press, 1993); Nicholas Thomas, *Colonialism's Culture: Anthropology, Travel, and Government* (Princeton N.J.: Princeton University Press, 1994).

The metropolitan *habitus* in Africa

It was this vision of Europe which the traveller performed with the spectacle of his disciplined body and in his demonstration of the European consuming and technological worlds. We can find the coordinates of this metropolitan *habitus* in the elements of the travellers' performances in front of Africans: the British American traveller Henry Morton Stanley demonstrated the firepower of his state-of-the-art carbine to the Zanzibari trader Tippu Tipp, while von Wissmann performed at Mdarabu what he had learned at the Prussian barracks square – the use of such guns by a disciplined body. The members of the East Africa Expedition of the German African Society demonstrated the »wonders of Uleia [Europe]« to the local population of Usagara and Unyamwezi: their equipment and scientific instruments. On his way through Africa, von Wissmann used the local fascination with printed pictures by distributing pictures from Stanley's books to traders and chiefs: »cheap tricks«, as Fabian called this, by which the traveller tried to impress and sometimes to intimidate the Africans.[28]

Not only were the »wonders of Uleia« a feature of the traveller's performances, but also were the mastery and control of these wonders by the traveller. Such a staged use of their equipment was rooted in a belief that mastery and control over these wonders constituted a difference between the traveller and the local people. Moreover, it came from the conviction that these ›wonders‹ guaranteed their survival and their scientific success. For Reichard the best way to travel included the use of the latest technological products that the industrial and scientific revolution had provided for travellers. Accordingly, he begins his *Suggestions for travel equipment in Eastern Africa* with an exhibition of European modernity, that included description of waterproof tents, canned food, the achievements of tropical medicine and the latest in scientific instruments.[29] But all this was worth nothing without the appropriate use of this technology by a disciplined body. Von Wissmann was convinced that there existed an important difference between Africans and Europeans. It was the »slower effect of transmission from the nerves to the musculature« among Africans that made it impossible for them to react quickly while facing changing situations. An early morning attack on a village near Lake Tanganyika served for him as an example of this. The star-

---

28 Richard Böhm & Herman Schalow, *Von Sansibar zum Tanganjika* (Leipzig: Brockhaus, 1888), pp. 23, 51; Hermann von Wissmann, *Unter deutscher Flagge quer durch Afrika von West nach Ost, 1880 bis 1883* (Berlin: Walther & Apolant, 1889), pp. 181, 200; Hamed bin Muhammed el Murjebi, »Autobiographie des Arabers Schech Hamed bin Muhammed el Murjebi, genannt Tippu Tip«, in: *Mitteilungen des Seminars für Orientalische Sprachen* 3,4 (1902/03), pp. 175–277, 171–155, in particular p. 61. See also Fabian, *Out of Our Minds*, op. cit. (note 21), pp. 108,122.

29 Paul Reichard, »Vorschläge zu einer Reiseausrüstung für Ost- und Centralafrika«, in: *Zeitschrift der Gesellschaft für Erdkunde* 24 (1889a), 1, pp. 1–80, in particular pp. 12, 36.

tled villagers were unable to resist von Wissmann and his few soldiers. For von Wissmann this scene was proof that the African was incapable of a »quick and energetic reaction of his body or emotions.« Here von Wissmann's language suggests his socialisation at the Prussian barracks square. This difference between Africans and Europeans would be obvious when it came to shooting when, according to von Wissmann, the ability of the European to react quickly would give him a decisive advantage over Africans or Arabs.[30] For the German this was not only a question of theory, but, as one can imagine, one of the more practical aspects of travelling and, later, when he became the first Governor of German East Africa, of colonial conquest. The colonial troops' favourite time to attack African villages was, not surprisingly, the early morning.[31]

But let me return to von Wissmann's time as a traveller, to a scene he describes when, in 1883, he arrived with one of Tippu Tipp's caravans in Mdarabu, a small village and residence of the Swahili trader Muinitwana. Von Wissmann's account of a welcoming feast, which the trading chief offered to Tippu Tipp, his trading partner and ally, turns into a scene where he fought a truly symbolic battle with some Arab or Swahili traders. The scene begins with a dance by some of Muinitwana's warriors, his *ruga-ruga*, dressed in »colourful clothes, with turbans and feather headdress, carrying nicely decorated guns and spears, with most wrapped in red flannel capes«. In ecstatic dances they mimicked attacks and the killing of enemies. Describing the scene to the reader, von Wissmann uses images of wild and frenzied behaviour to distinguish the body culture of the ›Other‹.[32] The scene seems to climax when two of Tippu Tipp's followers jump into the dancing circle:

> Now the two dancers jumped onto the veranda and continued with their exaggerated gestures, a wild expression on their faces. First, I thought they liked to impress me, but their blood-suffused eyes became even wilder and were fixed on me. Their spears almost touched me [...] When they came nearer and nearer to me, Tippu Tipp jumped up and tried to stop them.[33]

Some days before it was these two Zanzibari men with whom von Wissmann

---

30 All quotations from von Wissmann, *Unter deutscher Flagge*, op. cit. (note 28), p. 217.
31 Von Wissmann discusses this experience on Lake Tanganyika in his booklet Hermann von Wissmann, *Afrika. Schilderungen und Rathschläge zur Vorbereitung für den Aufenthalt und den Dienst in den deutschen Schutzgebieten* (Berlin: E.S. Mittler, 1895).This guide, which could be found on every military station in the colony, is one of the most important documents for understanding German politics of conquest between 1889 and 1903. See in detail my Pesek, *Koloniale Herrschaft*, op. cit. (note 1).
32 All quotations from von Wissmann, *Unter deutscher Flagge*, op. cit. (note 28), p. 289 [my translation].
33 Ibid. [my translation].

had a dispute over a shooting contest and he regarded the two men's dance as a provocation to his reputation. Therefore, he responded by dancing himself:

> I thought that now it was the time to run with the pack. I took my karabiner together with the bayonet and five cartridges, jumped over the balustrades and hinted to the people to leave the circle. The wild masses scattered away. I charged my gun and fired at a tree, moved some steps forward, went down on earth, fired again, etc. When all my cartridges were fired, I fixed my bayonet, moved forward and rammed my bayonet into the tree, in which all my five cartridges had found their target. Then shouting and cheering began which confirmed that I had found the right way to deal with the situation. All men, even the old robber chief, ran to the tree and admired my shots. This is the way in which all whites in Europe fight, I explained, and every German is able to do as I have done.[34]

Von Wissmann interprets this scene as an encounter between different body cultures. It is von Wissmann's language that hints at his own body culture and differentiates it from the African. According to his description, his performance had nothing to do with the ecstatic behaviour of the African dancers. He fired exactly five cartridges and all met their target. Moreover, he describes his movements – running, shooting, using the bayonet – in terms of exactness, precision and order. It is the routine skill of a drilled and rationalised body. This is perhaps one of the most striking examples of the performance of the metropolitan *habitus* at work. When he explains to the Africans that this was the way in which Europeans fight, he constructed his body as an embodiment of European or German culture, which came to the Africans only by way of his performance. Nevertheless, his Prussian warrior dance has its own ambiguities, mainly because it can be regarded as a warrior dance with its own ecstatic moments. Indeed, some years later, when von Wissmann was acting as a coloniser, he held a parade of colonial troops in Ubena on the northern shore of Lake Nyassa, and the local population interpreted this parade as a German warrior dance.[35]

That the traveller put so much importance on his appearance is not surprising. His body played a crucial role in ceremonial meetings with African chiefs. A drawing from von Wissmann's book indicates this role or the traveller's perception of this role (see Figure 1). What we see is the meeting between von Wissmann and Lukengo Muana during von Wissmann's first trip through Africa. The African chief is carried on a stretcher. His body is in the centre of a ceremonial parade of thousands of his followers. Von Wissmann appears as a counterbalance to the overwhelming crowd. His white uniform and a majestic posture highlight his presence. Only a few followers stand behind him – some

---

34 Ibid. [my translation].
35 Further information on the expedition of the ›Kaiserlicher Commissar Major‹ Hermann von Wissmann see: *DKB (Deutsches Kolonialblatt)* 1893, p. 453.

Figure 1: Wissmann meets chief Lukengo on his first travel through Africa.

are dressed; some are naked. The German flag is prominently displayed to the right of the picture.

In the ceremonial meetings with African chiefs, the metropolitan *habitus* became a symbol, but this *habitus* itself was full of ambiguities. Its performance was at least a performance of an idealised construct, which unfolded its glamour only as an antithesis to other body cultures in the contact zone of European exploration. Despite technological and scientific progress, and the successive establishment of a bourgeois culture and urbanisation in Germany, German society of the nineteenth century was far from being a modern society. The pre-modern rituals of the empire's aristocratic elites characterized this society as they did the urban entertainment culture of bourgeois middle classes. During the reign of Wilhelm II, Germany was subjected to a wave of ceremonies and feasts that were inspired by an idealized image of the mediaeval Hohenzollern regime.[36] What German travellers described in Africa as a backward political system, while using

---

36 Arno F. Mayer, *Adelsmacht und Bürgertum. Die Krise der Europäischen Gesellschaften 1848–1914* (München: dtv, 1984), p. 135; Rudolf Braun & David Gugerli, *Macht des Tanzes- Tanz der Mächtigen. Hoffeste und Herrschaftszeremoniell 1550–1914* (München: C.H. Beck, 1993), p. 292.

metaphors of mediaeval times, was not very far from their experiences at home in Germany.[37]

In the travellers' debates on the topic of hygiene, the features of the metropolitan *habitus* became obvious. Notions of rationality, self-control and discipline are used to describe this *habitus*. »For a healthy European in his best years«, von Wissmann wrote in his *Practical hints for travelling in Africa*, »the danger to life is not as great as is regarded by many, if he follows a rational lifestyle«.[38] The traveller has to pay great attention to daily hygiene, advised Jerôme Becker, who undertook several expeditions into the Congo for the *International African Association*. For him, hygiene covered a wide field. It included protective measures for the traveller's health, daily personal hygiene and recreation. The traveller's body has to be a disciplined one, which »thanks to a rational, theoretically founded and practically orientated education«, has to be used during expeditions in »a rational and methodical way«. Daily work was, for Becker, a part of daily hygiene and a »rational gymnastics« was the ideal way to achieve that goal. Moreover, it incorporated a moral concept. Work served as a protective measure for the health of the traveller and as a way to maintain his respectable appearance or, in other words, his claim to be a representative of European culture and civilisation.[39]

With regard to hygiene, we have an example from Carl Peters, the German adventurer and imperialist, who travelled in 1883 to Usagara to negotiate protection treaties with African chiefs. He performed his daily personal hygiene as a spectacle for the African members of his expedition:

Now this solemn scene took place, which so often astonished the Africans: I shaved my beard. I did this with almost ceremonial seriousness, because I knew what a great impression and influence this evoked amongst my followers, who looked on me with admiration.[40]

Peters' assumptions about the impressions his ceremony made through his performances tells us more about his self-conception than about the possible reactions of his African porters and guides. For him, the irreconcilable cultural difference between himself and the Africans was not least the product of performances of his daily hygiene, one of the »wonders of Uleia«. And, as Stephen

---

37 Richard Böhm & Ernst Kaiser, »Bericht über die Reise zum Tanganyika«, in: *Mitteilungen der Afrikanischen Gesellschaft in Deutschland* 3 (1882), 3, pp. 181–208, in particular p. 200; von Wissmann, *Unter deutscher Flagge*, op. cit. (note 28), p. 150.
38 Von Wissmann, *Unter deutscher Flagge*, op. cit. (note 28), p. 405.
39 All quotations from Jerôme Becker, *Über Ausbildungsanstalten für Forschungsreisende und Kolonialisatoren* (Antwerpen: Kockx, 1886), p. 22.
40 Carl Peters, *Gesammelte Schriften* (München: C. H. Beck, 1943), p. 297.

Greenblatt reminds us, it is only in this difference that awe and the wonderment emerge.[41]

The crisis of the metropolitan *habitus*

To maintain the metropolitan *habitus* during an expedition was a hard task for the traveller. It is therefore not surprising that we rarely have photographs of European travellers for the period they were in Africa. Most pictures we have of them are taken before their departure to Africa. Take for instance the book on Von Wissmann's second expedition to the Kassai River in 1883. Only a few of the more than hundred pictures show the travellers in African contexts. In most pictures, the travellers are not present or are hard to identify. In the first picture in the book, which was taken before their departure to Africa, we see them as representatives of a bourgeois culture – middle class suits, moustaches, and a dignified posture. Only one picture shows the members of the expedition dressed in traveller mode. Here we see that the solid-middle-class suits replaced by cotton travel suits, which remind me more of peasant clothes. Heavy boots had replaced the fine city shoes. The twisted moustaches had become long beards. This is quite a different image from that which we have seen before.

Reichard's *Suggestions for travel equipment in Eastern Africa* pays great attention to the clothing of the traveller. He recommends a practical and durable cloth for travellers. From his suggestions we get an image of how difficult it was to maintain the state of the cloth. Tall grass ruined his cotton trousers in a few days, he wrote, while local soaps and rain quickly frayed his clothing.[42] The consequences of travelling for the clothes and the traveller's appearance are made visible in two pictures of Count von Götzen while on his expedition through Africa in 1895. The first is a drawing which was published in his travel account. It shows a parade of the expedition. Order is the main topic of this picture: in rank and file the *Askari,* or armed guards of the expedition are lined up, and the tents and the equipment are arranged. The uniforms of Europeans and Africans are of a clean white colour. The other picture, a photograph, found no place in the publication. It comes from the pictorial archive of the German Colonial Society. Like the first picture, it shows a scene in an expedition camp. One sees Götzen and his comrade Erhard. Next to them are sitting two servants and porters of the expedition. The seating of the Europeans in the picture evokes

---

41 Stephen Jay Greenblatt, *Marvellous Possessions: The Wonder of the New World* (Oxford: Clarendon Press, 1992), p. 21.
42 Reichard, »Vorschläge«, op. cit. (note 29), p. 31.

a quite different image from the first and from the general impetus of Götzen's travel account.[43] The strains of the travel are inscribed in the facial features of Götzen and Erhard. Götzen's clothes are dirty and his socks ragged. The existence of this picture is not surprising, nor what it illustrates: the travellers' difficulties in maintaining their metropolitan *habitus*.

The metropolitan *habitus* was also undermined by food shortages and tropical illnesses. Due to food-shortages, Europeans were sometimes forced to sell part of their clothing and equipment.[44] The threat of becoming ill with tropical diseases hung like the sword of Damocles over every European traveller in Africa. In the last decades of the nineteenth century, Western innovations in tropical medicine had reduced the mortality rates of Europeans in the tropics. But knowledge about the causes and treatment of tropical illnesses was still limited. Overdoses of quinine and morphine and excessive drinking of alcohol, which was seen by many travellers as an appropriate treatment for many illnesses, caused the same kinds of disastrous consequences for their health as the illnesses against which they were used.[45] Often the travellers were brought to the limits of their physical existence and sometimes beyond. Of the four members of the East African expedition of the German African Society, only Reichard survived. Malaria and dysentery caused long periods of infirmity. Before Kaiser died of malaria, he was plagued by fever, paralysis and pain. Overdoses of quinine caused him sleeplessness and exhaustion. This had serious consequences for his expedition, since he was no longer able to maintain his role as the leader of the expedition. Many porters deserted and the expedition had to pause many times. In the last days of his life, he lay in bed and was washed and cared for by his porters and servants. The carefully observed bodily distance between him and the Africans had, in consequence, melted away. But it was exactly this bodily

---

43 See Gustav Adolf Graf von Götzen, *Durch Afrika von Ost nach West. Resultate und Begebenheiten einer Reise von der Deutsch-Ostafrikanischen Küste bis zur Kongomündung in den Jahren 1893/94* (Berlin: D. Reimer, 1899).
44 Von Wissmann, *Unter deutscher Flagge*, op. cit. (note 28), p. 152; Emin Pascha & Franz Stuhlmann, *Die Tagebücher von Dr. Emin Pascha* (Berlin: Westermann, 1927), p. 398.
45 Von Wissmann to »Ausführungskommission der Deutschen Antisklaverei-Lotterie«, Chinde 29.7.1892 (reprinted in Ausführungskommission des Deutschen Antisklavereikomites, *Die Akten der Ausführungskommission des Deutschen Antisklavereikomittes betreffend das v. Wissmann-Dampferunternehmen* (Koblenz: Deutsches Antisklavereikomitee, 1893), p. 384); Becker, *Ausbildungsanstalten*, op. cit. (note 39), p. 10; Reichard, »Vorschläge«, op. cit. (note 29), p. 39; Hermann von Wissmann, *Afrika. Schilderungen und Ratschläge zur Vorbereitung für den Aufenthalt und den Dienst in den Deutschen Schutzgebieten* (Berlin: Mittler & Sohn, 1903), p. 82. For the emergence of the tropical medicine in the nineteenth century see Roy M. MacLeod & Milton James Lewis, *Disease, Medicine, and Empire: Perspectives on Western Medicine and the Experience of European Expansion* (London ;New York: Routledge, 1988); David Arnold (ed.), *Warm climates and Western Medicine. The Emergence of Tropical Medicine, 1500–1800* (Amsterdam: Rodopi, 1996); Philip D. Curtin, *Disease and Empire: The Health of European Troops in the Conquest of Africa* (Cambridge New York: Cambridge University Press, 1998).

distance that the travellers regarded as essential for the maintenance of their role as expedition leaders.⁴⁶

Another example of the consequences of tropical illness for the metropolitan *habitus* is found in an account of von Wissmann's first journey to Africa. As a novice in the art of travelling, he had learned from his mentor, the traveller of long experience Carl Pogge, that all conflicts with African members of his expedition should be solved by negotiation, and not by force. Self-control and patience would be the main obligation of the traveller, since the success of the expedition depended on the cooperation of the porters and guides of the caravan. Nevertheless, when von Wissmann, plagued by fever, whipped porters with his *kiboko* (hippo-whip), such intentions quickly faded away. He described later his behaviour as irrational and a *faux pas* in his role as European expedition leader.⁴⁷

Such scenes may be found in many travelogues. Perhaps the most striking example is the fate of Rochus Schmidt, an agent of Peters' German East African Society, who made several expeditions to Usagara to negotiate protection treaties with African chiefs. On his return to the coast, he was attacked and robbed by local warriors. Schmidt was seriously wounded and was left alone by his porters in the forest. The metropolitan *habitus*, which Schmidt had celebrated prior to this in his many negotiations with African chiefs, was successively reduced to pure physicality. The contrast with the scenes some days beforehand could not be sharper. Schmidt was divested of his status which the ceremonies of negotiations and the expedition had secured for him, and crawled through the forest where even the Africans who were passing by paid him no attention. Only after days of an odyssey through the bush was he saved by local people who brought him to a mission station.⁴⁸

Mimicry in the contact zone

Despite his cataloguing of European travel technologies, Reichard was aware of the limits of this technology. This was first and foremost a practical issue. The

---

46 Paul Reichard & Richard Böhm, »Kaisers Reise von Gonda zum Rikwa-See, September - Oktober 1882, Auszüge aus seinem Tagebuch«, in: *Mitteilungen der Afrikanischen Gesellschaft in Deutschland* IV (1884), 2, in particular p. 162; Böhm & Schalow, *Von Sansibar*, op. cit. (note 28), p. 143; Reichard, *Deutsch-Ostafrika. das Land und seine Bewohner, seine politische und wirtschaftliche Entwicklung*, op. cit. (note 23), p. 305.
47 Von Wissmann, *Unter deutscher Flagge*, op. cit. (note 28), p. 116.
48 Rochus Schmidt, *Meine Reise in Usaramo und den deutschen Schutzgebieten Central-Ostafrikas* (Berlin: Engelhardt, 1886), pp. 24–25; Rochus Schmidt, *Kolonialpioniere. Persönliche Erinnerungen aus kolonialer Frühzeit* (Berlin: Safari-Verlag, 1938), pp. 66–67.

Figure 2: The members of the Kassai expedition of 1883 photographed before their travel to Africa.

traveller had to limit his baggage, and therefore, he had to carefully decide what was necessary and what was not. This becomes most visible in the question of food. After more than three years of experience travelling in Eastern Africa, he knew that food was perhaps the most vital key for the success of an expedition. Food was important for the health of the European and it was important for the loyalty, discipline and capability of porters. Concerning food, the traveller was well advised not to insist on prejudices; he had to adapt to local knowledge.[49] Despite the innovations of the European food industry in the conservation of food, the pressure to rely on local food remained. Not least, because the cooks for Europeans were mostly Africans. Therefore, Reichard strongly advised that the traveller also use local resources. He describes in detail edible and medicinal plants to be found and used in Eastern Africa. Many of them, he argues, are used by local people for the treatment of a variety of illnesses. Jerome Becker echoes this observation by stating that his Sukuma porters provided him with an accurate and rich knowledge about medicinal plants. Contrary to the European discourses of the nineteenth century, where African healers were mainly regarded as witchdoctors, he assumes that many *mganga* in Usukuma were truly medicinal experts. Stuhlmann, a German doctor, who accompanied Emin Pasha on his last expedition in 1891, draws a similar conclusion and compares the methods

---

49 Reichard, »Vorschläge«, op. cit. (note 29), pp. 12, 45, 60.

Figure 3: A drawing of the members of the Kassai expedeition together with Tschingenge and a certain Sagula.

used by his porters to treat cases of small pox with the latest insights of Western tropical medicine.[50]
Such insights opposed the assumption that Europeans by definition ruled over a superior knowledge. However, we can find fragments of such transfers of knowledge in other parts of Reichard's writings. Reichard often stresses the continuities between the caravan trader and the European traveller. The European could learn from the trader how he had to behave when dealing with his porters and with African chiefs.[51] The example of the German traveller Gustav Fischer, who, in order to manage his way to Mount Kilimanjaro, dressed himself as an Arab trader, might be an extreme example of such mimicry, but it shows that travellers had to appropriate local habits and practices in order to be successful.[52]

The metropolitan *habitus* contained a remarkable paradox. Although con-

---

50 Becker, *Ausbildungsanstalten*, op. cit. (note 39), p. 16; Reichard, »Vorschläge«, op. cit. (note 29), in particular p. 18; Franz Stuhlmann, »Forschungsreisen in Usaramo«, in: *Mitteilungen von Forschungsreisenden und Gelehrten aus den deutschen Schutzgebieten* 7 (1894), 3, pp. 225–232, in particular p. 85. For the Western discourse on non-Western medical knowledge see David Arnold, »Introduction: disease, medicine and empire«, in: David Arnold (ed.), *Imperial Medicine and Indigenous Societies* (Manchester: Manchester University Press, 1988), pp. 1–26, in particular p. 7.
51 Reichard, »Vorschläge«, op. cit. (note 29), in particular pp. 66–68. See also Becker, *Ausbildungsanstalten*, op. cit. (note 39), p. 25.
52 G.A. Fischer, *Das Massai-Land (Ost-Aequatorial-Afrika). Bericht über die im Auftrage der Geographischen Gesellschaft in Hamburg unternommene Reise von Pangani bis Naiwascha-See* (Hamburg: L. Friederichsen & Co., 1885), p. 3.

structed in Europe to be performed in Africa or elsewhere as a marker of difference, the metropolitan *habitus* was not always adjustable to the African context. The traveller acted in situations in which other body cultures and bodily practices were inscribed. Local rituals of blood brotherhood are an interesting example. In such rituals, the body was used and manipulated as a ceremonial symbol. In the contact zone of European exploration and the interregional caravan trade, blood brotherhoods were a common way of establishing political and commercial ties. While many travellers endured such ceremonies, many tried to avoid them by delegating the ceremony to their African guides or translators. Most travellers had to overcome a deep internal resistance. Not always was it blood that was exchanged, sometimes the ceremony included the eating of raw animal giblets. Nevertheless, rituals of blood brotherhood were always connected with the exchange of body fluids. For a European of the nineteenth century this was without doubt a great obstacle. For the British traveller John Hanning Speke the exchange of blood with an African was unthinkable. He replied to his African counterparts that for a Briton the expression of friendship was bodiless and limited to emotional manifestations or the exchange of gifts. In the many negotiations for protection treaties, which the German traveller Rochus Schmidt engaged in during his journeys in the 1880s, rituals of blood brotherhood played an important role. He endured the rituals, as he wrote, »with a sour look«, and insisted that his African counterpart washed his forearm before the ceremony – a rather helpless attempt to soothe the exchange of body fluids with hygienic procedures.[53]

The fact that, despite their disgust and internal resistance, the travellers endured the ceremonies indicates how dependent they were on local infrastructures. By exchanging their blood with African chiefs, they hoped to get what they needed for their own progress: guarantees of their safe-conduct, porters, food and water. Europeans tried to reduce blood brotherhoods to a lavish ceremonial nature, thus denying or ignoring their wider impact on establishing political relationships. Only a few explorers were interested in establishing permanent relationships with the chiefs; the majority simply traded their blood for supplies in order to continue on their way. This changed when Europeans began to become involved in the ivory and arms trade, or founded stations – half of them scientific, half of them early colonial projects. Perhaps one of the most successful European traders, Stokes, not only used blood brotherhoods for establishing ties with chiefs and trading partners, he was also among the few Europeans who married the daughter of an African.[54] During Reichard's expedition

---

53 Schmidt, *Kolonialpioniere*, op. cit. (note 48), p. 53; John Hanning Speke, *Journal of the discovery of the source of the Nile* (London: Dent, 1969), p. 261.
54 Ralph A. Austen, *Northwestern Tanzania under German and British Rule. Colonial Policy and Tribal Politics, 1889–1939* (New Haven: Yale University Press, 1968), p. 23.

to Unyamwezi, with the aim of founding a station, he became intensely involved in local diplomacy and had to hold several blood brotherhood ceremonies. Not always, it seems, did African chiefs meet the expectations of the Europeans. Being evidently disappointed, Reichard and his colleagues reported that the chiefs were only a little interested in the ceremonies but were more interested in the gifts. This view of the African chiefs has some plausibility: the increasing caravan traffic often contributed to a commercialisation of relationships between locals and strangers.[55]

Epilogue

Rituals of blood brotherhood in the contact zone of European exploration should remind us how ambiguous the situations were in which travellers interacted. The representatives of the metropolis or of Europe did not always act as such. It was not European modernity that came with these travellers to Africa, it was rather a vision of it, one that had to be performed in a contact zone. The traveller might have conjured out of his travelling boxes the newest wonders of European technology, but he was and remained dependent on local infrastructures, technologies and knowledge. For this short moment in history, when Europeans used the infrastructure of the East African caravan trade, they were, by the threat of their downfall, obliged to adapt to local knowledge and practices. As the example of blood brotherhoods shows, the travellers used the vocabulary of diplomacy which was common in the interregional caravan trade. Their bodies, constructed as an essential difference, acted in ceremonies that were expressions of »other« body cultures. The body itself was endangered by illnesses, hardships and conflicts with Africans. The resources which they needed for maintaining their metropolitan *habitus* were not always accessible. What Fabian describes as ecstasies of the travellers, i.e. the trespassing of intellectual frames in moments when their experiences were beyond the comprehensible, was not only a matter of discourse but also of their bodily practices.[56]

Moreover, this vision of modernity that German travellers celebrated in front of real or imaginary Africans was only one among others that were circulating in Eastern Africa at that time. Berlin might have been the inspiring metropolis for German travellers, but for many East Africans this role was clearly held by Zanzibar. It was not only an important commercial centre and the starting point for trading caravans and European expeditions; it was an intellectual and cul-

---

55 See in detail Pesek, *Koloniale Herrschaft*, op. cit. (note 1).
56 Fabian, *Out of Our Minds*, op. cit. (note 21), p. 8.

tural centre as well. It was there that all the consumer products that came to the African interior were trans-shipped, and it was there where the steamships from Europe, India and the Arab peninsula stopped. During the second half of the nineteenth century, Zanzibar rose to become a regional centre of Muslim scholarship, which maintained close and lively relationships with the religious centres of Cairo, Istanbul and Bombay. With the Muslim scholars came new ideas of religion, politics and society to East Africa. New cultural practices such as dances, fashion and culinary arts made their way into the African mainland from Zanzibar.[57] German travellers were well aware of the cultural and economic influence of Zanzibar in the African interior. Reichard describes Zanzibar as the »Paris« of East Africa, which haunted the fantasies of Africans. For them Zanzibar with its stone houses, electric street lamps, and metropolitan flair was the »city of wonders«.[58] Wherever the European traveller happened to arrive in Eastern Africa, he somehow lamented that the impact of Zanzibar was already present. Just as the German expeditions were a means of transferring and performing representations of modernity, caravans of Zanzibari and coastal traders brought with them their own imaginaries of historical change in the nineteenth century. As I have argued, both imaginaries were closely connected to each other. But to tell this story, this would need to be the subject of another article.

---

57 For Zanzibar as regional centre of Muslim scholarship and education see: B. G. Martin, »Notes on some members of the learned class of Zanzibar and East Africa in the nineteenth century«, in: *African Historical Studies* IV (1971), 3, pp. 525–545; Randall Lee Pouwels, *Horn and Crescent: Cultural Change and Traditional Islam on the East African Coast, 800–1900* (Cambridge: Cambridge University Press, 1987); Edward A. Alpers, »East Central Africa«, in: Nehemia Levtzion & Randall L. Pouwels (eds.), *The History of Islam in Africa* (Oxford: James Currey, 2000); Anne K. Bang, *Sufis and Scholars of the Sea. The Sufi and Familiy Networks of Ahmad bin Sumayt and the Tariqa 'Alawiyya in East Africa c. 1860–1925* (Ph.D. thesis, University of Bergen, 2000); for its commercial role in Eastern Africa see in particular R. W. Beachey, »The Arms Trade in East Africa in the Late Nineteenth Century«, in: *Journal of African History* 3 (1962), pp. 451–467; R. W. Beachey, »The East African Ivory Trade in the Nineteenth Century«, in: *Journal of African History* 8 (1967); Abdul Sheriff, *Slaves, Spices, and Ivory in Zanzibar : Integration of an East African Commercial Empire into the World Economy, 1770–1873* (London: James Currey, 1987); for Zanzibar as an origin of new cultural practices see: Terence O. Ranger, *Dance and Society in Eastern Africa, 1890–1970: the Beni-Ngoma* (London: Heinemann, 1975); Majorie Ann Franken, *Anyone Can Dance. A Survey and Analysis of Swahili Ngoma. Past and Present* (Ph.D. Thesis, University of Massachusetts, 1986); Laura Fair, »Dressing up. Clohting, class and gender in post-abolition Zanzibar«, in: *Journal of African History* 39 (1998), 1, pp. 63–94.

58 Reichard, *Deutsch-Ostafrika*, op. cit. (note 23), pp. 80–81.

Becoming Modern through Education

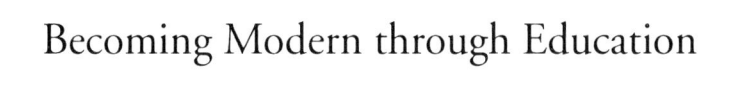

Modern Indians: the Training of Indigenous Teachers in Post-Revolutionary Mexico

Eugenia Roldán Vera

An article written in 1929 by an indigenous student from Chiapas who was training to become a rural teacher summarized what the »modern« Mexican teacher should be like:

The modern teacher must teach everything within his reach according to the level of his students, he should never inflict inadequate punishment, be selfish or act in a pretentious way towards local villagers. I have seen men who, when they go back to their own villages after studying in the city, become very self-important and do not even want to talk; they think they are superior to their friends and brothers ... [The modern teacher] should not show bad habits in his own land; the Indian who has been emancipated through his study should be kind and humble towards his fellow countrymen ... He shall never consider his job as a stronghold of power; he should simply be a social leader disinterestedly guiding his community.[1]

This student seemed to have appropriated the particular discourse of modernity proclaimed by the *Casa del Estudiante Indígena* (House of the Indian Student)– a state-funded institution located in Mexico City intended for the training of indigenous male teachers who were meant to go back to their own places of origin as ›agents of change‹. His view of the modern teacher entailed elements of a reformist pedagogy as well as of a code of conduct that was meant to prevent the teacher clashing with rural communities. This was indeed a peculiarly modern idea of teaching, as self-contradictory as any modern idea can be. According to the program of the *Casa del Estudiante Indígena*, this select group of indigenous students should grow accustomed to the needs and comforts of the urban world, but they should not reject their previous lifestyle completely; they should remain indigenous enough to want to go back to their villages and for their communities to accept them.

Now, how did this student from Chiapas come to express these ideas as his own? Were his views only an internalisation of what the school had taught him? What effect did the school have upon the habits and the ways of thinking of

---

1 Celestino Bravo P., »Tres factores que impiden el progreso y la civilización en nuestro país«, in: *El Indio: Revista de la Casa del Estudiante Indígena*, (September 1929), Num. 2, p. 20. (All quotations are my translations from the Spanish).

its – mostly mature – indigenous students? How did students' responses affect subsequent government programs regarding the indigenous population?

In this essay I examine the interaction between a state ideology of modernity, its agents and a small segment of the subjects to be modernised – a group selected from the indigenous population. My analysis focuses on one of the sites in which that interaction took place, the short-lived *Casa del Estudiante Indígena* (1926–1932). Assuming that modernity does not simply mean ›westernisation‹, but also involves a wide range of approaches to representing processes of social transformation and strategies for dealing with those processes (hence the ›multiple‹ character of modernity),[2] I analyse the emergence and constant reformulation of those representations and strategies in a particular school context. I understand the school to be a privileged site for the production and reproduction of modernity or a particular figuration of modernity, one which is deeply marked by a specific dynamic of constant negotiation between processes of control and processes of appropriation.[3] In this respect, with the example of the *Casa*, I argue that a significant aspect of the social transformation and mass mobilisation that characterised Mexico in the post-revolutionary period (1920s-1930s) consisted of a process of appropriation of the discourses of modernity and a refashioning of individual and collective representations according to the new elements introduced by these discourses. To the methodological question of whether the »subaltern« can speak clearly and distinctly apart from the state discourse that defines it,[4] I do not aim to define the »pure« Indian – as the authorities of the *Casa* did in their recruitment of students – but I consider the indigenous students and their process of self-representation in a relational manner, their identities being defined neither as the reflection of the state discourse on citizenship and nationalism nor as mere resistance against it, but as a variety of responses to it.[5] These responses can be traced in the administrative documents of the school – students' published and unpublished writings, their complaints, and student association initiatives, among others – which form the basis of my study. In my analysis I will first identify the strategies of control associated with the modernity narrative

---

2 Shmuel N. Eisenstadt, »Multiple Modernities«, in: *Daedalus*, 129, (2000), 1, pp. 1–29.

3 Justa Ezpeleta & Elsie Rockwell, »Escuela y clases subalternas«, in: *Educación y clases populares en América Latina*, ed. by María de Ibarrola & Elsie Rockwell (México: Departamento de Investigaciones Educativas, Centro de Investigación y Estudios Avanzados del IPN, 1985), pp. 195–215.

4 Gayatri Chakravorty Spivak, »»Can the Subaltern Speak?«, in: *Marxism and the Interpretation of Culture*, ed. by Cary Nelson and Lawrence Grossbergg (Urbana, Il: University of Illinois Press, 1988), pp. 271–313. See also Greg Grandin, »Can the Subaltern be seen? Photography and the Affects of Nationalism«, in: *Hispanic American Historical Review* 84, (2004), 1, pp. 83–111.

5 Tracy Lynne Devine, »Indigenous Identity and Identification in Peru: Indigenismo, Education and Contradictions in State Discourses«, in: *Journal of Latin American Cultural Studies* 8, (1999), 1, pp. 63–74.

and then I will examine the varied strategies by which students appropriated it and how they contributed to modifying the state's policies towards indigenous peoples.

A modernity project

For the state emerging from the revolutionary struggles of 1910–1920, the modernity project was related to both westernisation and nationalism. The state policies in the 1920s were concerned with the stabilisation of rural and urban masses that had been mobilised by the preceding social revolution. Such policies comprised a program for the integration of the masses (*incorporación de las masas*, in the language of the time) into an inclusive idea of nation and for their involvement in a national economic project that comprised the modernisation of agriculture and the industrialisation of the country. These policies were accompanied by the dissemination of secular ways of thinking that were supposed to make the people more productive and loyal to the state, and by the spreading of the rituals and symbols of national identity. The indigenous population, which comprised around 20 per cent of the country's total population, should thus be assimilated (*incorporación del indígena*) into the way of life of the mixed (*mestizo*) and white population.[6]

Education – and later agrarian reform – were conceived as the main means to achieve those goals, and the *Casa del Estudiante Indígena* was one of the institutions created by the educational reform programs of the 1920s. Funded jointly by the Ministry of Education and the individual state governments, its official purpose was to »bridge the evolutionary gap that separates the Indians from the present time, transforming their mentality, tendencies and customs, to make them join civilised life and to fully incorporate them into the Mexican social community«[7]. Yet the *Casa* was a rather extraordinary and expensive initiative: by taking a few hundred indigenous students out of their localities and bringing

---

6 In Mexico in 1928, out of a total population of fourteen million some four million people were considered to be Indians. Of them, more than one million did not speak Spanish. The indigenous population was made up of eighty different ethnic groups with forty-nine different languages. Engracia Loyo, »Educacion de la comunidad, tarea prioritaria, 1920–1934«, in: *Historia de la alfabetización y de la educación de adultos en México 2. De Juárez al Cardenismo. La búsqueda de una educación popular* (México: Secretaría de Educación Pública – Instituto Nacional de Educación para Adultos, 1990), pp. 339–411; in particular p. 360.
7 Secretaría de Educación Pública (SEP), *La Casa del Estudiante Indígena. 16 meses de labor en un experimento psicológico colectivo con indios, febrero de 1926-junio de 1927* (México: Talleres Gráficos de la Nación, 1927), p. 35.

them to a boarding school in Mexico City, it stood in contrast to the policy of expansion of rural schooling designed to take elementary schooling and teacher training institutions to peasant and indigenous regions throughout the country. The reason for this discrepancy in educational policies was the fact that the *Casa* was conceived first and foremost as an »experiment«. Its main implicit – only occasionally stated – objective was, in the words of President Calles, to »prove to the privileged classes of Mexico City that the Indians have a great capacity to educate themselves, if only the right conditions are given to them«[8]. As a »psychological experiment«, the institution had thus to legitimate the 1920s state ideology as »revolutionary«– affirming that, »with equal opportunities, Indians were as capable of progress as whites and *mestizos*«[9]. If the post-revolutionary state assumed as its main purpose the provision of those »equal opportunities«, an eventual failure of the »psycho-social experiment« of the *Casa* would bring under question the very foundations of the state.

The *Casa* was to gather Indians of ›pure‹ races aged 14 to 18 years from regions that were »not yet incorporated«, who were able to speak an indigenous language, and who were mentally and physically fit. These Indians were to live in the *Casa* for a few years, while attending regular primary schools in the vicinity, spending time in a variety of technical workshops (electrical, car mechanics), and taking part in national and local festivals. In this way the students would get to mingle with all the racial groups and social classes of Mexico City and eventually contribute to the »unification of the national soul«[10]. In the *Casa* itself the students had a routine of physical education, hygiene, group study and civic ceremonies. The students also acquired basic agricultural knowledge and skills in small industrial crafts – soap making, food preservation and tanning – that were considered useful for life in the countryside. After 1928 the students began to be trained as rural teachers, with a program similar to those of the normal rural schools. Regular festivals, theatre performances (by the students), public lectures and movie shows in the school theatre were meant to bring the surrounding neighbourhood in touch with the *Casa*, as well as bring in extra cash for the school's finances. In its design, arrangement and discipline, the *Casa representaed* (in its dual sense as reflection and as construction) civilisation and integration for everyone who had something to do with it: the indigenous

---

8 Memorandum from Rafael Ramírez to the Undersecretary of Education, 27 October 1930. Archivo Histórico de la Secretaría de Educación Pública (hereafter AHSEP), Escuelas Rurales DF, Internados Indígenas, Box 3, File 6214/36, docs. 1–2.
9 Enrique Corona to the Secretary of Public Education, 1 April 1927, in: AHSEP, Escuelas Rurales DF, Internados Indígenas, Caja 2, Exp. »Casa del Estudiante Indígena – Enseñanza«, docs. 23–27.
10 Manuel Mesa A., »Informe del visitador especial«, in: *Memoria relativa al estado que guarda el ramo de educación pública el 31 de agosto de 1932,* Vol. I (México: Talleres Gráficos de la Nación, 1932), p. 31.

students, the surrounding community, society in general and the government itself.

After a two to six year stay in the *Casa*, the indigenous students were supposed to go back to their places of origin, where they would convey what they had learned. Although at the beginning it was not the policy of the institution to train these students as teachers, they were at any rate expected to be ›agents of change‹ who contributed to the transforming of the habits of their countrymen, to make them healthier and more productive; encourage them to think rationally and be less superstitious; motivate them to speak Spanish, participate in sports, drink less alcohol; and, to turn them into good citizens. This was to contribute towards bringing the indigenous population out of poverty and integrating them into the mainstream of progress in the country.[11]

In the state narrative that led to the creation of this institution, the dominant view was that the indigenous population was asking for assistance so as to become civilised, even though Indians were not totally aware of their wants. As an example of how the government defined indigenous needs, one could cite the speeches of two indigenous delegates presented in 1922 at the first Congress of Cultural Missionaries (teachers appointed by the Education Ministry to travel to rural areas in order to train existing rural teachers and work towards the modernization of rural communities). In line with the tone of the whole congress, an *Otomí* Indian stated that, »If the Mexican government educates our races, developing our aptitudes, we will stop being a burden on the nation and will become agents for progress.«[12] According to a *Zapoteca* Indian speaking on behalf of »the *Zapoteca* race«: »I think the time of my redemption has come and that you – the missionaries – are in charge of wisely leading me with your example so that I can improve my social condition.«[13] Government officials used these kinds of discourses to legitimate their programs of indigenous incorporation.

The idea underlying the foundation of the *Casa* was, therefore, a typical modernity narrative with a homogenising, unifying purpose, based on the following assumptions: a) it defined the Indian race as being in a miserable state of ignorance and as suffering (even though the Indians were not aware of this; they needed to ›wake up‹); b) it made the Indians ask to be ›redeemed‹ from their state of ignorance; c) it made the government responsible for providing the means to produce indigenous agents working for the ›redemption‹ of their own people.[14]

---

11 For a detailed history of the *Casa*, see: Engracia Loyo, »La empresa redentora. La Casa del Estudiante Indígena«, in: *Historia Mexicana* Vol. 46, (1996), 1, pp. 99–131; Alexander S. Dawson, »›Wild Indians‹, ›Mexican Gentlemen‹, and the Lessons Learned in the *Casa del Estudiante Indígena*, 1926–1932«, in: *The Americas*, 57, (2001), 3, pp. 329–361.

12 Catarino Tovar, *Discurso que pronunciara en el Congreso de Misioneros* (Mexico: Dirección de Educación y Cultura Indígena, AHSEP, December 1922), Caja 21, Exp 19, doc. 1.

13 »Habla la raza zapoteca en uno de sus dialectos.« Ibid., doc. 4.

14 According to Walter Mignolo, modernity narratives are homogenising western world views that

However, this modernity narrative – like virtually every narrative of its kind – was not free of ambiguity. Indian folklore traditions (music, textiles, pottery) were considered of value to the Mexican culture, and Indio motifs were among the symbols of national identity promoted by the post-revolutionary government at the same time as official rhetoric referred to the assimilation of the Indian into a ›civilised‹ form of life. And whereas that rhetoric defined the Indian as in need of redemption by the civilisation provided by the post-revolutionary state, it at times also represented the Indian as a ›pure‹ creature that faced the risk of being corrupted by urban or *mestizo* forms of life. This ambiguity, typical of the concept of race in the modern world, lay at the core of the *Casa* and permeated its whole discourse. It further made possible the varied – even contradictory – appropriation of its policies by its students, teachers, officials of the Ministry of Education, and members of the public.[15]

As the speeches of the indigenous delegates in 1922 suggest, most indigenous communities had been historically exposed in one way or another to some kind of homogenising modernity narrative coming from a central authority – indeed, these delegates associated the modern rural teachers and cultural missionaries with the Spanish Christian missionaries of the sixteenth century. Nevertheless, life in the *Casa* was for all the students a powerful experience which influenced the shaping of their identities and caused them to develop *ad hoc* strategies to adapt to the trans-location they were experiencing. In what follows, I will discuss the particular impact that this institution had upon the students with regard to three distinctly modern values: awareness of their individuality, self-governance and realisation of their capacity to change themselves and to change reality.

Individualisation

In the *Casa* students were subjected to a process of individualisation. After a selection procedure that included a detailed enquiry about the family and social

---

are meant to be extended to all mankind: the expansion of Christianity (16th-17th centuries), the more secular civilising mission (19th century), modernisation and industrialisation (20th century), and the globalisation of liberal-democratic values (last part of the 20th century – 21st century). Walter Mignolo, *Local Histories / Global Designs: Coloniality, Subaltern Knowledges, and Border Thinking* (Princeton: Princeton University Press, 2000). See also Enrique Dussel, *1492. El encubrimiento del otro (Hacia el origen del »mito de la modernidad«). Conferencias de Frankfurt, Octubre de 1992* (Santafé de Bogotá: Ediciones Antropos, 1992). For a reflection on the modernity narrative in the definition of the »campesino« (peasant) in post-revolutionary Mexico, see Guillermo Palacios, *La pluma y el arado. los intelectuales pedagogos y la construcción sociocultural del »problema campesino« en México, 1932–1934* (México: El Colegio de México – Centro de Investigación y Docencia Económicas, 1999), pp. 15–16.

15 For a discussion of such ambiguity regarding the Indian race in Mexico, see Deborah Poole, »An Image of ›Our Indian‹: Type Photographs and Racial Sentiments in Oaxaca, 1920–1940«, in: *Hispanic American Historical Review* 84 (2004), 1, pp. 37–82.

background of the candidate (in the form of questionnaires filled out by rural education inspectors),[16] actions taken at the moment of their arrival further defined them as individuals and fixed them as Indians. They were given a surname if they did not have one; they were obliged to hand in the clothes characteristic of their community in exchange for western-style garments; and, their anatomical and physiognomic features were thoroughly measured. If a candidate did not meet the requirements of »Indigenousness« – certain racial features and/or knowledge of an indigenous language – he could be rejected.[17] Photographs of the students published in a 1927 school yearbook, show them in their initial state as having no name, and as mere representatives of an indigenous race. Photographs of their appearance six months later include a name and a surname, as well as details concerning their ethnic origin.

Moreover, the individual potential of each student was encouraged through all of the school activities. Although the academic demands of the *Casa* were not very high, students were subject to a meritocratic system in many of their tasks. Participation in sports was a core activity that lent itself admirably to such a system. Physical education was held up as an ideal at that time. With respect to the Indian, it was seen as having the power to redeem him from his natural »laziness« and to drive him away from his predilection for alcohol.[18] In the *Casa*, sports were one of the main instruments for social integration – especially after just joining the school when the students' command of Spanish was not good. School sports competitions were also meant to promote individual excellence. Writing competitions for the students in upper grades were also a common feature; selected texts were published in the school magazine *El Indio* and in the luxuriously presented book *La Casa del Estudiante Indígena: 16 meses de labor en un experimento psicológico colectivo con indios*.[19] The best students had the chance of becoming the bearers of the national flag at civic ceremonies,

---

16 There were three questionnaires: one on personal background, another on family background and a third on the geographic, social and economic characteristics of the region of origin. See for example the file of student Julián Etzana in: AHSEP, Escuelas Rurales DF, Internados Indígenas Caja 3, Exp. 6214/70.
17 The process of selection failed the first time because the request sent by the *Casa* to the governors of the states was interpreted by many as an opportunity for a subsidised education in the capital, and they sent the children of relatives and friends. Since the majority of candidates of the first round were not considered »indigenous« enough by the authorities of the *Casa*, a second selection process was launched, this time assigned to the Federal Inspectors of Education. See SEP, *Memoria que indica el estado que guarda el ramo de Educación Pública* (México: Talleres Gráficos de la Nación, 1932), pp. 26–27.
18 For an analysis of the role of sports in the transformation of the Indian in the rhetoric of the post-revolutionary government, see Keith Brewster, »Redeeming the ›Indian‹. Sport and Ethnicity in Post-Revolutionary Mexico«, in: *Patterns of Prejudice* 38, (2004), 3, pp. 213–231.
19 This book was published as part of an effort by the government of President Calles to prove that his social policies were working and give legitimacy to the government's revolutionary »revolutionary« project. Other departments of the SEP published similar volumes, all elegantly

and of having their hand shaken by distinguished visitors to the school (from ambassadors from foreign countries to the Mexican President himself).

Individualisation, however, was not supposed to exclude a cooperative spirit, something that was thought to be a virtue of the Indians, because of their communal life-style. However, as we will see, these two values often clashed.

»Self-governance«

The concept of »self-governance«, according to the school director, was to be promoted among students, both as individuals and as a group. As individuals, the particular discipline of the *Casa* was meant to make the Indians responsible for themselves. The director, Enrique Corona, described the school structure as an »evolutionary disciplinary system«, by means of which »the will of the students would be directed as long as they were not able to do so themselves.« This system was to »develop the »spontaneity«, »virility« and »responsibility« of students; »make them think and act with regard to the logical consequences of their acts; and, train them for freedom«. It was aimed at »forming free and self-sufficient men, sensitive to duty and capable of influencing the community for the good of all«.[20] This notion of self-responsibility applied above all to household chores, which, according to the original rules of the *Casa*, should be largely left in the hands of the students. Every student had to do his own laundry and ironing, and take part in house cleaning and dishwashing chores. These tasks were expected to be carried out with great humility and even »gratitude« in view of the benefits the students were receiving.[21] Beyond that, this system to teach self-governance did not mean a great deal – students were not free to go out of the house, and all of their activities were regulated and supervised – but the discourse about individual responsibility and freedoms was an important one.

With respect to collective responsibility, students were asked to take part in the school council and in a board created in 1932 to solve instances of behavioural problems; they were also encouraged to publish a school magazine and form literary or cultural organizations. As the director Enrique Corona commented regarding the »Cuauhtémoc« student association: »This society serves

---

printed and lavishly illustrated. Secretaría de Educación Pública (SEP), *La Casa del Estudiante Indígena,* op. cit. (Note 7).

20 SEP, *La Casa del Estudiante Indígena*, op. cit. (Note 7), p. 39; AHSEP, Escuelas Rurales DF, Caja 6, Exp. 24, doc 14.

21 Del artículo »La incorporación del Indio«, de »El Imparcial«:»... Las labores caseras, pegar botones, lavar los trastos, servir la mesa, regar los prados, cultivar la hortaliza, limpiar el estanque, barrer los diversos departamentos, arreglar las calles adyacentes, son siempre desempeñadas por ellos con puntualidad y presteza, pues su decoro y dignidad nativos les hacen comprender el desdoro de un incapacitado, y piensan que con esa laboriosidad corresponden el beneficio que reciben.« Cif. Ibid., p. 76.

me as an adequate means to put the students on the right track towards self-governance – based on honour, duty and responsibility, with corresponding rights – which is the system we promote in this institution.«[22]

The promotion of cooperation was also aimed at achieving collective responsibility. The *Casa* had a cooperative in which the money the students received from their state governments was invested, and through which the products made in the students' workshops were sold; the profits were used to buy materials for the *Casa* supplementing funds from the Secretary of Public Education (Secretaría de Educación Pública, SEP). Students were taught how to form and run such cooperatives so that when they returned to life in the countryside, they would have the means to help their communities become self-sufficient and independent. The cooperative as conceived by *Casa* staff was such that »from the very beginning students should get used to planning, through forming corporations for savings, investment and cooperation, in order to develop the habits of work, order, economy and organisation«. In this way, the students »will not get used to expecting everything from the government«[23].

Agents of change

The measures directed towards individualisation and self-governance were an important means by which to raise indigenous students' awareness of their capacity to change themselves. It was also important to turn this into an awareness of their capacity to effect change in others, and give them the desire to do so.

To make the Indians true ›agents of change‹, they were first made to construct a difference between themselves and their respective communities of origin. They were to perceive the positive effects that study, sports, healthy eating, bathing and daily combing of their hair had upon them. These were habits that did not exist where they came from. In an end-of-year ceremony, no less than the president of the country Plutarco Elías Calles reminded the graduates: »You have to remember how you were when you came here, how it was at your parents' place, full of poverty, where you only saw ruin and disgrace. Now I want… you to tell me what spiritual and intellectual differences there are between you and your parents.«[24]

Through the creation of this difference, the need for civilisation was to be

---

22 Enrique Corona, »Labores desarrolladas por los alumnos de la Casa del Estudiante Indígena, durante los meses de febrero, marzo y abril de 1929. Materias que reciben los dos grupos del Departamento Normal y todos los alumnos de la casa«, 30 April 1929. AHSEP, Escuelas Rrurales DF, Caja 3 »Internados Indígenas«, Exp. 6214/ 13, docs. 14–18.
23 AHSEP, Escuelas Rurales DF, »Internados Indígenas«, Box 3, File 6214 / 16, docs. 1–2.
24 Manuel Mesa A., »Informe del visitador especial«, in *Memoria relativa al estado que guarda el ramo de educación pública el 31 de agosto de 1932,* Vol. I (México: Talleres Gráficos de la Nación, 1932), p. 26.

inculcated. »It is important to create needs in the Indian« – said the director – »so that when he goes back to his land he will make an effort to improve his economic resources and be in a position to overcome poverty.«[25] Moreover, it was believed that the various tasks of daily life were in and of themselves a sign of civilisation, because they implied a constant renewal of the person who undertook them. Indeed, the monotony of rural life was considered one of the causes of the social and economic alienation of the peasant, and one of the reasons for his lack of motivation to improve his life. Actually, being »re-absorbed« by such a monotonous environment was one of the main risks indigenous teachers had to face upon their return to their places of origin. A rural teacher trained in the urban normal school wrote when faced with this reality:

A truly heroic spirit is needed in order not to be discouraged when one is confined by mountains, without newspapers, magazines and letters which bring information about life outside; without books and entertainment that give the spirit new strength; without talks and lectures about recent events ... The teacher should try by all means... to constantly renew himself, so that he can fight against the heavy mountain of the local environment, and avoid being re-absorbed by it. He needs a spiritual and intellectual agility to overcome the indolence accumulated amongst our peasants throughout the years.[26]

Therefore, the students trained in the *Casa del Estudiante Indígena* should grow to become flexible individuals, adaptable to different kinds of circumstances and able to perform a variety of roles. The very physical displacement they experienced in being transferred to the *Casa*, often from very far-away regions, was an essential element of the ›translocality‹ that should dominate their future lives, as well as being the beginning of a process of multiplication of roles that was seen as a positive aspect of their jobs.[27] What was expected from a rural teacher was far more demanding than that required of an urban teacher. It involved a multiplicity of roles: a rural teacher should be an intellectual and a moral leader of the community, a doctor, a father to the students, a kind of ›priest‹ and a political activist.

Finally, the desire to go back to their communities had to be stimulated. This was done through a number of measures: by allowing the students to preserve their indigenous languages (through the formation of societies where these languages were spoken); through the formation of student associations (the »Sociedad Cuauhtémoc«, for example, was meant »to keep alive in the students the pride of belonging to the rural masses and the firm purpose of serving their

---

25 Interview with Enrique Corona in: »Una visita al plantel de la raza autóctona«, *Excelsior* (no date), quoted in SEP, *La Casa del Estudiante Indígena*, p. 64.
26 Julia Ruisánchez, »Problemas que se presentan al maestro rural«, in: *El Indio*, Num. 2, (September 1929), p. 26.
27 On »translocality« as an essential component of modernity, see Eisenstadt, »Multiple Modernities«, op. cit. (note 2).

own races and regions of origin in the future«[28]); through the teaching of subjects such as »study of rural life« or »social organisation for the improvement of community life«; through inspiring lectures by intellectuals of the time; through writing competitions about the subject of returning home; and, through a number of patriotic rituals, songs and theatre pieces performed at festivals on the topic of home.[29]

Appropriation

To all these mechanisms of control set up at the *Casa*, the students responded, obviously, with a selective appropriation that involved both processes of resistance and empowerment. A large number of students did assimilate the ideals of individualisation, self-discipline and redemption from past backwardness, and became empowered in significant ways: they learned to organise themselves in ›modern ways‹; they formed alliances with organisations external to the school; they wrote petitions to the SEP authorities requesting certain materials for their self-improvement; and, they started their own magazine. Some of them even developed a desire for ›civilisation‹ that went in a direction that was not exactly the one intended by the authorities: having acquired technical skills that would allow them to get a job in the city, many graduates preferred to stay there and not go back to their communities. This forced the *Casa*, three years after its foundation, to change its approach towards the training of rural teachers, and to insist on the importance of going back. Other students rejected the institution and escaped, or refused to do anything until they were sent back home. Of the ones who stayed, some resisted participating in the cooperative (they refused the forced ›investment‹ of their money there); others raised complaints about the disciplinary regime; and, others collected signatures in letters to higher authorities aimed at denouncing the maltreatment of students by prefects or the director. Many reacted against the requirement that they do their own cooking and laun-

---

28 Corona, »Labores desarrolladas por los alumnos de la Casa del Estudiante Indígena«, 30 April 1929. AHSEP, Escuelas Rrurales DF, Caja 3 »Internados Indígenas«, Exp. 6214 / 13, docs. 14–18.
29 For example, the following oath was taken at the Monument of Independence by the students: »We, the students of the Casa del Estudiante Indígena, in our own names and in those of the Indian races of Mexico, swear solemnly before the remains of the Heroes of Independence, that we will return to our lands of origin and cooperate in the strengthening of our nationality, with work, with social justice, and, if necessary, with our lives.« Enrique Corona, »Informe de las labores desarrolladas en los meses de mayo a septiembre inclusive«, 17 October 1929. AHSEP, Escuelas Rurales DF, »Internados Indígenas«, Box 3, File 6214 / 13, doc. 20. I am citing Dawson's translation »›Wild Indians‹, ›Mexican Gentlemen‹«, op. cit. (note 11), p.349.

dry, which was supposed to make them self-sufficient and self-governed men. What is interesting about both the processes of empowerment and resistance is that students articulated their aspirations, demands and complaints within the frame of the discourse of modernity upon which the institution was based. It was within the parameters of that discourse that the Indians were defining their identities.

The first student magazine, a manuscript entitled *Inspiraciones del Indio* (»Inspirations of the Indian«) (1928) that did not get into print, reflected a need of students to express themselves and turn the teachings they were receiving into action: »We invite all our classmates to take part in its preparation, in order to show that we are also capable of writing and of expressing our ideas.«[30] In a way, this statement suggests that students had a desire to take things into their own hands and become the subjects of their own destiny. As a student suggestively wrote, »punctuality« is a habit that makes one »more or less respectable, because it shows that the person has authority, that is, that he is the owner of his own existence«[31]. Indeed in this first magazine, the articles were not edited by any teacher and were much more spontaneous pieces than those published in the rather official, printed magazine *El Indio* (»The Indian«), which appeared from 1929 onwards. *Inspiraciones* included essays that assimilated the dominant school discourse of redemption from backwardness: for example, a poem about the consequences of drinking *pulque*, a popular alcoholic drink; statements of intention concerning self-improvement and the determination to effect transformation in their home communities; and inspired compositions about life in the countryside. But it also had pieces expressing great sorrow. Poems such as »I do not want to live« or »The Poor« referred to the miserable condition of the Indian – either expressing a social concern or indicating the existential sadness experienced by the authors living in the *Casa*. Interestingly, the level of grief expressed in these texts is not typical of the students' writings published in school yearbooks. Clearly, the *Casa* was trying to convey a very positive picture of the transformation its students were undergoing, which included what the students were learning about how to articulate and communicate their deepest feelings in written forms taught at school. Indeed, the acquisition of these writing skills enabled the students to express different aspects of their identities, which they also learned to mobilise strategically to obtain benefits in certain circumstances.

The capacity of *Casa* students to represent themselves in a variety of ways is particularly evident in the documents written at the time of a conflict that

---

30 »Inspiraciones del indio«, 1 April 1928. AHSEP, Escuelas Rurales DF, Internados Indígenas, Caja 3, Exp. 6214/41, doc. 3. To my knowledge, none of the pieces written by the students in this magazine were included in *El Indio*. The latter included many official pieces and only few written by students themselves.

31 Ibid., p. 5.

broke out in this institution in 1932. At the beginning of that year a group of students sent a letter to the Minister of Education in which they protested against some of the school conditions and demanded the removal of the director and the prefects. The letter, which was signed by nearly a quarter of all the students, complained about the lack of school supplies and poor medical care. It denounced the school authorities for treating them »as if they were servants not students« by obliging them to do domestic chores: laundry, ironing, and dishwashing. The students also complained that the food was not varied and that they were »not given the freedom to attend the workshop of their choice«[32]. One may conclude that, what the authorities represented as dignifying tasks that would produce responsibility and humility in the students, were seen by some of the Indians as demeaning activities that debased their social status to that of servants – most of the Indians who lived in the cities were in fact servants. The conflict that this letter unleashed led to an investigation by the SEP, and to the formation of alliances between dissident students and external agrarian organisations (alliances that were anyway encouraged by the institution) so as to defend themselves against what they considered the »despotic« behaviour of the *Casa's* authorities. An internal inquiry as to the motives of all the students who signed the petition eventually led to the expulsion of dissident leaders and the removal of director. The damage caused by this revolt to the reputation of the *Casa* contributed to its closure later that year.

As part of their rhetoric of complaint, students often employed the discourse of the Indian living in poverty and needing to become civilised, whose backwardness prevented him from knowing how to behave. Adopting the government's language of modernity, they frequently referred to their villages as places where the people were »suffering an ancestral misery«, and suggested that only by means of a civilising education would they »be saved from their present suffering«[33]. Whereas this served in some circumstances to allow the students to portray themselves as the future agents of the salvation/redemption of their own communities, on other occasions they chose to use a rhetoric of demand (demanding to be helped) or of complaint. Thus, when conflict arose in 1932, the leading dissident students sought support from the governors of their respective states in the following terms: »Since the director of this institution ... does not give us enlightening lectures that may lead us on the good path, it is impossible for us, who are beginning our training as men of character, to suddenly become

---

32 AHSEP, Escuelas Rurales DF, Caja 6, Exp. 24, doc. 12.
33 »En mi pueblo hoy está padeciendo la miceria que más allá en los tiempos pasados venía sufriendo y comprendo que mi pueblo para que llegue a civilizar, es indispensable que tenga una buena escuela de enseñanza para bien de sus hijos, entonces salbará de lo que hoy sufre.« (Juan Solorza, winning text in a writing competition, SEP, *La Casa del Estudiante Indígena*, op. cit. (note 7), p. 132.)

the way he wants us to be.« They ended their letter by asking for »justice for the needy«.³⁴

By contrast with such sentiments emphasising marginalisation, other documents tended to underline the protagonist role Indians had played in the revolution. A letter in support of the dissident Indians sent to the Ministry of Education by the Alliance of Agrarian Communities emphasized that the officials should remember that the revolutionary fight was basically fought by »humble and honest peasants, the parents of these indigenous students who await, with all justice, the fruit to which they are entitled.«³⁵

To what were the students »entitled«? By the time this letter was written, the language of individual rights had to a considerable extent permeated the language of some of the indigenous students and that of their allies outside the school. The dissident students wrote: »We are being expelled/criticised because we truly defend our rights, and also the rights of the others;«³⁶ and the Alliance of Agrarian Communities opined that the students »should not be obliged to abdicate their rights as free men«³⁷ by submitting to the absurd requirements of the director or the school. The dissident students' motto was a modern one: »In the Name of Reason and Justice«. This contrasted with the comparatively more conservative, official motto of the *Casa*: »Hope, Fight and Succeed« (*Esperar, luchar, triunfar*).³⁸

So, if the director understood the purpose of disciplinary system of the *Casa* as being to form »free and self-conscious men«, freedom and self-consciousness were terms employed by indigenous students to protest against that same disciplinary system. The authorities also reacted within the parameters of the modernity discourse in which they were positioned, partly through the ambiguities of the notion of race. The way in which the director explained what had happened was by describing the leaders of the revolt as »a group of *mestizo*« who had either been admitted into the school by mistake or as a consequence of the recommendations of influential people. The assumption was that *mestizos* were less pure and more prone to desire an urban lifestyle. Consequently, these students were »individualists« who had »preferred to satisfy disorderly appetites of a material nature and follow careers that have nothing to do with the rural environment.« He blamed the *Casa* for not having done enough to develop a »co-

---

34 Francisco Valenzuela and Franco V. Aguilar to Macario Gaxiola, governor of the state of Sinaloa, 30 June 1932. AHSEP, Escuelas Rurales DF, Caja 6, Exp. 21, doc. 35
35 Filiberto Villarreal, secretary of the Alianza de Comunidades Agrarias de la República to the Secretary of Public Education, 27 July 1932. AHSEP, Escuelas Rurales DF, Caja 6, Exp. 14, doc. 4.
36 Letter from Valenzuela and Aguilar to Macario Gaxiola, 30 June 1932 (note 32).
37 Letter from Villarreal to the Secretary of Public Education, 27 July 1932 (note 33).
38 AHSEP, Escuelas Rurales DF, Caja 6, Exp. 21, doc. 1.

operative spirit«[39]. On another occasion their lack of discipline was attributed to their having been in contact with urban life. One of the students who signed the dissidents' petition stated that he had done so because on one occasion the director had taken away his scarf, arguing that he should not be »snobbish« (*fifí*), and that a scarf was not necessary in the countryside where he came from. The director was of the opinion that some of the students were getting too used to the comforts of ›civilised‹ life. Indeed, the way in which the *Casa* director's superior, the head of the department of rural schools, made sense of the students' complaints against their maltreatment by the prefects ran along similar lines. He suggested that »maybe it is because of their contact with metropolitan life that students had become vain, arrogant and even disrespectful«[40]. The implications of this were that Indians in their natural state were humble, kind, respectful and willing to serve, which were the qualities most praised by visitors to the house – qualities which reproduced the prejudices people held concerning the proper behaviour of a subjected race.

Not all the writings of the indigenous students referred, however, to the modern values they had learned at the *Casa*. Many students were also ready to invoke their traditional values as something positive. A text written by Matías Zempoaltécatl entitled »To you, my sister«, described the ideal virtues that an Indian woman should have, while introducing the modern qualities that she should embrace:

> You are quiet, honest, maybe because of your lack of [modern] culture; how saintly you are; how pure are your actions, a thousand times better than the manners and actions of others who presume to be educated. You have not violated the way you dress, you have not profaned your long black hair, you have not added to your pupils the artificial beauty of make up … You remain still immaculate, your features are purely those of our old Mexico; you are not ashamed of being Indian, Mexican … You are the pure source of folklore … [Yet] you need freedom, you have to get rid of the rude yoke without drifting away from your woman's path; for if you get rid of your yoke, our homes will change, they will be the model, the basis of our future nation.[41]

We are here dealing here with a gendered discourse in which the woman is expected to be keeper of tradition and to embody more conservative values than the men. Still, this is a discourse that at the same time gives value to ›indigenousness‹ and expresses the need to change what ›indigenousness‹ means: Indians are repositories of a wise and pure culture that should be preserved, but they can also

---

39 Corona, »Informe«, January-May 1932. AHSEP, Escuelas Rurales DF, Caja 6, Exp. 24, doc. 13.
40 Rafael Ramírez to the SEP's Chief Administrative Official, 7 November 1929. AHSEP, Escuelas Rurales DF, »Internados Indígenas«, Caja 3, file 6214 / 16, Exp 1–2).
41 Bravo, »Tres factores que impiden el progreso y la civilización en nuestro país«, op. cit. (note 1), p. 7.

become agents of their own transformation into something better. Is this ambiguity a contradiction resulting from an indigenous assimilation of the modernity project of the state? In my view, all these writings should be read also as a strategy of self-representation resulting from the need of indigenous subjects to adapt to a variety of circumstances in order to survive in a rapidly changing society. By locating traditional values in the body of the woman, they can relieve some of the anxieties they held regarding their entrance into the ›civilised‹ world.[42]

Modernity, Multiple Representations and Change

Life at the *Casa* brought about significant changes in the self-representation of its indigenous students. Their reactions were not mere expressions of resistance against the imposition of a state ideology; they were above all the result of processes of adapting not only to change, but also to something that modernity discourse considered to be one of the features of modern civilisation: variability in life. In a sense, the variety of tasks they were made to carry out the multiplicity of physical and intellectual activities reinforced by the number of different outfits they had to change into in one day (sports, military and school uniforms; the clothes of workers, farmers or »Indians« in a theatre play) – suggests that students were constructing their identities in a rather performative way.[43] They were not only the spectators of an urban, ›civilised‹ society, but they were also acting out roles within this society and becoming models of civilisation for others. This insistence on performance made them learn to represent themselves in various ways according to different circumstances. In effect, this was part of their training in adaptability. When the students expressed themselves, either in a school essay, a speech, a petition or a complaint, they employed, depending on the situation, either the language of the suffering Indians who needed assistance or a language that vindicated the important role that Indians played in modern society in general. They might employ a language that asserted traditional indigenous values or a language incorporating modern values using the rhetoric of individual rights and freedoms as a way to deal with some of the anxieties derived from experiencing accelerated change.

Modernity at the *Casa del Estudiante Indígena* was more than a fluid and mul-

---

42 For the gendering location of tradition in indigenous representations, see Grandin, »Can the Subaltern be seen?«, op.cit (note 4), pp. 94–95.
43 On the performative construction of identity, see Judith Butler, *Bodies that Matter. On the Discursive Limits of ›Sex‹* (New York: Routledge, 1993); Judith Butler, *Excitable Speech. A Politics of the Performative* (London: Routledge, 1997).

tiple discourse used by all those involved in the institution. It was also a tool used to adapt to and make sense of a situation of rapid social change. Whereas the state's modernity project both adapted, and reinforced itself through, this »experiment«, the indigenous subjects actively responded to it and developed their own means to understand the changing world and to define their place within it. They learnt to represent and empower themselves in the variety of new social and political situations they had to face, and to mobilise those aspects of their identity that suited particular circumstances. Furthermore, they internalised the modernising rhetoric and started to play out the tradition-modernity dichotomy in order to gain the upper hand in the symbolic representation of backwardness of life in rural areas. Through the use of this rhetoric they managed to subvert some of the aspects of the social order by causing the authorities to abandon this type of educational experiment and create other types of schools for teachers in rural areas, where the students had much less contact with urban life.

If we assume that a typical feature of modernity is its capacity to generate multiple ways of representing social change, by enabling its students to develop the skills for dealing with the features and ambiguities of a rapidly-changing world, the *Casa* definitely succeeded in making its indigenous students »modern«. Although no study has been done of the further trajectory of the graduates of this institution who did go on to become rural teachers, other studies of the training of indigenous teachers in twentieth-century Mexico show how those teachers developed strategies to adapt and subvert the modern and homogenising discourses they were exposed to during their training. When they went back to the local realities of rural areas, they often developed representations of the social order that totally contradicted official representations (though articulated through the conceptual elements they had learnt during their training); and which even led them to take part in rebellions against the government in defence of what they considered ›traditional‹ indigenous forms of life.[44] This phenomenon does not mean that the modernisation of the Indians through education in post-revolutionary Mexico ›failed‹; on the contrary, it is revealing of the variability of interpretations that the modernity project can generate.[45] Only by means of an inclusive and variable notion of modernity is it possible to understand the full complexity of the particular appropriation of it by a significant segment of the indigenous population.

---

44 See Natividad Gutiérrez, *Nationalist Myths and Ethnic Identities. Indigenous Intellectuals and the Mexican State* (Lincoln and London: University of Nebraska Press, 1999).
45 On the plurality of interpretations as inherent in modernity, see Ibrahim Kaya, »Modernity, Openness, Interpretation: A Perspective on Multiple Modernities«, in: *Theory and Methods* 43, (2004), 1, pp. 35–57.

Representations of Modernisation and Vocational Education in Argentina at the Beginning of the 20th Century

Verónica Oelsner

Introduction

Argentina, a former Spanish colony on the La Plata River in South America, experienced major infrastructural transformations after becoming independent in 1816. The declaration of independence from Spain was followed by a period of profound political struggle. When the political panorama became stabilised around 1860, the ruling classes embarked upon the promotion of various measures to convert the old colonial territory into a modern nation state.[1] As a consequence, the country began to participate more actively in the international market and received a significant level of foreign investment in infrastructure. Also the immigration of European workers was strongly promoted to sustain productive growth. The resultant economic and demographic development was without precedent. The area of cultivable land grew from 0.58 million hectares in 1869 to 24.32 in 1914; during the same period, exports increased from 30.8 million *pesos oro* to 501.8 million. As a result of immigration policies Argentina received some 7.5 million people between 1870 and 1914.[2] These remarkable incremental growth statistics point to further dramatic transformations, such as the demand for new labour skills, the formation of new social groups, the dete-

---

1 The first stages of Argentine independence were very turbulent. The antagonism between two opposing political factions, the *unitarios* and *federales*, resulted in a long series of civil battles from 1820 to between various bands of people and provinces. After the defeat in 1853 of the federalist Juan Manuel de Rosas, who as Governor of the province of Buenos Aires represented the country between 1830 and 1853, and the victory of the *unitarios* of Buenos Aires in 1861, the conflicts abated. A new phase in Argentina's development began, in which the ruling classes were no longer preoccupied with in-country fighting, but were now able to concentrate on the building up of the foundations of a modern nation state. See Tulio Halperín Donghi, *Una nación para el desierto argentino* (Buenos Aires: Centro Editor de América Latina, 1982).
2 Nevertheless, a significant number of these immigrants did not stay long. The net increase in the number of immigrants for the period 1870–1914 was 3.1 million people, which nonetheless represents a very large number, especially taking into account that, at the beginning of this period, the census of 1869 counted 1.9 inhabitants in total. See Ernesto H. Kritz, *La formación de la fuerza de trabajo en la Argentina: 1869–1914* (Buenos Aires: Centro de Estudios de Población, 1985).

rioration in living conditions of some groups, and the emergence of new social claims.

In the context of this modernisation process, consideration began to be given to vocational education. Diverse actors were involved in the early discussions and plans arising from them. Included among them were members of the Ministry of Education and the Ministry of Agriculture leaders of non-state organizations, such as the Society for Industrial Education, the engine driver's union, the Salesian religious order of Don Bosco, and philanthropic societies. According to their varying affiliations, actors emphasized the different functions and potential benefits of vocational education. It could foster industrial development, help the working classes to become financially independent, or discipline the new social groups and, in that way, contribute to the maintenance of social tranquillity.

This article aims to explore the relationship between imagined functions of vocational education and diverse perceptions of modernisation in Argentina at the beginning of the twentieth century, as they appeared in proposals and debates during the period of institutionalisation of the first vocational schools. The argument of the article is twofold. First, it is proposed that the different functions ascribed to vocational education were related to the different perceptions and concerns that the different actors involved had about the processes and consequences of modernisation. Secondly, drawing upon the ›multiple modernities‹ perspective,[3] it is suggested that the different functions associated with vocational schools resulted from a particular Argentinean figuration of modernity, one that was different from configurations of modernity in European contexts, where modernisation first emerged.[4]

The ›multiple modernities‹ approach emphasizes the existence of culturally specific forms of modernity shaped by distinct cultural heritages and socio-political conditions.[5] The main idea that is shared here is that these different paths of modernity are the result of different starting points.[6] Given the colonial past, the region around the La Plata River lacked of its own previous structures or

---

[3] Among others representative articles, see Shmuel N. Eisenstadt, »Multiple Modernities«, in: *Daedalus* (2000), Nr. 129/1, pp. 1–29; Shmuel N. Eisenstadt, »Vielfältige Moderne«, in: *Zeitschrift für Weltgeschichte* 2 (2001), pp. 9–33; Dominic Sachsenmaier & Jens Riedel (eds.), *Reflections on Multiple Modernities. European, Chinese and Other Interpretations* (Leiden, Boston, Köln: Brill, 2002); Gerard Delanty, »An Interview with S.N. Eisenstadt: Pluralism and the Multiple Forms of Modernity«, in: *European Journal of Social Theory* (2004), Nr. 7(3), pp. 391–404.

[4] Shmuel Eisenstadt, »Some Observations on Multiple Modernities«, in: *Reflections on Multiple Modernities*, ed. by Dominic Sachsenmaier & Jens Riedel (Leiden, Boston, Köln: Brill, 2002), op. cit. (note 3), p. 27.

[5] Shmuel Eisenstadt, Jens Riedel & Dominic Sachsenmaier, »The Context of the Multiple Modernities Paradigm«, in: *Reflections on Multiple Modernities* ed. by Dominic Sachsenmaier & Jens Riedel (Leiden, Boston, Köln: Brill, 2002), op. cit. (note 3), p. 1.

[6] Prasenjit Duara, »Civilizations and Nations in a Globalizing World«, in: *Reflections on Multiple*

models of vocational education that could be taken as a starting point.[7] Because the expansion of arts and crafts in the colonial territories contradicted the interests and economic policies of the Spanish crown, Spanish authorities repressed all kinds of handicraft development.[8] Likewise, they strictly banned every attempt to build trade unions, which sought to protect the meagre arts and crafts industries.[9] The apprenticeship system, based on the European model, had in fact been implemented at the La Plata River, but only weakly and in a maladapted form, in order to obtain a cheap labour force and not to train it.[10] For that reason, institutions for defining and setting professional standards, and monitoring the granting of professional qualifications – institutions such as the European guilds – were not available in the region. Consequently, in Argentina around 1900 when modernizing attempts were in full swing, vocational education was a yet uncharted field. In that context, diverse actors with different concerns and understandings could get involved in the debate and the task of shaping vocational education.

This article begins with some consideration of representations of vocational education as a tool for modernisation. It then highlights representations of vocational education and modernisation at the time when the debate about vocational education first took off and when the first institutions were built. In so doing, the contributions of three of the most important actors involved in this debate and institution building are explored. Finally, the article summarises and contrasts the dominant representations of each group, emphasizing the multi-

---

Modernities ed. by Dominic Sachsenmaier & Jens Riedel (Leiden, Boston, Köln: Brill, 2002), op. cit. (note 3), p. 79.
7 As Mariluz Urquijo has pointed out, the region at La Plata River lacked of an »authentic guild tradition«. See Mariluz Urquijo, *La industria sombrerera porteña: 1780–1835. Derecho, sociedad, economía* (Buenos Aires: Instituto de Investigaciones de Historia del Derecho, Editorial Dunken, 2002), p. 87.
8 As Quiroz has affirmed, handcraft professions were merely »tolerated«. See Francisco Quiroz, *Gremios, Razas y Libertad de Industria. Lima Colonial* (Lima: Facultad de Ciencias Sociales, Universidad Nacional Mayor de San Marcos, 1995), p. 9.
9 Up until the end of the 18th century, and along with the official opening of the La Plata River region to free trade, which inundated the local market with imported products, there were only a few attempts to establish trade guilds, with the aim of helping artisans to defend their livelihoods. These attempts were suppressed on each occasion – justified on the basis of liberal argument in support of free trade. See José M. Mariluz Urquijo, *Estado e industria* (Buenos Aires: Ediciones Macchi, 1969) and José M. Mariluz Urquijo, *La industria sombrerera porteña, 1780–1835. Derecho, sociedad, economía* (Buenos Aires: Editorial Dunken, 2002).
10 See Lyman L. Johnson, *The development of slave and free labor regimes in late colonial Buenos Aires, 1770–1815*, occasional paper no. 9 (Latin American Studies Consortium of New England, University of Connecticut, University of Massachusetts, Brown University, 1997) and Hilda Sábato & Luis A. Romero (eds.), *Los trabajadores de Buenos Aires. La experiencia del mercado: 1850–1880* (Buenos Aires: Editorial Sudamericana, 1992), p. 178.

plicity of meanings they expressed as well as the role of Argentina's particular configuration of modernity in shaping such developments.

Representations of Vocational Education in the Context of Modernisation

At the beginning of the twentieth century, several governmental as well as nongovernmental actors such as the already mentioned Ministries of Education and Agriculture, the Society for Industrial Education, the engine driver's union, Don Bosco's Salesians and philanthropic societies were involved in decision-making about the institutionalisation of vocational education as a way of facing up to what they identified as the challenges experienced in Argentina due to the modernisation process. The idea that vocational education had modernising potential was not completely new. Some proposals in this direction had already been made, all of them attempting to promote the economy and the progress of Argentina, but they were not taken up. Among these was the initiative of Manuel Belgrano (1770–1820), still in colonial times, to create professional schools, based on the new ideas circulating in, and the institutional models available in, Spain where he undertook legal studies.[11] But his modernising plan did not match the colonial interests of the Spanish Crown and were rejected. A further failed attempt was a proposal in 1870 to establish »Departamentos de enseñanza profesional de agronomía« (Departments for Professional Agronomic

---

11 Belgrano was a *criollo*, a son of Spaniards born at La Plata River, who held important appointments in the local colonial government. His eight-year long residence in Spain, where he studied law, exerted a great ideological influence on him. He read, amongst others, the works of Spaniards like Foronda, Arriquíbar, Campomanes, and Jovellanos, but also Rousseau, Condillac, Locke, Genovesi, Turgot, and D'Alembert. Some of these writers emphasized technical training as one of the means to get Spain out of its economic backwardness. Once back in South America, Belgrano became one of the most important exponents of the Enlightenment and helped to establish a number of different public institutions. See Comité Argentino para el Bicentenario de la Revolución Francesa, *Imagen y recepción de la Revolución Francesa en la Argentina* (Buenos Aires: Grupo Editor Latinoamericano, 1990); Rodolfo E. Pastore, & Nancy Calvo (eds.), »Cultura colonial, ideas económicas y formación superior ›ilustrada‹ en el Río de la Plata. El caso de Manuel Belgrano«, in: *Prohistoria* 4 (2000), pp. 27–58; Rodolfo E. Pastore, »Formación económica de la élite intelectual rioplatense en el marco de la España ilustrada: el caso de Manuel Belgrano«, in: *Spagna Contemporanea*, 19 (2000), Nr. 18, pp. 33–48; and Eduardo Acero Sáez, *Crónica de la formación profesional española. Tomo primero: La formación profesional desde el comienzo del aprendizaje artesanal hasta finales de los años sesenta* (Madrid – Fuengirola: Ediciones Técnicas y Profesionales, 1992).

Education) and to set up mining schools.[12] The person making the proposal was the president of the country, Domingo Faustino Sarmiento (1811–1888), who largely took US-American institutions as the model.[13] The establishment of an »Escuela Nacional de Artes y Oficios« (National School of Arts and Crafts), was proposed by the Minister of Instruction Dr. Manuel Pizarro (1841–1909) in 1881,[14] based on the French *Ecole d'Arts et Métiers*, but it also failed to gain acceptance.[15]

It was only around the turn of the century, in the context of growing concerns about newly-experienced social and economic changes and the challenges attributed to what was labelled as ›modernisation‹, that proposals for vocational schools proliferated and were eventually implemented. As was the case in other countries, at the end of the nineteenth century, vocational education began to be seen more and more as a possible instrument for economic and social transformation.[16] Nevertheless, as mentioned in the introduction, the preconditions for

---

12 Details of the proposal to develop these schools can be retrieved from the *Memorias* of the Ministry of Education. See Ministerio de Justicia, Culto e Instrucción Pública, *Memoria presentada al Congreso de 1873 por el Ministro de Justicia, Culto e Instrucción Pública* (Buenos Aires: Imprenta de La Unión, 1873).

13 Sarmiento was an educator, statesman, journalist, and writer. He began his professional career at the age of 15, as a teacher in a rural school, and very soon became a legislator in his province of San Juan. He was also director of the National Council of Education, governor of his province, as well as president of the country. He had previously spent more than three years in the USA attending pedagogical congresses, from which he took away many ideas for the educational programmes he was to later propose. See Alberto Gerónimo Mosquera, *Sarmiento: jurista y universitario* (Buenos Aires: Dunken, 2003).

14 Ministerio de Justicia, Culto e Instrucción Pública, *Memoria presentada al Congreso Nacional de 1881 por el Ministro de Justicia, Culto e Instrucción Pública* (Buenos Aires: Imprenta de la Penitenciaría, Imprenta de la Penitenciaría, 1881), pp. 87–88.

15 For Pizarro, as well as for many other Argentine politicians and intellectuals of that time, France represented a much admired political and cultural model. Especially after becoming independent from Spain, which was from then on demonized as the origin of most of the Argentine problems, a new reference society was needed. France was the model, the ideal, which many Argentine politicians and intellectuals looked to, in their endeavour to modernise their society and political institutions. Pizarro was Minister of Instruction during the first part (until 1882) of the first presidency of Julio A. Roca (1880–1886). Under the motto of ›peace and administration‹, this liberal-conservative government introduced major changes in Argentina: amongst others, the separation of church and state. As a firm catholic and defender of the position of the church against the government, Pizarro did not last long in his function as education minister. He was replaced in 1882. See Comité Argentino para el Bicentenario de la Revolución Francesa, *Imagen y recepción de la Revolución Francesa*, op. cit. (note 11).

16 See, for instance, Herbert Kliebard, *School to Work: Vocationalism and the Struggle for the American Curriculum, 1876–1946* (New York: Teachers College Press, 1999) for the United States; Thomas D. Curran, *Educational Reform in Republican China: the Failure of Educators to Create a Modern Nation* (Lewinston, Queenston, Lampeter: The Edwin Mellen Press, 2005), in particular chapter VII, for China; Agustín Escolano Benito, *Educación y Economía en la España Ilustrada* (Madrid: Ministerio de Educación y Ciencia, 1988) for Spain; Frank Safford, *The Ideal of the Practical: Colombia's Struggle to Form a Technical Elite* (Austin & London: Uni-

thinking about the form and aims of vocational education differed from those in other countries.

The actors involved belonged to diverse sectors of society, represented varied interests, and thus concentrated on different aspects. As a result, their ideas about the capabilities and functions of vocational education in a modernizing context differed. The outcome of their engagement in this field was the establishment of more than ninety schools within about two decades. These institutions had different orientations, types of qualifications, and were organized by diverse supporting groups. In what follows, various understandings of vocational education and its potential in enhancing the future of the country, the conditions for labour and production as well as the social and political circumstances will be outlined. Three of the most important institutional promoters of vocational education were the National Ministry of Education, the Society for Industrial Education, and the engine driver's union La Fraternidad.

The National Ministry of Education: Vocational Education as an Instrument of Social Control in a Modernising Society

From the end of the nineteenth century onwards, several liberal-conservative politicians repeatedly proposed the introduction of a vocational orientation into the formal educational system. Vocational education was considered essential in educating and disciplining the masses of people, who could not afford to enter higher education. It was seen as offering an alternative for a major portion of the student population aspiring to enter the ›Colegios Nacionales‹ (national secondary schools), which were directed towards preparing students for university, and were, at that time, the only educational path available after primary school.

The promoters of these reform attempts did not seem to associate vocational education with possible benefits for the productive sector or the economy, which was still largely based on the exporting of raw materials (meat, leather, and grains) and the importing of finished products with practically no local production content. It seems that they rather saw a vocational orientation within the school system as a means of controlling the existing social order, which was being jeopardized by the social transformations resulting from modernisation, such as the growing middle class, which was demanding more political participation, as well as the formation of an organized working class, which was beginning to articulate its dissatisfaction with labour conditions.

Education, which since national independence in 1816 had been seen as a key instrument to bring Argentineans out of »barbarism« so as to become a mem-

---

versity of Texas Press, 1976) for Colombia; María C. Heuguerot, *El origen de la Universidad del Trabajo del Uruguay: »una colmena sin zánganos«* (Montevideo: Ed. de la Banda Oriental, 2002) for Uruguay.

ber of »civilization«, which was »more advanced« in other parts of the world,[17] had became general and »encyclopaedic«[18] in orientation. National secondary schools, erected during the second half of the nineteenth century, focused almost exclusively on the humanities, since they were meant to fulfil the political function of preparing the next generation of leaders and bureaucrats, who were expected to bring the country forward.[19] This educational model satisfied these expectations for some decades, but already by the end of the nineteenth century, it had begun to be perceived as deficient, especially in the light of the economic and social transformations the country was undergoing. Politicians began to see the need for a more practical education stream as an alternative to these elite-orientated schools.

As part of efforts to modernise the country, during the entire nineteenth century, and especially during its last decades, the Argentinean government promoted European immigration in order to increase the population as well as to boost the economy through the supply of »industrious« people.[20] The resultant waves of, »mass immigration«, mainly from Italy and Spain, dramatically transformed the social structure within a few decades.[21] On the one hand, a working class had begun to organize itself and to articulate common demands by holding strikes and sometimes also engaging in acts of violence.[22] On the other hand, an emerging middle class attempted to get involved in the political

---

17 Torcuato S. Di Tella, »La controversia sobre la educación Argentina: Sus raíces«, in: *Revista mexicana de sociología* 28 (1966), Nr. 4, pp. 855–888.
18 This term was used in pejorative manner to indicate the marked tendency to focus on abstract knowledge in the curriculum.
19 Juan Carlos Tedesco, *Educación y Sociedad en la Argentina (1880–1945)* (Buenos Aires: Ediciones del Solar, 1993, 2nd edition).
20 See Tulio Halperín Donghi, »¿Para qué la inmigración? Ideología y política inmigratoria y aceleración del proceso modernizador: el caso argentino (1810–1914)«, in: Richard Konetzke & Hermann Kellenbenz (eds.), *Jahrbuch für Geschichte von Staat, Wirtschaft und Gesellschaft Lateinamerikas* (Köln-Wien: Steiner, 1976), pp. 437–488.
21 See Fernando Devoto, *Historia de la inmigración en la Argentina* (Buenos Aires: Sudamericana, 2003).
22 The European workers brought not only their industrial skills. They also brought their experiences with labour movements and their exposure to related ideas circulating in Europe at the time. It was European immigrants who disseminated socialist and anarchist ideas amongst workers and who led in the organisation of labour movements and protests (José Panettieri, *Las primeras leyes obreras* (Buenos Aires: CEAL, 1984), p. 7; Hilda Sábato & Luis A.Romero (eds.), *Los trabajadores de Buenos Aires. La experiencia del mercado: 1850–1880* (Buenos Aires: Sudamericana, 1992), p. 267). These protests multiplied especially during the last decade of the nineteenth century to reaching a peak around 1903–1904 (Julio Godio, *El movimiento obrero argentino* (Buenos Aires: Legasa, 1987). See also Verónica Oelsner, »Die europäische Einwanderung in Argentinien (1810–1914): Ideal, offizielle Förderung und Auswirkungen auf die argentinische Arbeitswelt«, in: *Themenportal Europäische Geschichte* (2007), URL: http://www.europa.clio-online.de/site/lang__de/ItemID__254/mid__11554/40208419/Default.aspx.

life of the country, by creating a new political party[23] and by seeking employment in the public service. Thus, they aspired to have access for their children to the humanities-based national secondary schools, which were seen as the doorway to public administration careers. For all these reasons, around the turn of the century some (mainly conservative) politicians began to deliberate on how to implement vocational education.

The diversification of education towards professional instruction was supposed to be the great remedy. As to the working class, vocational education would tame the masses, equipping them with work-related knowledge and discipline, which should also allow them to improve their economic situation and, in that way, to come to better terms with their own social condition. Vocational schooling would also keep the growing middle class away from the secondary schools and university, designed to educate the ruling class, and consequently would keep the middle class away from politics and governmental functions.[24]

However, none of the proposed plans was to be successfully implemented. These were generally interpreted as attempts to reduce the number of national schools or the number of national school students. The debate over the proposed reforms was constantly focussed on the social and political consequences of restricting access to general education. There was much less debate about the training structures being proposed. Historically, manual labour had been disdained, while academic careers were seen as a noble endeavour and as the way of advancement up the social scale. Because humanities-based education was widely held in such high esteem, the majority of the democratic oriented politicians did not want it to be reformed; they did not want to see restraints on access to social and political advancement that national schools facilitated. Consequently, all the reforms seen as threatening the existing structure of formal education were repudiated. Nevertheless, the arguments brought forward by the advocates of reform provide insights into understandings circulating at that time of the social dimensions of modernisation as well as of vocational education as an instrument to respond to it.

In 1899, Minister of Education Osvaldo Magnasco[25] (1864–1920) presented

---

23 This party was called Radical Civic Union and it took over government in 1917.
24 See Tedesco, *Educación y Sociedad*, op. cit. (note 19); Roberto H. Albergucci, *Educación y Estado. Organización del Sistema Educativo* (Buenos Aires: Editorial Docencia, 1996); Roberto A. Miranda & Osvaldo M. Iazzetta, *Proyectos políticos y escuela 1890–1920* (Buenos Aires: Ediciones Matética S.A., 1982); Guillermina Tiramonti & Claudio Suasnabar, »La reforma educativa nacional en busca de una interpretación«, in: *Revista APORTES para el Estado y la Administración Gubernamental* (2000), Nr. 15.
25 Magnasco was born in Argentina, in the northwest province of Entre Ríos. Besides being Minister of Instruction, he was a jurist and professor at the Faculty of Social Sciences at the University of Buenos Aires. He wrote articles and books on military codes, penal law, international relationships and education.

a proposal, in which he pleaded for the abrogation of encyclopaedism and the reorientation of education along utilitarian lines.[26] The majority of the national secondary schools would become practical schools – for the teaching of arts and crafts, agriculture, industry, mining and commerce.[27] His argumentation was much more focussed on political and social considerations of how to deal with the masses, rather than on concrete technical or economic shortcomings. In a speech given in Parliament in 1900 defending his bill, he proclaimed that practical schools were needed

[...]to face or solve no less than a threefold problem; socially, the orientation of our generations to paths of labour; politically, the materialization of Alberdi's[[28]] formula: pacification of aspirations through industry, which represents the pacification means par excellence; and economically, to bring national production out of the ruts in which it is today.[29]

Magnasco's project was firmly supported by José B. Zubiaur[30] (1856–1921), an experienced educational authority, who was a determined opponent of general humanities-based education. In his own words, national schools

[...]served virtually to do no more than to train bad office employees and worse *politiqueros* [pejorative term for unprofessional politicians]. If we were to restrict their number and replace them with practical industrial schools, as Minister Dr. Magnasco has rightly proposed [...], we would not only disseminate skills, which Argentine youth lack in

---

26 The complete text can be found in *Diario de Sesiones de la Cámara de Diputados* (Buenos Aires: 1899), pp. 641–662.
27 Consejo Nacional de Educación, *El Monitor de la Educación Común*, Band XVII (Buenos Aires: 1899–1901), pp. 798.
28 Alberdi was one of the most important intellectuals and politicians in Argentina in the nineteenth century. As a jurist and a writer, he exerted a great influence on the formation of Argentine institutions. His work *Bases y punto de partida para la organización política de la República Argentina*, written in 1852, served as a basis for the formulation of the first national constitution in 1853. In this book, he postulated European immigration and industrial activities as the most effective means of bringing civilisation. See Juan B Alberdi, *Bases y punto de partida para la organización política de la República Argentina* (Buenos Aires: [1852] 1915).
29 Congreso Nacional, *Diario de Sesiones de Cámara de Diputados* (Buenos Aires: Compañía Sudamericana de Billetes de Banco, 1900), p. 1245. This and all following quotations were originally in Spanish. All translations have been done by the author of this article.
30 Zubiaur was a jurist. He entered the Ministry of Instruction at the age of twenty-five. He also served as a teacher at secondary level, a rector of National School, a member of the National Council of Education, and an inspector of middle schools. As director of the Department of Public Instruction at the national Ministry of Instruction, he travelled and represented the Argentine government in Europe. Aspects of his experience abroad were reflected in his books: *The Prevention of Crime through the Education and Correction of Children, Overview of the Education in the Argentine Republic, The Practical and Industrial Instruction in the Argentine Republic* (English translation of book titles).

practice, but we would also contribute to lowering educational costs as well as reducing its catastrophic results.[31]

For Zubiaur, »practical and industrial education« would not »represent a magic wand, which changes the state of affairs«, but it should be, »without doubt, one of the most powerful elements, which contribute to its modification«[32]. His main point of criticism addressed the narrow orientation of secondary school education as well as the general ambition to obtain ›doctoral degrees‹. From Zubiaur's point of view, practical and industrial training would

[…]reduce the number of people, who, without intelligence and vocation, are seduced by the effortless success of an elementary, deficient and superficial preparation as well as by the allure of a *doctoral* degree, which represents the highest form of ambition, are attending national schools, which are simply university-oriented institutes and are productive of employment-mania.

Nevertheless, the opposition in parliament declared the project undemocratic and successfully rejected it.

A few years later in 1905, similar ideas were proposed by a member of parliament, Emilio Gouchón[33] (1860–1912). He referred to the need to expand the educational avenues on offer after primary school. For this purpose, he proposed the establishment of different educational trajectories – many oriented towards vocations – within the existing school structure. Amongst other things, he proposed that a two year long course of »enseñanza primaria especial« (special primary education) be introduced, which Gouchón also called a »professional« course. He presented it as an intermediate »gear« between primary and secondary school. In reality, it was post-primary tuition, which would offer only applied subjects and which had no connection with other educational facilities. He described his proposal as follows:

In favour of the large number of children, who complete primary school every year but cannot or don't want to go to secondary school, I propose the establishment of agricultural, mining, mechanics or commercial schools with two-year courses, whose goal would be the preparation of foremen for agriculture, mining or mechanics as well as commercial employees, with a training and culture superior to the average person in the population.[34]

---

31 José B. Zubiaur, *La enseñanza práctica e industrial en la República Argentina* (Buenos Aires: Felix Lajouane Editor, 1900), p. 387.
32 Zubiaur, *La enseñanza práctica,* op. cit. (note 31), p. 386.
33 Gouchón was a lawyer, politician and, a member of the Civic Radical Union. He was a member of parliament between 1898 and 1912. Apart from educational topics, he wrote about issues related to immigration into Argentina. One of his books was entitled »Notes on colonization and immigration«.
34 Congreso Nacional, *Diario de Sesiones de la Cámara de Diputados* (Buenos Aires: Establecimiento Tipográfico »El Comercio«, 1905), p. 130.

His main motivation in putting forward this bill was to solve the political and social problems, which he saw as a consequence of the prevailing system of »catalogue education«, which, in his view,

[...]defoliates everything and deepens nothing, which burdens the mind without developing intelligence, and which instead only causes an irreparable debilitation and an irremediable aversion to work.[35]

The new curriculum and school structure should combat the dominant preference for humanities-based education, the general aspiration for civil service posts (the so-called ›employment-mania‹), as well as the distaste for manual occupations:

With this bifurcation I aim to contest the intellectual mediocrity, the superficial spirit and the presumptuous ignorance, which arise from the habit of generalizing everything instead of learning things correctly. [...] In place of cowardly generations, we would have doughty and proud generations; in place of parasites, we would have producers.[36]

This bill failed too. However, some of these ideas were taken up again in 1916 by the Minister of Education Carlos Saavedra Lamas (1878–1959), although with only temporary success. In his speeches and essays, he referred to what he indicated as the great problems of the educational system, which should be solved through the creation of an intermediate vocational school. These problems were primarily social ones concerning secondary schools. He emphasized its limited university-focus and its ›encyclopaedism‹ which, in his opinion, led to a twofold neglect of: 1) vocational aspirations, and 2) adequate education for the majority of the population, which attended no more than primary school. In the words of Saavedra Lamas, »submerged in encyclopaedism«, the secondary school did not offer anyone efficient preparation, neither for life nor for special schools and universities.[37] Particularly affected by this problem were, according to him, sixty per cent of the children, who »only get primary education, which is insufficient to both earn one's living and to be useful to society«[38] and, as a result, threatened to disturb the social order:

Our National School completes the gradual and automatic exclusion, which begins in primary school, and leaves a new group of individuals behind with no practical orientation in life, no skills for a remunerative and honourable job. That way, they become

---

35 Congreso Nacional, *Diario de Sesiones*, op. cit. (note 35), p. 131.
36 Congreso Nacional, *Diario de Sesiones*, op. cit. (note 35), pp. 131–132.
37 Carlos Saavedra Lamas, *Reformas orgánicas en la enseñanza pública. Sus antecedentes y fundamentos* (Buenos Aires: Imprenta Argentina »Jacobo Peuser«, 1916); Carlos Saavedra Lamas, *El gobierno educacional. Discurso del Ministro de Justicia e Instrucción Pública Doctor Carlos Saavedra Lamas en la apertura de cursos de la Universidad de La Plata el 25 de abril de 1916* (Buenos Aires: Imprenta de Coni Hermanos, 1916).
38 Saavedra Lamas, *Reformas orgánicas,* op. cit. (note 38), p. 7.

confused losers, who either jump on the bandwagon of employment-mania or lag behind in unproductiveness.[39]

To battle against these problems, he proposed an intermediate level between primary and secondary school, which had to be attended by all students before being enrolled in secondary education. This planned »intermediate school« would provide students with manual skills, which they could use later in life. It was envisaged that it would also arouse an interest amongst students for vocations by offering them various »professional« courses, thereby reducing the flow of students aspiring to enter secondary schools. The new intermediate level would »complete general education, put an end to encyclopaedism, and enable students to have a vocation«. The encouragement of a vocational stream would later »make possible an alternative to university-oriented and technical studies«[40].

In 1917, a new political party, the Radical Civic Union, took over power in Argentina. Its members perceived such attempts to introduce alternative streams into the educational system as attempts to deny non-elite members access to secondary schooling and political participation. Consequently, they immediately abolished Saavedra Lamas' reform, returning to the old educational structure.[41] Instead of the intermediate school offering vocational education within the formal educational system, they decided to establish Schools of Crafts and Arts, which would be separate from the formal school system, as proposed by Manuel Pizarro many years earlier in 1881.

Society for Industrial Education: Vocational Education as a Way to Foster Industrialisation

The ›Sociedad de Educación Industrial‹ was founded in 1900 by Dr. Norberto Piñero (1858–1938), a lawyer who held several governmental positions as well as a chair at the Faculty of Law at the University of Buenos Aires. The declared aim of the Society was to build vocational schools to promote industrialization. Members of the new Society were to all become »advocates for the Society and for the creation of technical and professional schools and an industrial museum«[42]. Piñero saw the establishment of such schools as part of the »solution of the economic and educational problems«[43]. On the one hand, professional schools

---

39 Saavedra Lamas, *El gobierno educacional*, op. cit. (note 38), p. 26.
40 Saavedra Lamas, *Reformas orgánicas*, op. cit. (note 38), p. 28.
41 In fact, it was the unrestricted access to secondary school and university education, that had enabled this group to get involved in government. Thus, they rejected every official attempt to set up a vocational education stream prior to, or as an alternative to, secondary schooling.
42 Horacio C. Rivarola, *Sociedad de Educación Industrial. La acción de Norberto Piñero en la enseñanza industrial* (Buenos Aires: Talleres Gráficos de la Cía. Gral. Fabril Financiera S.A., 1952), p. 9.
43 Rivarola, *Sociedad de Educación Industrial*, op. cit. (note 43).

could contribute to bettering the situation of the lowest strata in the population. On the other hand, such schools would provide the preconditions for Argentina to become an industrialised country. Piñero himself was convinced that this would happen:

[...][B]ecause of its international position, its geographical situation, the fertility of its soil, the variety of its climate and skies, its natural forces, Argentina will be a manufacturing country in the future. It is on its way already. The energy now propelling it forward points to a fruitful future. Its industrial factories will be as potent and important as its agricultural and livestock industries. And they will employ as many people as possible.[44]

However, as he saw it, for this development to take place it was necessary to overcome a number of obstacles. These included: 1) the absence of the transmission of professional skills necessary for the elementary practice of any occupation as well as the incapability of the state to implement such training, 2) the significant preference of youngsters for theoretical studies, 3) as a result, the lack of qualified Argentine workers or their inferiority in comparison with European immigrants, and 4) the lack of interest from industrial management circles, who thought that vocational training was an excessive luxury for Argentine industries. In his opinion, some of these obstacles could be solved through the establishment of vocational education and training and its dissemination among the worker stratum. This would provide industries with qualified manpower. He saw it as crucial

[...]to establish institutions, in which youngsters will be able to get the necessary technical and practical education, to prepare the workmen and journeymen that modern industry requires.[45]

The Society aimed at concretely managing »parts of the big educational problem« by offering a new educational path, which was »practice-oriented regarding its means as well as its goals«. Like Saavedra Lamas, the Society intended to gradually transform the character and bias of instruction for the masses after primary school and, thus, to transform »the preferences of the popular stratum, redirecting it from exclusively theoretical studies and an aspiration for decorative diplomas«[46]. Each of the Society's technical coursesshould provide the students with a profession or a trade coupled with an awareness of his own autonomy as a worker, since »a profession makes an individual his own owner, it orientates life, and it promotes independency«[47]. But above all, the professional quali-

---

44 Norberto Piñero, *Sobre Educación e Instrucción* (Buenos Aires: Jesús Menéndez Librero Editor, [1911]1927), p. 125.
45 Piñero, *Sobre Educación e Instrucción*, op.cit (note 45), p. 120.
46 Piñero, *Sobre Educación e Instrucción*, op.cit (note 45), p. 123.
47 Piñero, *Sobre Educación e Instrucción*, op.cit (note 45), p. 124.

fication of workers should also foster the development and growth of nascent industries. That is why, Piñero, the president of the Society, expected industrial entrepreneurs to support the schools financially:

> It would be appropriate, if members try to expand the list of society supporters and, above all, to raise the interest of industrialists and those who need good workers. Since they will benefit from the results, it is only fair that they participate in the effort.[48]

With the main aim of recruiting and preparing workers for industry, the Society established special schools with a clear technical and professional orientation. Its first project in 1900 was a school for mechanical and electrical apprentices. The second was an evening technical design school, which was opened in 1902 and which had a cross-professional orientation targeting workers from diverse occupational branches. Later, a school for chauffeurs and car mechanics was established (in 1908) as well as a school of radio communication (in 1913), which trained workers for the post office and the army. Many other establishments followed. The members of the Society opened, reformed and closed schools, according to their criteria for what they considered as the needs of industry and the degree of success of such schools in achieving their aims.

The Engine Driver's Union La Fraternidad: Vocational Education as a Mechanism to Face the Professional Challenges of Modernisation

Newly founded trade unions in Argentina also showed some interest in education and they developed different activities in this field.[49] But it was the exception that concentrated on purely vocational education and training. In general, they offered political education as well as literacy courses, in order to foster the »enlightenment« and material progress of workers.[50] The engine driver's union La Fraternidad (The Brotherhood), however, represented one of these exceptions and it developed the most important of the vocational training programmes offered by unions at the time.

The engine driver's union La Fraternidad was established in 1887. The sig-

---

48　Sociedad de Educación Industrial, *Memorias del Directorio* (Buenos Aires: Talleres de la Compañía General de Fósforos, 1905), p. 3.

49　The first trade union in Argentina was created in 1857 by typographers. Others followed mainly after 1880, with the waves of migrants coming from Europe, immigrant European anarchists, communists and socialists played a decisive role in establishing labour unions. For an overview of labour organization in Argentina, see, among others, Edgardo J. Bilsky, *Esbozo de historia del movimiento obrero argentino: desde sus orígenes hasta el advenimiento del peronismo* (Buenos Aires: Fundación Simón Rodríguez, Editorial Biblos, 1988) and Julio Godio, *El movimiento obrero argentino* (Buenos Aires: Editorial Legasa, 1987).

50　See Dora Barrancos, *Educación, cultura y trabajadores (1890–1930)* (Buenos Aires: Centro Editor de América Latina, 1991) and Dora Barrancos, *La escena iluminada. Ciencia para Trabajadores 1890–1930* (Buenos Aires, Plus Ultra, 1996).

nificant role in the transportation of livestock for export, and in railways in particular, provided advantageous conditions for the vigorous development of this labour union. In 1895 it had 164 members, after a year, 762 members, and in 1903, nearly 1800.[51]

La Fraternidad cared about its professional reputation and standing, and concerned itself with shaping a well-defined profile for the engine driver. Many articles in the union paper concentrated on the machinist and the challenges of his daily work activities, on problems in employment procedures, on training and the need for new schools as well as libraries for affiliates. As described in the union's periodical, the profession of machinist was a hard one, in which one was exposed to coldness, rain, sun, storms, fire as well as dangers and even mortal accidents. Thus, the job required a conscious and very attentive execution and also lot of coordinating skills related to the control of engines.[52]

From the point of view of the union leaders, the priority was the establishment of professional schools aimed at the »intellectual and professional progress« of machinists in general.[53] The instruction in schools should improve their professional reputation and professional situation as well as enable them to adapt to the rapid change-over from one type of engine to another as technology improved. A union member wrote in 1914:

> To teach personnel the technical knowledge of the profession is one of the tasks to which the greatest effort should be dedicated. In that way, nurturing the intellectual growth of members of the union is complementary to the work of organizing and promoting the union.[54]

In successive articles, union members expressed similar ideas, emphasizing also the challenges of technological advance and, accordingly, the importance of workers' capabilities and skills. One union member wrote:

> The union leadership must care for the future of the union, because its progress should go hand in hand with modern evolution. The union has to improve intellectually and professionally along with the progress in engine technology[...] that way, it will soon be possible to train professionals with great technical skills. This will increase the brilliance of the profession and uproot the vulgar idea that this is just a simple manual occupation done without training and responsibilities.[55]

In another article it was suggested that:

---

51 Mónica R. Gordillo, *El movimiento obrero ferroviario desde el interior del país (1916–1922)* (Buenos Aires: Centro Editor de América Latina, 1988).
52 This very heroic depiction of the profession can be found in issue number 20 of the publication *La Fraternidad* (1909).
53 La Fraternidad, *La Fraternidad* (1909), N° 26, p. 2.
54 La Fraternidad, *La Fraternidad* (1914), N° 100, p. 5.
55 La Fraternidad, *La Fraternidad* (1917), N° 155, p. 3.

our task should give us the impulse to conquer new horizons. If machines become more complex, or more simplified or if they require greater responsibility, the nerve, which is controlling them and getting them moving, should also develop accordingly. And it should be something more than a machine, more than a mechanism, that is able to give them, with talent and specialised techniques, not only impetus but also the breath for a longer life, because in doing so, the worker will achieve the status of indispensability, will be considered essential, and he will not have, even at his bleakest hour, the sad idea of the possibility of being replaced. [56]

The members of the engine driver's union viewed vocational education as a way to face rapid technological change: to stay current, become more professional, to foster a better reputation, and, that way, to preserve their occupation. Indeed, all proposals for vocational education for machinists involved a focus on the technical aspects of their profession. Such facilities would expand all over the country and also be recognized by the State as official machinist training courses.[57] The first academy was created in the city of Buenos Aires in 1890. Further establishments would follow after 1907: two new schools were founded in the province of Buenos Aires in 1908 and shortly after that, five more in the same and in other provinces. New waves of expansion took place in 1913 and 1920. By the year 1943, the trade union claimed to have 220 schools.[58] Union members have eagerly supported these schools even until today.

Vocational Education as a Means to Engage with Modernity

Advocates of vocational education at the beginning of the twentieth century in Argentina saw it as a means to confront the changes, problems and challenges posed by the modernisation processes that the country was undergoing. The discourses examined here reflect the worries, ideas and aspirations of those at the forefront of this movement. Vocational schools were seen as a helpful institutional means to deal with and to foster modernisation, in part by replacing old structures, but mainly by venturing into uncharted territories. Early advocates – including Belgrano and, later, Sarmiento and Pizarro – saw specialised schools as an essential medium for promoting and developing production in industry, agriculture, mining and commerce, and also for supporting the moral and material progress of the region, following the path taken by more modern

---

56 La Fraternidad, *La Fraternidad* (1917), N° 156, p. 2.
57 Jorge Larroca & Armando Vidal, *Rieles de lucha: aporte para la historia del sindicalismo argentino* (Buenos Aires: La Fraternidad, 1987).
58 La Fraternidad, *La Fraternidad* (1943), Nr. 766.

countries.[59] Towards the end of the nineteenth century, as economic changes and the social consequences were becoming evermore pervasive, voices calling for vocational schools proliferated. Along with the multiplication of actors involved in the field, discourse on the relationship between vocational schools and modernisation took on a wider spectrum of issues.

As shown in this article, in some cases, vocational schools were primarily associated with the social aspects of modernisation, such as changes in the social structure, imminent democratisation of the political system, and struggles for restricting or enhancing the social and political participation of new social groups. The reforms intended by politicians, all labelled by historians as conservative, seemed to concentrate mainly on the establishment of alternative educational paths for new social groups who were demanding access to secondary schools actually created for elites. They also seemed to target the dissemination of a work-related ethic among the masses as a means of safeguarding the social order. In other cases, as in the case of the non-governmental organisation, the Society for Industrial Education, vocational education was also related to perceived social and political changes and problems. In fact, the teaching of professional skills was to take place among the lowest classes of society, in order to ensure individuals the means of earning a living, and thus preventing disturbances to the social order. Nevertheless, the Society concentrated primarily on the perceived needs of industry – establishing, reforming or closing schools, according to what it considered as demands of the productive sector. From its perspective, Argentina possessed the preconditions to become an industrial country. The spread of vocational education among the masses would provide the quantity and quality of manpower needed to support industrialisation. In the case of a third group of actors, the machinists' union, vocational education was neither related to social control nor seen principally as a means of fostering modernisation. Rather, its major concern was how to deal with the challenges of modernisation, which were seen as threatening the profession. Therefore, the main goal was not to foster modernisation but to adapt to it. Professional reputation and improvements in technical skills had to be safeguarded in order to avoid becoming obsolete workers.

Clearly, there was a multiplicity of meanings associated with vocational education as a result of the particular figuration of modernity in Argentina. This country, with its colonial structural and symbolic heritage, entered on its own modernisation programme, starting from very particular base-line conditions. The peculiarity of Argentina was that vocational education, as well as other modern institutions, did not have strong precedents or existing structures that could

---

59 As Shmuel Eisenstadt affirms, in the process of modernisation of Latin American countries the ›external‹ reference points were always central and decisive. See Shmuel Eisenstadt, »Vielfältige Moderne«, op. cit. (note 3), p. 22.

be modified or replaced. This is in contrast to Europe where modern vocational training developed from already established guilds and their apprenticeship systems. In Argentina, vocational education represented a new field, in which various actors with different interests were able to get involved. And, given the lack of an established tradition in the vocational education field, they had ample freedom to develop a wide variety of ideas as well as to materialise those ideas in the form of institutions with different aims and structures. Given such base-line conditions, the door to potential possibilities for the institutionalisation of vocational education was more open and allowed different actors to shape it through their diverse interpretations of local problems, priorities, and the future to be achieved.

Ethic and Ethnic Identities

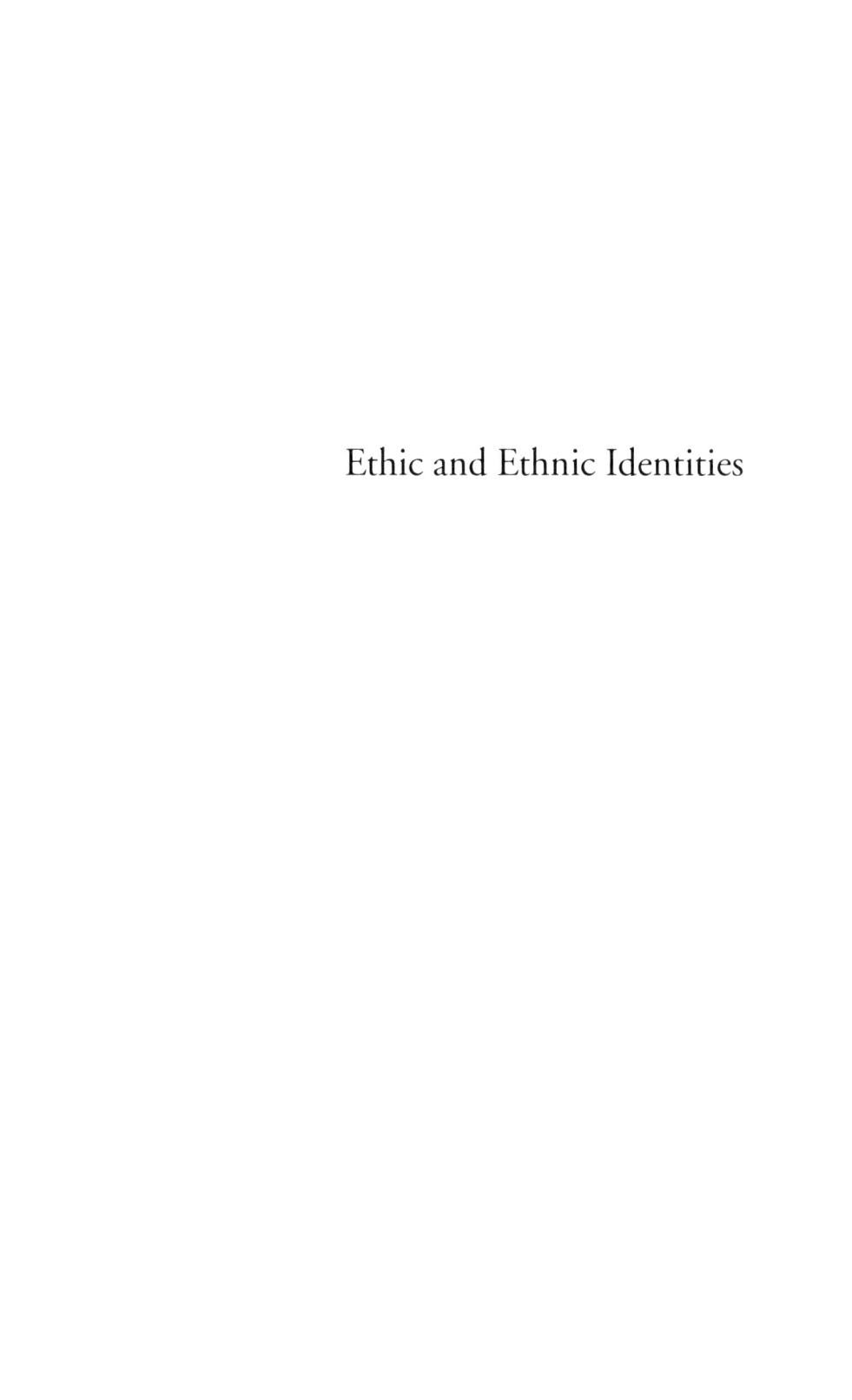

Modernity and the Problem of Secular Morality in Tibet

Vincanne Adams

Modernity

As the organisers of this volume have argued, debates over the theorisation of modernity have historically focused on (1) questions of a singular modernity in which post-colonial readings of history as achieved or unachieved homogeneity (that is, modernity as a result of colonial/ postcolonial encounters that indirectly hoped to homogenise), or on (2) questions of plurality that explore the nature of modernity as a set of specific »cultural« modes of thought and engagement in relation to civil society (the template being enlightenment, with its commensurate notions of science, rationality, empiricism and secularism), and asking how different »modes« co-exist but define, by their differences, different forms of »modernity« or incommensurate ways of being »modern« in the world.[1] Questions about particularity, specificity and locality of modernity are, as they suggest, answered in part by ethnographic investigation of the effects of such things as technology transfer, economic globalisation, the politicisation of identity and biology, but also in empirical data that show how various »cultural« modes of engagement co-exist and interrelate, even as processes of colonial or postcolonial change occur. Speaking of these particularities and specificities in terms of »figurations« provides a useful means of troubling this bifurcated dialogue and promoting an exploration of how modernity is always in the process of being »figured« in unique ways despite its desires for universalist points of reference.

In this essay, I explore the figuring of Tibetan modernity by way of an exploration of the problem of »morality« in the Tibetan Autonomous Region of the People's Republic of China. My focus is on what Tibetans' experiences of rapid social change over the past fifty years – a particular kind of socialist secular modernization – can tell us about how we theorise and explain modernity in general. In looking here, and focusing on questions of morality and secularism, I do not mean to suggest uniformity of opinion or experience among Tibetans.

---

1 I am grateful to Mona Schrempf, and participants at this workshop, for providing valuable feedback on this work.

On the contrary, many Tibetans hold different views of modernity, engage differentially in its projects of secularisation, and in some cases, have a good deal of ambivalence about these processes. I do not suggest a romantic view of a Tibetan Other, who holds fast to religious sensibilities in distinction to a modern secular observer. Rather, I suggest that one of the things accomplished by efforts to become secular and modern is that people are asked to become self-conscious of the fact that they have religious cultural ideals; Tibetans are confronted with the idea that the normal way they do things, and their normal ways of »knowing« the world, are questionable or at least distinguishable from other ways of being and knowing truth in the world they now live in. That this phenomenon exists in some part, among some Tibetans, is not to suggest that it exists uniformly for all Tibetans, but in acknowledging that this is true for at least some Tibetans, I hope to also show that we can think of modernity as a process of subjective configuration and refiguration – that is, of reflecting on how one knows oneself in relation to the world.

In what follows, I first take us to a rural part of Tibet, to explore ethnographically what it is that some Tibetans might tell us and teach us about ours and their modern lives.

Tibet

In 2004, I accompanied a team of Tibetans and foreign medical professionals to a rural village about four hours east of Lhasa.[2] We were on our way to meet the township health worker who was in charge of prenatal check-ups. We also had another mission that morning. A week earlier, we had been asked to help an elderly nomad woman who was sick with stomach pains, losing weight rapidly, and was now vomiting pus. Her family had constructed a makeshift tent on an open lot next to the clinic. We finished our check-ups at the clinic and ventured into her tent at the request of her daughter. Realizing she was severely ill, we made room for her in our Land Rover and, arriving to the county hospital several hours away, took up a collection of Yuan from everyone in our team (foreigners and Tibetans) in order to pay for her hospitalisation.

Now, a week later, we stopped to check on her, and the hospital doctors gave us the sad news that they believed she had stomach cancer and could not help her. Stomach cancer was common among rural Tibetans, a fact that many of our colleagues assumed was associated with high rates of infection from Helicobactor

---

2 I acknowledge that some of this research was conducted under the support of One HEART, a private non-profit organisation devoted to women's health in the TAR.

Pylori bacteria which produced ulcers and, when left untreated for many years, was thought to cause stomach cancer. Our patient had guessed her diagnosis was serious and was worried that she would die in the hospital, so asked to be brought home.

We drove a rocky vomit-filled two hours back to her roadside encampment, and as we rounded the corner and saw the tents of her family and fellow nomads, we noticed a dreadful site on the side of the road. A yak had been killed by a truck passing in the night. It was sprawled out sideways, its neck broken, blood visible in its nostrils had flowed out onto the roadway. Another animal was standing at its side, draped neck, licking the forehead of its dead companion. I could hear the collective gasping in our car. Here we were, bringing home this elderly woman to her family, ostensibly to let her die. Passing this augur of death right at the place where we were to deliver her silenced us. We guessed that the family would immediately know that we were bringing her back to die as well.

Inside her tent, we sat with her three daughters, two sons, and their spouses and children. Two monks were well into their second day of prayers on her behalf at a makeshift shrine set up near the kitchen fire. Fifty butter lamps were lit and burning. The monks chanted. We sat, holding back tears, incapable of holding any sort of long conversation. At last, another daughter, the youngest, arrived and, unlike her older siblings who remained stoically silent, she collapsed loudly into her mother's lap, weeping and sobbing.

It was an uncomfortable few hours of long glances and sad faces. As we left, we discreetly palmed more money into the mother's hands, which we assumed would be used to help pay for her funeral. The whole thing indelibly etched on our minds the reality of our limits as foreign and local medical experts, who, even with a hospital visit, could not prevent her death.

We left the family and returned to town where we had scheduled meetings with the rural health workers to observe their pre-natal check ups. It turned out that the first patient we met was the woman whose yak had been killed the night before – the very one we had found on the side of the road. We expected her to be distraught, but to our great surprise, she was quite happy. We asked how this could be, given that she had lost her yak the night before, a considerable financial loss to her and her family. She didn't focus on the yak. Instead, she said that on her last visit to the clinic she was told that her baby was breech position and that her delivery would be dangerous. She had worried for months about her health and her unborn child. But today, to her great delight, she was told that the baby had rotated and was now in a good position for delivery, therefore she was out of a great deal of danger. She attributed this good fortune to the loss of her yak. You see, the health worker explained, »she believes that the death of the yak has ›burned off‹ the bad karma that would have manifested in the possible death, or dangerous delivery, of her child. She believes that this prevented her from a worse fate«. Despite the loss of a small fortune in the death of this animal, its death had produced a beneficial result for her.

The story could end here, with it's insights about the logic of karma and safe motherhood that beg a discussion of alternative modes of »knowing« in the modern world, but there is another more interesting finale. A year later, we returned to the same nomad settlement, and as we rounded the corner and saw tents (this time on the other side of the road) we found, at our first tent, the same family whose mother we had escorted to and from the hospital. We spoke with three of the daughters for about an hour studiously avoiding mention of their mother, knowing that talk of the deceased is considered dangerous. Then, as we were bringing the conversation to a close, one daughter said, »Oh, it is too bad mother could not be here to see you«. We thought she meant, because she is dead. But then she said, »Mother is in the township selling vegetables today«!

With surprise and joy, we learned that this woman we had thought would not last the month after we last brought her back from the hospital was, in fact, alive and well! The daughters told us she had been very sick for another month after we left and then she got better. We looked at one another with disbelief and then it gradually dawned on us that we had been doubly mistaken – first in thinking we could help her and couldn't and then in assuming she was beyond help when in fact she was cured by what seemed like a miracle. Had the doctors misdiagnosed her? Had she had a spontaneous remission? The daughters explained it to us: the money we had left at our last departure was used for more ritual services from monks which, according to her daughters, kept her alive. Without missing a beat in the movement that would have required a reflection on the fallibility of our modern medical repertoire or our sense of impotence in the face of what looked like obvious mortality, the daughters revealed to us that there might be another way to »explain« the achievement of their mother's extended life. It is this sense of our own inadequacy, and the recognition of a difference that must be accounted for, that arises from encounters with modernity like this that I will explore in the rest of this chapter.

History and Modernity

Although most rural Tibetans have undergone nearly sixty years of efforts to modernise (not including those efforts begun before the advent of Chinese socialism), some things have not changed for many of them. Many Tibetans still assume that prayers and faith provide the basis for reason and empiricism, rather than assuming these two sets of things are competitors. So, what exactly does modernisation mean, for many rural Tibetans?

In its most dramatic forms, modernisation in Tibet has meant adjusting and accommodating a host of infrastructural, governmental changes enacted at the level of individuals, villages, counties, regions, in agriculture, kinship relations, health and health care, education and governance. To some extent, there is an ethnic politics to this dynamic, as Mona Schrempf[3] points out, and I have suggested another way of exploring these dynamics in Lhasa[4]. Goldstein maps the political issues involved in this dynamic well[5], and he provides ample evidence of the history behind these politics, noting that the problem is not simply one in which Tibetans are positioned against Chinese[6]; on the contrary, both Chinese and Tibetans can be found on both sides of the modernisation, Sinification, political spectrum. Many Tibetans see efforts to modernise as part and parcel of »Sinification« and not simply modernisation. This is true in part because most of the modernisation in Tibetan regions has been ushered in by the Chinese state (or the Autonomous Region governance infrastructure working under Beijing's direction). The dynamics of ethnic politics in most Tibetan regions, however, suggest that the problems that arise from the push toward secularisation in some ways bring up more important and more fundamental concerns for Tibetans and these concerns are not tied only to the Chinese state.

The part of modernization that I want to focus on, in this chapter, is that which has required Tibetans at various historical times more than others to be self-conscious about certain things, that is, about anything that could be construed as »superstitious« – beliefs about spirits, pollution, or even more fundamental beliefs like karma and the beneficial force of prayers. Efforts to eradicate »folk« beliefs and later, religion, were initially part of China's great push to achieve a form of secular, socialist modernity within a very short period of time, despite the official effort at first to allow Tibetans to modernise at a slower, more culturally sensitive pace than other regions.[7] By the time of the Cultural Revolution, religion was viewed as an »oppressive« force, and although official rhetoric at various times legitimised the religions of Buddhism and Taoism, in practice, it was mostly and most often seen as needing to be entirely eliminated in order to enlighten peasants to their rightful place as unmystified, unexploited laborers in a socialist utopia. Over the years, however, such political efforts became

---

3 See Mona Schrempfs text in this volume.
4 Vincanne Adams, »Karaoke as Modern Lhasa, Tibet: A Western Encounter with Cultural Politics«, in: *Cultural Anthropology* 11 (1996), 4, pp. 510–546.
5 See Melvin Goldstein, *The Snow Lion and The Dragon: China, Tibet and the Dalai Lama* (Berkeley: University of California Press, 1999).
6 See Melvyn Goldstein, *A History of Modern Tibet, 1913–1951: The Demise of the Lamaist State* (Berkeley: University of California Press, 1989).
7 Goldstein, *The Snow Lion and the Dragon*, op. cit. (note 5).

entangled in other political agendas, including efforts to eliminate the perceived political »splittism« of Tibetans.[8] Religious devotion, although »legal« in China now, is still awkwardly tied into problems of political dissent in Tibet, or so the government believes, making expressions of religious devotion politically problematic.[9] No matter what the politics of its engagement, however, the effort to eradicate »belief« in Tibet has been only partially successful.

Belief in karma and spirits have been problematic in China's push to modernisation for a number of reasons: not only were religious and folk beliefs portrayed as false-consciousness-producing oppressive ideology in the Marxist model of sociality advocated by Mao, but they also did not fit well with the rational insights of any version of secular modernity,[10] let alone a socialist one. Religious and folk beliefs were portrayed as »unenlightened« in the modern European rationalist sense of the term »enlightenment«. Thus, today, many Tibetans who have been educated in colleges both in China and abroad in non-socialist countries express rather uniform sentiments about the problems of »belief« among »backward and uneducated rural Tibetans«. They castigate beliefs as problems that hinder villagers' development and participation in the rapidly modernising state. Tibetans who cling to these beliefs, they say, are simply uneducated about the truth – about the objective and scientific truth that undergirds a materialist, rationalist view of truth. Villagers do not make use of advice from local health care providers because they believe spirits caused their disorder and that lamas and monks can cure them. They spend precious resources on butter and tsampa that they offer to deities in monasteries, rather than on saving their money for their health insurance payment that will guarantee them emergency and routine medical care at local clinics. They naively believe that household deities will flee if exposed to things like blood of childbirth because it is polluting, ensuring that women are sent to dirty places like the cowshed for their deliveries, instead of to local clinics or hospitals. For many modern Tibetans, the problem of religious beliefs is a problem that reveals »failed« or »not yet achieved« modernisation. As Pigg[11] notes for Tibet's neighboring Nepalis, villagers know that this is how not only most Chinese officials and foreign aid workers, but also many urban educated Tibetans feel about them. But for these villagers, now made to feel self-conscious about their beliefs, matters of life and death are not governed by such simplistic forces as bacteria and insurance plans.

---

8 Ibid.
9 Vincanne Adams, »The Sacred in the Scientific: Ambiguous Practices of Science in Tibetan Medicine«, in: *Cultural Anthropology* 16(2001), 4, pp. 542–575.
10 Goldstein, *A History of Modern Tibet 1913–1951*, op. cit. (note 6).
11 Stacy Leigh Pigg, »The Credible and the Credulous: The Question of ›Villagers‹ Beliefs in Nepal«, in: *Cultural Anthropology* 11 (1996), 2, pp. 160–201.

Religious and or »folk« beliefs are seen as foundational to successful participation in modernisation. That is, belief-based ways of knowing the world provide better explanations of the empirical modern world and its dangers, and ways to avoid these dangers, than materialist empirical or scientific explanations arriving through socialism and western modernisation efforts.

In the interstitial spaces between the »modern« Tibetan and his or her (often rural) counterpart who is called »not yet« modern we might find forms of modern subjectivity that exemplify a »figurative« approach to modernity more generally. In the gap between those who »believe« in different ways – between those who know the empirical validity of a world in which karma works as a force more compelling and no less powerful than gravity to ensure the healthy deliver of a baby, or in which benevolent spirit entities recruited through supplication of skilled monks can keep a dying mother alive, and those who »know« equally empirically that beliefs like this are irrational and need to be eliminated for a healthy, prosperous life – it is in this gap we find clues as to what it really means to be modern and what might be entailed in sustaining it.

Moral Secularism

The figuration of modernity presented by these ethnographic realities is tied to an understanding of the place of »the moral« in modernity. It is, in part at least, precisely the idea held by many Tibetans that there is a moral foundation of the empirical world that is under assault in China's rapid push to modernity.

Few would argue that the rise of modern secularism in and through various institutions, among the most important of which is perhaps »science«, has entailed a grappling with questions of morality. In many historical accounts of the rise of European enlightenment as a foundation for modernity in a global sense, the so-called religious modes of knowing the empirical world had to be made »invalid«. That is, religious ways of knowing truth had to be seen as oppositional to modern scientific ways of knowing truth because religious truth was corrupted by moral judgment.[12] Even Max Weber[13] devoted considerable attention to explaining how it might be possible for a religious ethic to survive under conditions of modern secular rationality. In the end, he noted, at its most perfected form, modern rational bureaucracies were like »iron cages« trapping

---

12 See Steven Shapin & Simon Schaffer, *Leviathan and the Air Pump* (Princeton: Princeton University Press, 1989) and Bruno Latour, *We Have Never Been Modern*. (Cambridge: Harvard University Press, 1993).
13 Max Weber, *Protestant Ethic and the Spirit of Capitalism* (NY: Routledge, 2nd edition 2001).

the human soul and killing its spirit. This achievement of rationality was perhaps also its greatest failure. Normality came to stand in for morality. Morality became indexed in performative acts of secular capitalist enterprise which, ultimately, took the rational measures of economic science as the index of success. Secular morality here was tethered to the world of economic gain, rather than to other-world social relations with benevolent or malevolent forces. The spirit of modern capitalism was a spirit stripped of the fundamental principle informing a prior religious epistemology: that morality was the measure of and precondition for a life lived well; instead, economic gain took its place, indexing its morality in financial achievement, but at great cost.

Likewise, Foucault, following Kant, theorised that the rise of modern secularism required a shift in the way morality is connected to truth. Foucault (and I quote Paul Rabinow here) »argued that until the seventeenth century, it was widely, perhaps universally, held that to know the truth one had to be virtuous, that is, capable and worthy of knowing. Descartes's philosophy constitutes a cultural break of major proportions. Descartes's views amounted to saying: ›To accede to truth, it suffices that I be any subject which can see what is evident ... Thus, I can be immoral and know the truth.‹ I believe that this is an idea which, more or less, explicitly, was rejected by all previous cultures. Before Descartes, one could not be impure, immoral and know the truth. With Descartes, direct evidence is enough. After Descartes, we have a nonascetic subject of knowledge. This change makes possible the institutionalisation of modern sciences«.[14]

In other words, the suggestion is that modern secularism, exemplified in the institutions of science that claim to hold rational and objective insights on the world, emerged in part by way of an enforcing of moral neutrality – or more strongly, to the rise of the idea that truth was itself unconnected to morality. Being modern means, to some extent in this analytic, being able to hold in abeyance certainty about the moral underpinnings of one's knowledge of the empirical world. Even in Weber's rational bureaucratic modernity, morality becomes subordinated to the figurations of science, economics, and financial audit that are not inherently driven by a moral compass but rather by the compass of the accumulation of capital. Modernity, in this framing, asks that we see truth as something that could be known outside of its moral implications and moral conditions of possibility.

---

14 Michel Foucault, »On the Genealogy of Ethics: An Overview of Work in Progress Interview with Paul Rabinow and Hubert Dreyfus«, in: *The Foucault Reader*, ed. by Paul Rabinow (New York: Pantheon, 1984), pp. 340–372 cited in Paul Rabinow, *Essays on the Anthropology of Reason* (Princeton: Princeton University Press, 1996), pp. 137–138. I have used this passage in another text that approaches this problem from a slightly different angle, see Vincanne Adams, »Saving Tibet? An inquiry into Modernity, Lies, Truths, and Beliefs«, in: *Medical Anthropology* 24 (2005), pp.71–110.

It would be obviously wrong to conclude that secular modernity is attendant upon the absence or loss of morality, as Weber argued. The rise of so-called secular states, especially the socialist models, are premised in some sense on a moral proposition – that it is more beneficial to the masses to be secular than religious because secular ways of knowing truth are »better«. That is, they are more promising than religious epistemologies in the effort to establish objective truths which can be of use in establishing a mode of governance in a society organised around the ideal of benefiting the masses. Ultimately this is a moral proposition. The rise of modern secularism did not eliminate morality at all. On the contrary, it simply refigured subjectivity in relation to it. That is, it is not that morality is lost in the shift to modernity, but rather that secularist modernity asks people to think of morality – of what it means to be moral – in new ways.

Chinese secularist socialism in particular espoused a rhetoric of morality to enforce its push to modernity. Adopting socialist positions on the benefits of one's labor, one's occupation, one's fertility, one's eating habits, living habits, marital habits, and so on (there was really no domain of public or private life that escaped inclusion), was discursively framed as a moral undertaking. Efforts to realign society »for the good of socialism« meant, indirectly, that it was not simply the most rational and effective economically but that it was morally correct to adopt the socialist flag and carry forward with its mission. In this equation, moral propositions here were affirmed by a secularist view of truth,[15] but truth is not »known« by way of those moral propositions.

The adoption of secular moralism, however, entails an erasure too. Secular moralism proposes a way of being moral that is tied to »objective truth« and not to religious belief. This means, more importantly, separating one's sense of knowing, of certainty, from one's moral compass. That is, secularism demands recognizing that morality is not an arbiter of truth, and so, morality can float freely on the side of truth and judgment about the world in an empirical sense.

Tibetans and Modernity

What can Tibetans' experiences and concerns under this particular figuration of modernity tell us about the condition of modernity more generally, or about the problem of moral secularism in particular? Listen to the words of a middle-aged Tibetan who worked in a government office in Lhasa:

---

15 One might read the missionary zeal of the red guards, the cultural revolution, and so on, in this light – that is, that participants felt they were on a moral mission to benefit others.

Look around and see where we are. We have all these things here that represent Tibetan culture, but they are fake and they aren't used for the things they were intended to be used for originally. We have wealth and the living standard has gone up but the quality of our morality and our life and of our *rlung* [»wind«] has gone down. We are more restless. Before people were happy to have enough money to get by, eating tsampa and appreciating what they had. Now we are eating popcorn and drinking beer, things that are made in factories and are not healthy. There is a sense of restlessness and it manifests in our physical health. [...] We have more *rlung* more »whispy« character, not grounded [...].[16]

It is also related to loss of religion. I'm a government employee and when I am sitting in my office, I think about the fact that we have fallen off the path. Which path? *Chos lam*, the path of religion, dharma. Now, before when I started working in this office in 1989, things were simpler. Less cars, and we would go home for lunch and cook our food with family and we maintained a connection to home and family. Now we just eat food cooked by others and we sit around with our co-workers and eat things made in factory. If you look at the teachings of Gyalwa Rimpoche (His Holiness the Dalai Lama), he talks about the benefits of being on the dharmic path. And we are losing that.[17]

I found that one of the most common ways that Tibetans talk about the struggles they have had with modernisation is in terms of their sense that, not entirely surprisingly, the world has become a place where morality is troubled. I heard this in commentary at the hospitals when doctors worried about the morality of young women whose sexual compasses seemed morally adrift because of the intersecting demands of reproductive programs and efforts to sexualise women (e.g., seeing sexuality as a biological event and also seeing themselves as modern by way of their sexual prowess, both of which undermined traditional sexual sensibilities).[18] I witnessed it in middle-aged women whose physical disorders, such as growths in their uterus and ovaries, were seen as consequences of this moral decline, explained as a combination of imbalances between the wind humor (related to poison of desire) and bile humor (related to poison of anger/aversion). It was seen in patients who were asked to participate in a modern clinical study, using randomisation, and they wondered why we would want to do a study of Tibetan medicine in ways that required us to »lie« or »keep secret« who would get medicines and who would not. It was, for these patients, wrong in a moral sense, despite our efforts to explain the benefits of being able to »know« in this manner, the true effects of the medicines we were testing. Modern science appeared distinctly immoral, when explained in those terms. It was present in

---

16 Rlung, here refers to the »nyeba« or »poison«, sometimes translated as humor, called »wind«. But it also refers to the imbalanced condition arising from excess »greed«.
17 Translated by Sienna Craig.
18 See Vincanne Adams, »Moral Orgasm and Productive Sex: Tantrism Faces Fertility Control in Lhasa, Tibet, China«, in: *The Moral Object of Sex,* ed. by Adams & Pigg (Duke University Press, 2005).

Tibetan's concerns that their children were doing well in school, becoming modern, but also, they said, becoming »green mind« (*lepa changu* – i.e. in Wylie: *klad pa ljang gu?* – *klad pa* has quite a physical meaning, i.e. »brain«, way of thinking perhaps?) which translates to something like »redneck« or not immoral but amoral in a way that does not make sense because it is not motivated by the moral principles of their religious ideals.

I think it is fair to say that one of the differences between those (including Tibetans) who are trying to secularise Tibet and their counterparts who hold hard and fast to »religious« perceptions and actions is in the way that morality comes to play a role in deciphering not only how to behave (in a moral sense) but also how to actually »know« the world in ways that are certain.

Traditional Tibetan approaches to the empirical world are premised in large part on being able to comprehend that empirical world as a moral universe. This is visible when we are talking about the basis of disease, the flourishing of crops, the karmic induced death of a yak to save a mother or infant, for example. The ability to know why these things occur is embedded, for many rural Tibetans (and many urban Tibetans I would add) in the idea that morality provides the basis for the empirical world. So, for example, many Tibetans will explain that the possibility of life itself, that is of enlivening the fetus with its spark of life (*srog*) is possible because of the moral accomplishments of past lives. That is, the very possibility of life itself is contingent on a moral accounting of effects of actions, thoughts, speech from past lives. These Tibetans also know that the ripening of karma in events that explain the death of animals, the fruitfulness of crops or even the loss of wealth are all premised on the fact that there is a moral force operating temporally and causally in the universe.

These ways of »knowing« the universe in relation to the moral engine that enables life itself are fundamentally troubling to a secular epistemology. Because the things we do and say arise from moral possibilities, morality can't be seen as extraneous or constant. It cannot be seen as an extraneous set of choices in relation to truth (that is, do you use your knowledge in morally virtuous or unvirtuous ways?). Karma is an incontrovertible force that operates because the universe is a moral universe. It is not something that can be set aside and held constant while truth is pursued. Morality is the objective basis for truth. It is the very basis upon which the empirical truth can be known. Secular modernity thus appears to some Tibetans as a problematic possibility. It asks Tibetans to reflect on their religious way of knowing with skepticism, to entertain the proposition that this might be wrong and that there are better and more valid ways of knowing the world.

Morality in practice: A Problem of Moral Secularism

Morality, as a domain of the ethical, might be seen not as a set of paradigmatic rules and ideals but as a set of experiential or lived practices[19], what Rose has called »regime of living«[20]. In particular, morality could be seen as the translated and lived experiences of trying to express ethical ideals. But I think morality can also be theorised, as Kleinman[21] has argued, as phenomenological and experiential; it is »that which we get passionate about«. Moral actions feel different than ordinary actions for many of the same reasons things that are sacred are different from things that are »mundane«; moral action distinguishes itself by the ways it is different from other action. In the case of Tibetan notions of morality, I think the »way it feels different« is in its ability to be distinguished by the fact that its effects carry an impact on others beyond oneself. Moral action is action that is carried out with some sense of obligation and concern for the effects of that action on others. This fundamental view of morality is not exclusive to Tibetan Buddhism, but it is key to it.

In addition to this notion of morality, Tibetans also bring another understanding of morality to the forefront: knowing morality means not simply knowing that it exists as an ethical possibility but actually bringing it into existence through actions and intentions. When Tibetans talk about this kind of behavior, they express it in terms of the so-called *sems*, or »sentient mind«. This, they note, is located in the heart, not the brain. It is closer to our notion of »conscience« in so far as it ties sensibility to a moral compass. When people feel compassionate, it comes from their *sems*. A more literal notion of »consiousness«, *rnam shes*, is used to talk about the mind stream that connects one life to the next through rebirth. *Rnam shes* is the ›container‹ of one's moral accounts, but *sems* is the guiding force that directs one toward or away from moral action in life. In any case, it is compelling to also note that the location of the *sems* in the heart conveys the sense that it, as would be true in many Western cultures also, that it concerns things about which people feel passionate. The idea that the »heart knows« is emergent in the description Robert Desjarlais[22] provides for what he, quoting his Sherpa informants, calls the »heartmind«. It is a way of saying that the heart (with all the entailments of its passions) *is* the mind.[23]

---

19 Aristotle, *The Nichomachaean Ethics* (Oxford: Oxford University Press, 1998).
20 Nicholas Rose, *Governing the Soul: the Shaping of the Private Self* (London: Routledge, 1990).
21 Arthur Kleinman, »›Everything That Really Matters‹: Social Suffering, Subjectivity, and the Remaking of Human Experience in a Disordering World«, in: *Harvard Theological Review* 90/3 (1997), pp. 315–335.

22 Robert Desjarlais, *Body and Emotion: the Aesthetics of Illness and Healing in the Nepal Himalayas* (University of Pennsylvania Press, 1992).
23 I am sure that not all Tibetans could articulate this version of morality. Many would, in fact,

Finally, I note that the idea that morality is not only in the ethical ideal that guides it but also in the expression of actions in relation to others directs us to its performative dimensions. Thus, one of the reasons Tibetans have felt such great loss in the repressions of their religious culture, and also in its reformulations that have been seen in efforts to revitalise Buddhism in the Autonomous Region, is that the performative part of religious culture – the thread that ties a mode of being in the world to feelings of being morally correct – has been curtailed. Tibetans simply are not allowed to fully express themselves in moral activities that are distinctively religious, and instead they have tried to find ways to express that devotion in secular contexts. (Of course, this course of action is in some sense already built into Buddhist culture, but I think seldom as important as in the context of a rapidly secularizing world.) When they do express moral devotion through secular practices, they often come up against obstacles that are not simply a result of the absence of religion, but more significantly obstacles that challenge their fundamental notions of truth, empirical fact, the reality of things like karma, or even the karmic basis for life itself.

If »ways of knowing« truth are being challenged in Tibet today, we might ask again why it is that Tibetans feel that this sense of morality can't find a home in a socialist secularist China? I think it is because, in part at least, of the problem of moral secularism itself. Moral secularism asks for morality as an optional possibility, not as a foundational basis upon which the world exists. It is not so much the repression of religion by the Chinese state then but rather a host of efforts to fundamentally change the way Tibetans know how to relate to their world. If you see the world and in some sense know the world as a morally-composed universe, it might feel radically wrong, even immoral, to assume that you could know truth in other ways. If the world exists because of the moral foundations upon which it rests, then suggesting that the empirical world exists despite such foundations will seem wrong in a moral sense. The laws of karma (*las*), for example, would have to be actively disbelieved.

Often, we hear Tibetans who are working at high levels of the government say that they believe that many of the reforms of modernisation are beneficial to many people, even they say, like the dharma – *chos* like in essence – and yet find themselves at a loss in explaining why religious approaches to such reforms are not tolerated. »Superstitions and backward ways are detrimental« they say. Reli-

---

entertain notions of karma and use the term in ways that suggested a more surface nod to ideas of religion, while holding fast to other and newer scientific and western notions of truth. Moreover, I think that for most Tibetans the idea of defining morality like this, as opposed to simply »knowing« that some things are right in the sense of »virtue« while others are wrong, in the sense of them being non-virtuous, would be unusual. However, as with other culturally-embedded ways of being that emerge from the fact that historic Tibet was a religious culture, the idea that many Tibetans do think about these things as that which one does get »passionate« about is not surprising.

gion, they say, is an inadequate basis for ensuring things like »fairness«, »equity«, »justice« – the lexicon for morality in a secular world. But, for a Tibetan whose first concern is with compassion – a way of being that is not driven by poisons of attachment, aversion or ignorance – things like »fairness«, »equity« and »justice« are only possible because of the fact that there are compassionate beings, or the fact that the world exists in some sense because the moral force of karma keeps ensuring the rebirth of fallible beings. To suggest that things like »fairness« are possible if one »opts« for being moral – putting truth to moral purposes – is to invert the relation of causality. It suggests the world is objectively without a moral foundation – that the role of morality in creating these possibilities – is optional, even though one could »opt« to achieve them for moral good. To a traditional believer, that view makes sense but misses some fundamental premise for its possibility. It feels all wrong. No longer legitimised within religious contexts for performative action, claims on morality feel inadequate and, ultimately, illogical. And they don't work to resolve the fundamental problem of how to »explain« the world, whether it is in the survival of a mother with a terminal diagnosis, or the good fortune brought by a dead yak.

Conclusion

In the end, the problem of secular morality – whether socialist communist, capitalist, or neoliberal – is that it asks people to believe in the moral possibilities of secularism without providing an adequate framework of truth for doing so. The framework for secular truth must always refer back to itself alone, not to a morally bound way of knowing the world. I don't think this is only true in Tibet, but rather in many so-called secular nations, where there is not an absence of religion but rather growing religious fervor because of the fear of loss or actual absence of that sense or way of knowing. Scientific truth claims are used stand in for moral certainty in secularist approaches to the world. And in this view, modernity always entails a sense of loss and gain, and a projection toward a future that will somehow solve the problems entailed in feelings of »loss« in the present. But, it is perhaps just this sense of loss that is aroused by a transformation, especially in those places where the transformation is enforced by the state and by development efforts and so on. This transformation is in the ways that people know truth – provoking feelings of loss under conditions of modernity. Thus, we see that the problem of religion never disappears in modern regimes (no matter what political structure) and the constant desire among modern subjects to recuperate the religious in their lives, and perhaps the ongoing need for fundamentalist religious movements in many places – not least of which is perhaps the new urban centers of China.

If theories of modernity that rest either on the possibility of universalist forms of sociality, or the possibility of historically contingent engagements of »different modernities« both need each other and ask us to explore the nuances of particular and local experiences of »the modern«, then what might we theorise from this evidence? The Tibetan case, I think, suggests the possibility of social critique.

In the first instance, it suggests that methodologically, it is important not to assume homogeneity of form that would depict a romantic and »traditional« Tibetans holding fast to religious views of the world as against a modern secular rationalist who cannot contemplate the possibility of sacred notions of truth or moral foundations of an empirical universe. That would reiterate an older and linear reading of modernity and modernisation. Rather, what the Tibetan case suggests is the need to read through the back and forth of processes of modernisation that force persons to reflect critically on their ways of knowing and being in the world. That is, their experiences of modernization – however uneven, heterogenous and incomplete, provide, because of this unevenness, a means of reflecting on other universalizing pretenses of modernity. This method suggests an approach to modernity as a »configuration« process – a means of configuring and refiguring one's place in the world and one's relationship to it that is uneven and often incomplete.

In the second case, the hope for a secular epistemology – a way of knowing truth that is uprooted from its moral foundations – is at the core of efforts to modernise and perhaps the most important element of modernisation that inspires this kind of reflexive configuring and refiguring among Tibetans. And, their experiences of this refiguring are, not surprisingly, disturbing to some of them. In portraying their unease with the processes, I do not suggest that secularism is undesirable. That they offer a social critique of secularism does not mean that secularism is worthy of critique in and of itself. On the contrary, a certain and fixed aspiration toward secularism (even though always incomplete) is one of modernity's greatest accomplishments. But Tibetans perhaps offer us a way to look critically at that achievement, and instruct us to the possibility of its erasures and displacements that come inevitably along with »trying to be modern«. These insights may be of use in challenging materialist approaches to liberal humanism, social critique and modernization theory.

Modernity requires a specific kind of reflection on one's »difference«. For Tibetans, this difference is found in their ability to see morality as at the foundation of the empirical universe, not separate from it. This »difference« is able to be either »romanticised« as a past that has been or is being lost, or it is »demonised« as the obstacle to successful development, something that Tibetans must overcome to be rational and modern. In their own words, however, modernisation sometimes feels like an assault on their notions of morality because it enables a self-reflection that leads to either romanticism or demonisation. Either way, it is seen as problematic. The assault comes in part from direct efforts to undermine religion or religious practice, although that is not where its greatest impact is found. On the contrary, that sort of assault usually just solidifies resolve and commitment. Rather, this assault comes from more subtle channels and less visible routes, through medical practices, notions of what makes crops healthy, what keeps a mother alive, what it means to have good fortune and so on. These important »ways of knowing the world« are things that many Tibetans begin to question under secular modernisation, and when they do, they sense that what is lost in this questioning about truth is the moral certainty about truth, about how they know truth. In this sense, Tibetan insights offer a way to critically read the processes of »configuring« modernity that occur in this region, and also perhaps in other places in the world where similar tensions and processes are occurring.

Planning the Modern Tibetan Family in China

Mona Schrempf

> Maybe there are two quite distinct mythical origins of the ideas of ›reality‹. One is the reality of representation, the other, the idea of what affects us and what we can affect.[1]

Introduction

The general question I approach in this essay is how two different realities of life in the Sino-Tibetan borderlands of China's Qinghai Province are related and have been negotiated by Tibetan women and their families since 1982. One reality is that of family planning as *the* emblematic state project of Chinese modernity with its public slogans, administrative institutions and local implementers. The other reality is a much more contested and less researched one: the experience and negotiation of family planning's biopolitical intrusion into minority families and, in particular, the private lives of targeted women. In comparison with their Han-Chinese contemporaries, Tibetan women have had to suddenly adapt to a culturally adverse idea of contraception, and one that contradicts their fundamental cosmological concepts of karma and rebirth, in particular in the case of abortion. Furthermore, previously unknown biomedical contraceptive technologies were often forcefully delivered in a condescending manner and in a language that most women did not understand, or without thorough explanation and advice. Birth control also entered Tibetan lives in an ambiance of mistrust about the motives of the state, following a recent and sometimes violent colonization in Tibetan areas and the imposition of a whole range of subsequent modernizing projects. In this paper, I argue that Tibetan women's experiences with, and understandings of, family planning need to be situated as part of a more general struggle to find a Tibetan figuration of modernity in which Tibetans must negotiate their own subjectivity in relation to the greater forces of socio-cultural, economic and political transformations in China. The few academic studies on women's reproductive behaviour, childbirth and surveys on fertility rates among Tibetans in China do not deliver a comprehensive

---

1 Ian Hacking, *Representing and Intervening. Introductory topics in the philosophy of natural science* (Cambridge: Cambridge University Press, 1983), p. 146.

picture of family planning as an everyday life experience. They demonstrate, however, the great variety of implementation practices and experiences in different Tibetan areas (for example between TAR and Qinghai Province), sometimes even within the same township. In order to find out on what these differences depend, I primarily collected personal accounts of the experience of family planning from rural Tibetan women as part of their life stories, along with accounts by those who implement the policy at the local level.[2]

Everyday expressions one hears nowadays, such as »Peoples' minds have changed« (*bSam blo 'gyur song ni red*), represent a more positive contemporary Tibetan attitude towards the two (or three) child-policy for minority nationalities (*minzu*) in China. This has not always been the case; in the 1980s there was in fact a fundamental fear of family planning among women. Poor medical practices and technologies were used, and sterilisation and abortion campaigns were secretly implemented (extending into the 1990s in some cases). Today, modern amenities are only available to those rural women whose families can afford to educate them, who have a job and a salary, and who can choose between living in a new apartment or moving in with their husband's parents, if they wish so. In other words, those who have the luxury of choosing a modern lifestyle can profit from it. However, the prevalent labour-intensive farming and pastoral subsistence economies in Tibet, require strong, hard-working women and more children in order to make a living. In the end, it seems to be a battle between two different ways of life – the ›Tibetan‹ or the ›Chinese‹ way, although it is a complex issue, as I will show in this essay that cannot be separated from negotiating different figurations of modernity which are closely intertwined with asymmetric power relations and identities.

»In front of the door, there are plenty of livestock. Around the fire pit there are many sons.«[3] (Local Tibetan proverb)
»Having a few children in good health means to enjoy a happy life.«[4] (Government slogan in Tongren, Tibetan Autonomous Huangnan Prefecture, 2005–6.)

The above sayings project diametrically opposed views as to what it means to

---

2 I thank first and foremost my assistants and informants for their trust and effort to convey their experiences to me. Furthermore, Vincanne Adams for her comments on the oral presentation of this paper, and Stuart Blackburn, Deborah Johnson, Vincent Houben and Toni Huber for their valuable critique on the many versions of this essay.
3 Tib. *Sgo kha rgyu yis bkang yod. Go kha bu yis bkang.* Cf. a traditional Chinese saying: *Duozi duofu* »Many sons means lots of luck.« It is clear that both traditional rural Chinese and Tibetan (farming) societies share the same ideal and in relation to modern family planning, share similar problems in terms of social pressures by other family members put on young couples to have at least one son.
4 Tib. *Nyung skye legs skye byas te tshe gang bde skyid skrun dgos*; Chin. *Shaosheng yousheng, xingfu yisheng.*

Figure 4: »To control population growth is to increase the quality of the population.« (Tib. Mi 'bor 'phel tshad tshod 'dzin dang/ Mi 'bor spus ka je legs su gtong dgos. Chin. Kongzhi renkou zengzhang tigao renkou suzhi). Government slogan on road signs in Tongren, Tibetan Autonomous Prefecture of Huangnan.

have a prosperous, happy ›quality‹ life when it comes to the size of one's family. The first saying is an orally transmitted proverb and represents traditional Tibetan cultural values and experiences, based on a subsistence economy and life as farmer and/or nomad where many sons and plenty of livestock (i.e. property or wealth) are seen as mutually advantageous and reinforcing.[5] In addition, those families with many sons, who were able to defend their own household or the village, have always maintained a high social status. The second set of sayings are state family planning slogans which are publicly displayed on billboards and posters, sometimes including depictions of traditional icons such as Tibetan Buddhist statues, monasteries or other items linked with Tibetan culture, to attract the passer-by's attention. They are written in both Chinese and Tibetan and promote economic growth, health, and quality and happiness of life by hav-

---

5 The inversion of this saying seems to have come true in that government policies are now limiting herd sizes among Tibetan pastoralists – ostensibly for environmental reasons – who thus can no longer sustain large families.

ing fewer children. Yet, the state slogans also imply the opposite threat – health hazards, lower quality of life and economic hardship for big families.

The above examples belong to two different cultural productions in the Sino-Tibetan borderlands of Qinghai Province, the region which Tibetans call Amdo where a significant Tibetan population lives in what is a modern Chinese state. However, Tibetan communities in China have their own quite different means and strategies by which to engage with modernity, while also trying to maintain their socio-cultural identities. By contrast, the state media publicly represent Tibetans as being a ›poor‹ and often ›backward‹ minority, an ethnic ›Other‹ who has yet to achieve the state project of modernity. As Rabinow and Rose have pointed out, the biopolitical role taken on by state family planning through organised birth control in countries such as China, India and throughout Latin America is focused on general truth claims about enhancing economic growth by limiting the reproduction of the poor as a prerequisite to modernisation.[6] Tibetans (and China's rural population in general) are made to believe that by adhering to family planning, socio-economic progress and ›quality‹[7] of both the population as a whole and of individual lives – in other words the main goal of China's modernity – will occur as a consequence. In fact, some modern Tibetan couples voluntarily have only one child so as to be able to afford the high costs of a good education (connected with ›quality‹) and health services that can amount to several average salaries per year. However, the way in which Tibetans engage with the state representation of family planning by adapting to, resisting or reconfiguring it, and how they thereby create their own figurations of modernity, is conditioned by complex and inter-subjective relations.

In the area of my fieldwork, the Tibetan Autonomous Prefecture of Huangnan (Chin. Huangnan Zangzu zizhizhou, Tib. rMa lho Bod rigs rang skyong khul), Tibetans make up about 66 per cent of the overall population, including both farming and nomadic communities who are often additionally involved in trade.[8] Tongren (Tib. Reb gong) County is the most ›developed‹ among the four counties of Huangnan Prefecture, bearing the prefectural seat of Tongren town

---

6 Building on Foucault's concept of biopower, Rabinow and Rose identify three key elements of biopower, i.e. »knowledge of vital life processes, power relations that take humans as living beings as their object, and the modes of subjectification through which subjects work on themselves qua living beings – as well as their multiple combinations«. Cf. Paul Rabinow & Nikolas Rose, »Biopower Today«, in: *BioSocieties* 1 (2006), pp. 195–217, in particular pp. 209, 215.

7 Concerning ›quality of population‹, Sigley argues that what makes out the »strength« of the Chinese state has a lot to do with the image of China in the world, and that it been shifted to a new »emphasis on the physical, mental, and moral attributes of the citizen-subject that are necessary to ensure national survival and revival« (Gary Sigley, »Liberal Despotism: Population Planning, Subjectivity, and Government in Contemporary China«, in: *Alternatives* 29 (2004), pp. 557–575, esp. p. 565.

8 In Huangnan Prefecture there are 142.360 Tibetans, based on a census in 2000 (http://en.wikipedia.org/wiki/Huangnan_Tibetan_Autonomous_Prefecture). See also Huangnan

as its main government administrative centre.⁹ There are winners and losers of recent modern development in the area. Some Tibetan families of near-by Rong bo village lost their houses to road construction, while Tibetan farmers from adjacent Sachi (Tib. Sa dkyil) village who owned land lying close to Tongren town have profited by selling it to the government for urbanisation purposes. Recently, Qinghai as well as other areas of the Tibetan Plateau have become the focus of the »Opening of the West« (Chin. Xibu da kaifa) campaign targeted at fostering economic progress in this comparatively poor region of China.¹⁰

Family planning has far-reaching and relational impacts on virtually all aspects of life: on individual, collective and state levels; in physical, reproductive, moral and gender terms; and, on the professional, socio-cultural, political and economic domains. Except for these latter four, most of the other aspects have not been thoroughly analysed, hence our understanding of family planning policies and their campaigns has been mostly limited to a ›top-down‹ perspective. Moreover, locally implemented campaigns stimulate a range of responses and strategies among their targets, ranging from resistance, avoidance and trickery to compliance, with potential for social empowerment but may also result in physical suffering. This ›ambivalence‹ of experiences needs to be contextualised ethnographically in order to understand why, and in which ways, different family planning subjectivities come about. I collected the personal, biographical accounts of Tibetan women from rural farming communities, and related them to each other as well as to accounts by family planning cadres working at the prefecture level down to those operating in individual villages. In addition, I gathered accounts by maternal and child health care doctors and public health officials (both at county and prefecture level); by barefoot doctors in *xiang* (i.e. village level) clinics; by former and present village leaders; and, by private traditional

---

Gaikuang (ed.), *Huangnan Zangzu Zhizi Zhou Gaikuang* / engl.: *A Survey of the Huangnan Tibetan Autonomous Prefecture* (Xining: Qinghai Renmin Chubanshe, 1985).

9 Since 2006, Tongren town has been connected with Xining, Qinghai's provincial capital, by a new highway requiring just two and a half hours drive. There is no doubt that distance to a county seat or prefectural town does intensify closer surveillance by and bigger exposure to Chinese state modernity. Thus, for example, the official ›spirit-medium‹ (Tib. *lha pa*) of a village in Rebgong is married with a Chinese woman. They moved to Xining. Interethnic marriages, especially between Tibetans and Chinese, are looked down upon by Tibetans, and couples who remain in rural areas have to face quite a lot of discrimination.

10 Qinghai Province entails five Tibetan autonomous prefectures (TAP) and one mixed Tibetan Mongolian prefecture with Tibetans occupying over 97 % of the total land area of the province. Whereas Han (53%) and Hui (16%) are living in concentrated urban areas around Xining and Haidong, Tibetans represent the largest minority group in Qinghai with 22% of the overall population. They remain mostly rural or live in small towns. By the mid 1990s, over two thirds of Qinghai's counties were defined as »poverty stricken«, and had the worst economic performance in the whole of the PRC. (David Goodman, »Qinghai and the Emergence of the West: Nationalities, Communal Interaction and National Integration«, in: *The China Quarterly* 178 (June 2004), pp. 379–399, in particular pp. 379, 381.)

Tibetan medicine practitioners.[11] The resulting representations are treated as ›social facts‹.[12] By taking family planning programs among rural Tibetan farmers in Qinghai Province as an example of the state's project of modernity, I also examine the ways in which Tibetans negotiate body, gender, place, agency and identity within the Chinese nation-state and in relation to state modernity. The main questions I ask are: what have been Tibetan women's experiences of family planning in the last 25 years and how do the women themselves represent them? What impact does family planning have on the lives of different families? What kind of agency are Tibetan women able to create through birth control; and how, in general, do they understand social change as impacting upon modern Tibetan family life?

Family Planning, Representations and Realities

Much has been written by both Western and Chinese scholars about China's controversial one-child-policy.[13] Family planning, which is integral to the state project of modernity, has been criticised as »the very ground for constructing

---

11 Because of the sensitive topic, I depended on local intermediaries in order to get into contact with my informants – thus I was able to interview Tibetan women and some of their family members between ages 17 and 84 in several different locations. Without their invaluable trust, patience and assistance, data gathering would have never been possible. To preserve the necessary anonymity of all my informants, their names and the exact locations of my fieldwork have to remain suppressed. My fieldwork sites encompassed two farming villages (Chin. *xiang*) close to the prefectural cum county town, and two were further removed. In this article I have focused on my material in farming areas that slightly differs from my findings in neighbouring nomadic areas in such a way as farmers tend to be more exposed to condensed places of modernity such as towns and thus be more influenced by state modernity. Household surveys were conducted to test the difference in numbers of children per couple since the 1980s in comparison to before. There is a clear change since at least 1985, in having fewer children, mostly two, max. four.

12 See Paul Rabinow, »Representations Are Social Facts: Modernity and Post-Modernity in Anthropology«, in: *Writing Culture, The Poetics and Politics of Ethnography*, ed. by James Clifford & George E. Marais (Berkeley: University of California Press, 1986), pp. 234–261.

13 There is an abundant literature on family planning in China, mostly among the Han population, i.e. analysis on policies, population control, economy, education and demography. Most relevant for my own work are studies on biopolitical dynamics, gender and modernity, see, for example, Ann Anagnost, »A Surfeit of Bodies: Population and the Rationality of the State in Post-Mao China«, in: *Conceiving the New World Order: the Global Politics of Reproduction*, ed. by Faye Ginsburg & R. Rapp (Berkeley: University of California Press, 1995); Susan Greenhalgh, »Planned births, unplanned persons: Population in the making of Chinese modernity«, in: *American Ethnologist* 30 (2003), 2, pp. 196–215; Susan Greenhalgh, »Science, Modernity, and the Making of China's One-Child-Policy«, in: *Population and Development Review* 29 (2003), 2, pp. 163–196. Only few works have dealt with the particular situation and reactions

political authority in the post-Mao period«,[14] and worse, as an issue of either the »genocide« or »cultural survival« of Tibetans.[15] Even after more than 30 years, it continues to be a hotly debated topic of human rights and global concern because of female foeticide and the strong sex-ratio imbalance, which this has caused, as well as the future economic and social implications of the changing demographics of China's population. However, inside China, family planning is represented as a *sine qua non* for national, socio-political, economic and environmental progress and development. At the same time, the state's claimed rationale links science, population and modernity as a powerful tool for both legitimising and exercising state control through family planning. Yet, this seems not to be a process unique to China alone. According to Rabinow and Rose, from the 1970s onwards human reproduction became a national and supra-national problem worldwide, a »bio-political space par excellence«.[16] Close connections between demography and economics were put forward as the prime reasons for this trend, being legitimised by 'scientific' statistics and quantitative truth claims, and made feasible through birth control technologies administered by newly created state medical institutions. Especially in densely populated countries like India and China, which in the 1970s began attempts to ›catch up‹ economically with the West, family planning became a national concern of the utmost importance for economic progress. Whereas state control and the institutionalised implementation of birth planning in China officially began during the early 1970s, with the first »later – longer – fewer« (Chin. *wan – xi – shao*) policy, prior to 1982 it was not strictly implemented in the Tibetan areas of Qinghai.[17] Greenhalgh, drawing on Foucault's notion of governmentality,[18] has convincingly shown that China's family planning policy and its aims are not reflective of a pre-existing re-

---

of minorities in that respect, and even fewer with local ethnographies of family-community-state interactions.

14 Anagnost, »A Surfeit of Bodies«, op. cit. (note 13), p. 29.
15 See the report »Tears of Silence. Tibetan Women and Population Control« from May 1995 (http://www.tibet.com/Women/tears1.html, retrieved 05.05.2008) by The Tibetan Women's Association (TWA) that is part of the Government of Tibet in Exile. Several arguments are brought forward on why and how China's population control is detrimental to the survival of the Tibetan population and culture as a whole. Next to an increased Chinese migration into Tibetan areas, it is argued that about 5–10% of the Tibetan population being monks and nuns is already not producing any offspring. Furthermore, abortion is represented as possibly the »most frequent form of birth prevention«, a claim, however, that my data does not verify.
16 Rabinow and Rose, »Biopower Today«, op. cit. (note 6), p. 208.
17 See Greenhalgh, »Planned births, unplanned persons«, op. cit. (note 13), p. 201. However, I have evidence that at least for cadre families in Huangnan Prefecture, Qinghai Province, family planning was already implemented in Sept/Oct 1980.
18 Defined by Greenhalgh (»Science, Modernity, and the Making of China's One-Child-Policy«, op. cit. (note 13), p. 164) as »a combination of governing and political rationality«, being a critical analysis of governmental policies and programs.

ality, but that it is creating a »new demographic and policy reality by shaping what is thinkable in the domain of population«.[19]

What has been lacking in much of the academic analysis to date, is an understanding of the ways in which family planning as a state project has impacted powerfully on rural family life, and especially on women's lives, perceptions of their bodies, gender roles and lifestyles. Few academic studies tackle the experiences of family planning at the level of implementation looking at the impacts on the people being targeted. Even fewer study the impacts on minorities in China.[20] Some studies have been undertaken in the Tibet Autonomous Region (TAR) focussing on Tibetan maternal and childbirth experiences; issues of morality, religion and sexuality; on demographic change and surveying fertility rates in both rural areas and Lhasa city.[21] However, the conclusions drawn in these studies of socio-physical suffering among Tibetan women that can be traced to their social, political and economic disadvantage as a Tibetan minority in China, are not apparent in my findings from Qinghai. Rather, I found that Tibetan women came under immense pressure where modern state, traditional family and individual expectations all came into collision.

Methodologically, it is difficult to quantify the situation on the ground. Rather it is necessary to do qualitative research on the different subjective ex-

---

19 Ibid., p. 164.
20 For example, survey and focus group data analysis undertaken by the China Family Planning Association and other official institutions result of course in positive outcomes of the family planning policy for women, such as being satisfied with having two children, enabling them a better education and less economic hardship. However, it is acknowledged that through family planning there is additional pressure on women to negotiate between pressures of state and society, i.e. being expected to bear at least one son to continue the family lineage (Karen Hardy, Zhenming Xie and Baochang Gu, »Family Planning and Women's Lives in Rural China«, in: *International Family Planning Perspectives* 30 (2003), 2, pp. 68–76).
21 The situation between rural and urban TAR is already very different, and again different from my data collected in Qinghai. Goldstein's detailed longitudinal survey shows, in contrast to my data, neither a coercive family planning practice nor the collection of fines for excess children among rural Tibetans (both farmers and nomads), nor even a general two-child-policy implementation until 2000, but rather a flexible one of advisory character (cf. Melvyn C. Goldstein et al., »Fertility and Family Planning in Rural Tibet«, in: *The China Journal* 47 (January 2002), pp. 25–39). Vincanne Adams, in contrast, has found that in urban Lhasa, TAR, between the late 1980s and throughout the 1990s, family planning was clearly strict: two children for ordinary couples, and one child per couple in urban work units (Vincanne Adams, »Moral Orgasm and Productive Sex: Tantrism Faces Fertility Control in Lhasa, Tibet (China)«, in: *Sex in Development. Science, Sexuality, and Morality in Global Perspective*, ed. by Vincanne Adams & Stacy Leigh Pigg, (Durham & London: Duke University Press, 2005), pp. 207–240, in particular p. 228). On childbirth practices from Tibetan lay and a modern biomedical NGO/ Chinese public health perspective including rather positive attitudes of Tibetan women towards contraception as well as abortion, see Jennifer Chertow, »Gender, Medicine and Modernity: Childbirth in Tibet Today«, in: *Harvard Asia Quarterly* 7 (autumn 2003), 4; also Vincanne Adams et al., »Having A »Safe Delivery«: Conflicting Views from Tibet«, in: *Health Care for Women International* 26 (2005), pp. 821–851.

periences of individuals, families and communities. In contrast to the widely disseminated public state representations of family planning, individual as well as collective family planning experiences among Tibetans have no clearly discernable representation – they usually remain invisible and unheard. Neither secretly executed family planning campaigns nor individual experiences of birth control are publicly represented, nor can they be captured by household surveys. Also, both official implementers and targets are usually reluctant to talk about ›what really happened‹ on the ground. Therefore, personal experiences of family planning in the reported life stories of Tibetan women and families are the only method by which to approach questions about policy implementation on the ground from the point of view of different subjectivities and an understanding of agency in everyday life.[22]

On the level of policy representation, there are some facts about family planning which are obvious in the area of my fieldwork. Among the rural population, Tibetan farmers are permitted to have two children, whereas since 1982 nomads may officially have three.[23] Tibetan officials living in major urban areas of China are required to have only one child, whereas other government employees or cadre couples living in minority areas are required to space the births of their two permitted children by at least four years. Additionally, annual birth quotas, that are based on local population statistics, can regulate maximum permitted births in local government units (Chin. *dan wei*), and at the level of village or nomadic encampments (Chin. *xiang*). Children born in excess of these quotas have to be paid for, usually through fines or, in some cases, with pressure for sterilisation after the third child. Local officials – family planning personnel and village leaders – additionally determine the urgency and strictness of implementation at the village level. Married couples need certificates from family planning personnel in order to gain permission for stopping contraception, to get medical services, and even for wanting to have a child at a certain time. Family planning policy also regulates the age of marriage; women are required to be at least

---

22 According to De Certeau, subjectivity is a process of translation between a plurality of experiences, different versions of history, and religion in everyday life (see Valentina Napolitano & David Pratten, »Michel de Certeau: Ethnography and the Challenge of Plurality«, in: *Social Anthropology* 15 (2007), 1, pp.1–12, esp. p. 5. Whereas subaltern ›resistance‹ has been a focus in social sciences recently, I understand Tibetan women's feelings and expressions of loss or actual sickness as well as compliance and satisfaction with birth control as acts of agency vis-à-vis modernity.

23 Concerning the number of children allowed per couple, cf. Jennifer Chertow on the two-child policy in urban TAR (Tibet Autonomous Region), and for Tibetan nomads *and* farmers on the three-child policy (Chertow, »Gender, Medicine and Modernity«, op. cit. (note 21). According to Eric Mueggler, who did fieldwork in a rural minority area of Southwest China, a maximum of two children was the limit, with three permitted only if a previous child was classified as mentally or physically ill. See Eric Mueggler, *The Age of Wild Ghosts. Memory, Violence and Place in Southwest China* (Berkeley: University of California Press, 2001), p. 286.

22 and men 24 years of age. Unmarried women are not supposed to have sex, let alone children. They are often denied (or are too ashamed to ask for) government sponsored contraception, which includes free abortions, thus putting them further into a socially and economically hazardous position. All this is in stark contrast to the open-ended and non-exclusive traditional household, where generally speaking even illegitimate children were living with and accepted by the main householder, and where birth control was apparently unknown and anyway rejected for moral and karmic reasons (and still is in many cases today). However, Tibetan name-giving practices for female newborns in the past reveal a certain gender bias against many daughters, as the names »Two is Enough« (Tib. gNyis chog) or »Stop« (Tib. mTshams gcod or mTshams chod) demonstrate. They indicate the wish of parents to have no more daughters after this child.[24] It is evident that traditionally, and in contrast to sons, to have many daughters is of no interest to parents since they leave the household and cannot continue the family lineage (at least this is true for Tibetan farming communities). In this respect, daughters are similar to sons who become monks, as this Tibetan saying demonstrates: »Daughters and monks are both outsiders«.[25]

Today, fertile married women, and their families more generally, are the main targets of family planning. Even though they are now familiar with the different methods of family planning employed by the state, many are concerned about their health and bodily integrity because of bad experiences with birth control technologies and personnel. In particular, Tibetans are very aware of the fact that there is a big gap between the state representation of family planning with all its restrictions, fines and punishments or awards, and the actual practice of implementing family planning on the ground. Thus, since their incorporation into the Peoples' Republic of China, Tibetans seem to have created their own bifurcated view of reality. Sometimes, during moments of openness, they speak of having »two mouths« (Tib. *kha gnyis*);[26] one for official purposes with which they say what they are expected to, and one for private opinions and thoughts, and to express personal experiences. When speaking about ›the government‹ – and sometimes, by extension, ›the Chinese‹ population in general with whom they live as neighbours – Tibetans feel strongly about what or who is »authentic« or »true« (Tib. *ngo ma*), and whom they can trust; and what is »false« or »fake« (Tib. *rdzun ma*), and whom they cannot trust. Generally, because of the state's

---

24 Geoff Childs, »Names and Nicknames in sKyid grong«, in: *The Tibet Journal* 28 (autumn 2003), 3, pp. 17–28, in particular pp. 23, 26. He also mentions two more references that show that this custom does not seem to be a specific regional issue but a phenomenon that is found across the Tibetan cultural sphere.
25 Tib. *Bu med dang grwa pa gnyis phyi mi red*. Cf. the notion of inside and outside and its positive or negative connotations in the following paragraph.
26 The opposite, *kha gcig* (»one mouth«) indicates belonging to the same group/class/community, i.e. those who share a cup together.

pressures to conform in terms of thought, morality and behaviour, and because of the many past promises concerning equal treatment for minority nationalities that the state has not kept, government policies and promises are often labelled ›fake‹ by Tibetans in terms of their morality and integrity.

Who you can trust is simply a matter of survival. Trusted people are regarded as »insiders« (Tib. *nang mi*). These can be family or household members and their close friends, members of the same village (Tib. *sde ba*) or one's »homeland« (Tib. *pha yul,* »fatherland«) who often happen to be relatives, and members of the same tribal affiliations. »Outsiders« (Tib. *phyi mi*) are all those who do not belong to, or are not closely affiliated with, the category of insiders. They are perceived as potentially ›polluting‹. Chinese doctors involved in family planning are regarded as outsiders, for example, but so are female Tibetan family planning officials living in the village. No wonder they are commonly referred to as »spies« (Tib. *myul ma*). They are both employed by the government and intrude into the most private individual domain of reproduction. As Eric Mueggler has put it, through birth control the state transformed itself »from [an] abstract external Other to [an] abstract internal Other«.[27] Inside-outside is a major organising principle of a socio-cultural, value-laden and spatial concept that is closely connected with who one can trust and who one can not.[28] In this way, Tibetans perceive two different worlds or realities that are crucial for their identity construction and social behaviour.

The state representations of family planning on one hand, and that of personal experiences on the other, are connected by a ›gap‹ – as Vincanne Adams (this volume) refers to it – between different beliefs. This gap is the space where different representations and experiences – of state, ethnicity, family, gender and moral issues – are negotiated. This process of negotiating modernity coincides with Tim Oakes' notion of ›true‹ or ›authentic‹ modernity. He defines this as »a tense and paradoxical *process* through which people produce, confront, and negotiate a particular kind of socio-economic change«.[29] ›Authentic‹ modernity, according to Oakes, is also connected with issues of identity and (local) history, issues that are particularly important for Tibetans because of the associated socio-political implications. However, this is a subjectivity that needs to be understood as being bound up with a second concept – what Oakes calls ›false modernity‹, i.e. China's national representation of modernity as a ›state to be reached‹ through modernisation. In the following, I will expound on China's

---

27 Mueggler, *The Age of Wild Ghosts.*, op. cit. (note 23), p. 287.
28 Throughout my fieldwork and on numerous occasions, I realized the huge difference it makes to know and be affiliated with an insider or not, concerning the openness and trust interviewees bring forth towards a foreigner. On this point see also: Chertow, »Gender, Medicine and Modernity«, op. cit. (note 21).
29 Tim Oakes, *Tourism and Modernity in China* (London: Routledge, 1998), in particular p. 7.

state modernity and on the processes of social change on the ground in the context of which Tibetans negotiate gender issues, ethnic identity and local history as well as ›Chinese‹ modernity.

Negotiating Different Modernities

China is obsessed with planning a state modernity, calling it »progress« (Chin. *jinbu*; Tib. *sngon thon*, lit. »coming forward«), »development« (Chin. *fazhan*; Tib. *'phel rgyas*, lit. »increased flourishing«), and »population quality« (Chin. *suzhi*; Tib. *spus tshad*, lit. »quality rate«). The most direct way to success in terms of these goals or ideals, at least in quantifiable terms from the state's perspective, is via family planning.[30] It is socialist in its normative and structural character, calling upon all its citizens to help build a prosperous and ›civilised‹ nation, and promising a better life for all those who comply and actively participate in the restructuring process.[31] It is a ›Chinese‹ modernity in the sense of it being based upon the propagated cultural norms, values and goals of the Han majority.[32] It is modern and socialist because of its scientific manner of homogenising and standardising to ensure both economic and moral progress. In a recent campaign, even different lifestyles become homogenised in the name of development, progress and recently also environment: newly planned ›socialist villages‹ restructure ›chaotic‹ farming and nomadic areas into uniform rows of living units with the acclaimed goal of ensuring a better infrastructure, access to schools, health care, water and electricity. Through resettlement and governmental restructuring, ethnic groups like the Tibetans with their traditional way of life as farmers or nomads are purportedly transformed from »backward« (Chin. *luohou*) into modern and civilised citizens – whether they want or not.

---

30 The Tibetan equivalents for the Chinese terms of ›progress‹ etc. express the alien as well as constructed character of these modern terms.

31 Cf. Greenhalgh on the anthropology of modernity and modernist discourses of ›development‹ as a discursive construction and technology (using, for example, surveys, census and family planning programs), i.e. as a ›field of power‹. The difference between capitalist and socialist versions of modernity, eventhough both settle on ›progress‹ and ›development‹, she describes as follows: »At least theoretically, socialist modernity is a comprehensively planned modernity, organized and executed by the state« (Greenhalgh, »Planned births, unplanned persons «, op. cit. (note 13), in particular p. 198).

32 According to Ong, Chinese modernity is based on notions of culture and nation that were made synonymous with the Han race, propelled forward by a type of capitalism with Chinese characteristics, yet clearly held in its boundaries by Chinese morality (Confucianism and socialism), historiography and territory. Aiwha Ong, »Anthropology, China, and Modernities: the geopolitics of cultural knowledge«, in: *The Future of Anthropological Knowledge*, ed. by Henrietta Moore (London [u.a.]: Routledge, 1996), pp. 60–92.

Family planning has been used as a vehicle to attempt to force a Chinese figuration of modernity onto Tibetans. It has, however, triggered an unintended reaction and fostered, instead, a particular view of modernity among Tibetans, one that can be called a ›Tibetan modernity‹.³³ This entails not only a reassertion as well as reinterpretation of certain traditional cultural values and meanings in the modern context. It also generates a Tibetan figuration of modernity that is based upon negotiations between self-reflective ethnic identity, local history and Chinese modernity that is quite different from that of the Han Chinese and of the urban population in general. Among Tibetans, what is often perceived as ›authentic‹ is that which is close to Tibetan values of pride, honesty, trust and their own local cultural history. The latter is a rather neglected topic in terms of the different homogenising nationalist agendas of both the Chinese and the ›Tibetans‹. However, it is crucial to understand the role of local cultural history in identity construction. Many Tibetan communities in Qinghai have revived their local traditions after Deng Xiaoping's reforms in 1980. The region of Rebgong, the main area of my research, provides a good example of this. Rebgong's inhabitants have written and published local histories in Tibetan, not just concerning important monasteries, but also detailing local folk religion and customs. Mountain god festivals with spirit possessions, famous schools of *thanka* painting and important monasteries have all been revived. These are partly supported by the government, but are mainly funded through private financing and voluntary labour investment by local communities. Furthermore, fertility rituals, such as the wearing of a charm in order to conceive – preferably a son, or circumambulating a fertility temple praying for becoming pregnant , have become increasingly popular practices. Nevertheless, I do agree with Oakes that rather than juxtaposing tradition and modernity, the insistence on ›tradition‹ and ›authenticity‹ among ethnic minorities in China »are themselves modern sensibilities, and that (authentic) modernity is not the careening, progressive counterpoint to these ideals, but is rather the tension filled project of building a sense of identity – that is, a truly liberating subjectivity – in a chronically unstable and ever changing world«.³⁴

So what does ›modernity‹ mean at the local level for rural Tibetans? One seeks in vain for a colloquial term for ›modernity‹ which they might use. Instead, they speak of »fundamental change« (Tib. *'gyur ldog*), meaning a marked difference from their past, which is perceived as ›traditional‹. In terms of Tibetan

---

33 I disagree with Chertow's economically oriented definition of Tibetan modernity that is too simplistic: »Tibetan modernity is marked by changes introduced through commodities, technologies, movement between sites and shifts occuring with the infusion of new forms of capital into the economy combined with state regulated industries ...« See Chertow, »Gender, Medicine and Modernity«, op. cit. (note 21).

34 Oakes, *Tourism and Modernity in China*, op. cit. (note 29), in particular p. 7.

thinking, modernity or ›change‹ is generally perceived as both an ongoing and a sudden thing, marking a time of »before« (Tib. *sngon chad*) and »after« (Tib. *gzhug nas*). Local history and thinking is structured along this time line. The biggest change *per se* is usually understood as the Chinese victory over rebelling Tibetans throughout Amdo in 1958, an event that radically changed the power relations between the Chinese state and the Tibetans. However, this cannot be openly mentioned because of the public discourse of ›peaceful liberation‹.[35] In the perception of many Tibetans belonging to the older generation, Chinese modernity was abruptly imposed as the ›one‹ and ›only‹ modern reality after 1958. For Tibetans, to ›retrieve‹ and preserve their cultural traditions through supporting their recent revival have been a means of ethnic agency, the only one ensuring a survival of their culture. My informants over 50 years of age often expressed their feelings of having been subjected to and excluded from Chinese modernity, but also their desire for their children to take part in it so as to get a proper education which was denied their generation, mainly due to the Cultural Revolution. In their view, ›progress‹ as postulated by the state carries an ambivalence and potential threat because they have experienced the times ›before‹ and ›after‹ and still remember their experiences of the major and forceful changes induced by the Chinese state.

›Change‹ is also characterised by learning »new concepts (thoughts, ideas)« (Tib. *'du shes gsar ba*) or »new knowledge« (Tib. *shes bya gsar ba*) that was introduced through the school, work unit, public education and propaganda, which includes family planning campaigns. Among rural Tibetans, ›change‹ is generally located outside of the village (though changes are, of course, happening inside, all the time, mainly due to outside influence). As Duara has rightly pointed out, the depiction of tradition and modernity is a *discursive* representation, i.e. *a way of* thinking about the past, present and future that is crucial for identity building.[36] This is definitely an important analytical point that differentiates Tibetan and Chinese (state) figurations of modernity. Minority nationalities in China are especially sensitive towards their own local histories and cultural traditions since these have either been neglected or misrepresented in national histories by the Han Chinese state. Nevertheless, Chinese modernity remains something to

---

35 Thus, in Amdo Tibetan historical documents written after that time, ›change‹ becomes synonymous with Cultural Revolution. Politically sensitive terms such as Chinese ›occupation‹, ›take-over‹ or even Cultural Revolution are – understandably so – avoided terms inside China until today since they represent counter-narratives against the Chinese state's nationalistic historiography and propaganda and could become dangerous if mentioned in the wrong context.
36 Prasenjit Duara, *Rescuing History from the Nation* (Chicago: The University of Chicago Press, 1995), p. 90.

be sought after, and something that is difficult or impossible to gain access to, or engage with, while remaining ethnic ›Others‹.[37]

These tensions are played out especially in education, which is now compulsory and free of charge until ninth grade in Tibetan areas. The school system is the site where Chinese modernity is taught to the next generation and where ›population quality‹ is purportedly reproduced.[38] Rural Tibetans – farmers and increasingly nomads – have thus entered condensed spaces of Chinese modernity that profoundly influence their daily lives and even lifestyles. Already the choice for either a ›Tibetan‹ or a ›Chinese‹ primary school seems to determine children's future access to modernity. Tibetan medium schools mostly lack a sufficient education in Chinese language, which means that their students will usually fail entry examinations to higher education or chances for government jobs. Sending a child to a Chinese medium school usually translates into good job opportunities, but also can result in a cultural loss of Tibetan language and identity. Young Tibetans thus grow up without learning how to read or write their own mother tongue, and, if their parents do not educate them, they will likely learn nothing of their culture and local history. Next to education it is the increasing urbanisation of both faming villages and nomadic settlements that produces condensed locations of state modernity. Rural Tibetans who visit or move to a new township enter a space of Chinese modernity with concrete and glass buildings, luxury goods, restaurants and government offices that can make their own lifestyles appear ›backward‹, and undesirable. One might argue that this is the course of global modern life and of colonial or state relations between majority and minority groups; and, it is one that is often welcomed by the poor and uneducated, seemingly giving them hope of finally gaining access to modernity and the wealth that it promises. Additionally, Western modernity has an alluring effect on young well-educated Tibetans from both rural and especially urban contexts. Access to it is gained through the acquisition of English language skills and many would like to work in a Western NGO, or even better, to study abroad.[39]

There is an important gendered aspect to Tibetan modernity transmitted through modern education, in that education can empower Tibetan women as agents where family planning matters and marriage are concerned. Many young Tibetan women feel anxious about traditional forms of virilocal marriage, in

---

37 Cf. Louisa Schein, *Minority Rules: the Miao and the Feminine in China's cultural Politics* (Durham: University Press, 2000).

38 Rachel Murphy, »Turning Peasants into Modern Chinese Citizens: »Population Quality« Discourse, Demographic Transition and Primary Education«, in: *The China Quarterly* 177 (March 2004), pp. 1–20.

39 The issue of Western modernity among Tibetans is a complex one since it is also heavily influenced by Tibetan exile politics, and the mutual fascination with the mythos of Tibet or the West.

which they must leave their parents behind and move into their husband's family household where they must not only care for their in-laws but also their own new family. Better education and birth control can lead to employment and emancipatory economic independence for young Tibetan women, and allow an escape from the family expectations and heavy workload typical of married life. On the other hand, gendered modernity can also represent additional alienation for those who still live a more ›traditional‹ lifestyle. A Tibetan woman farmer with three children who recently moved her family from her husband's village to the prefecture town due to her new government job reported that she suddenly felt like an ›alien‹ (i.e. ›backward‹) among her colleagues and friends in town. This was because she had ›so many‹ children compared to them, and while she had always given birth at home in the village, this was something now perceived as unusual for a woman working and living in town where all births occur in hospitals. Such conflicts demonstrate that even within rural areas, the setting of village or town and of education/profession determines how much modernity counts as a normal, desirable or undesirable way of life.

Local History and Modernity

Since local histories are very diverse in Tibetan areas, and because they play a big role in ethnic identity construction and the way in which modernity is played out, I will briefly outline the local history of the region in which I conducted my fieldwork. Qinghai Province is a multi-ethnic border zone whose long geopolitical history is one of border wars and fluctuating shifts in power between Tibetans, Han Chinese and other ethnic groups, and thus is quite different from the history of Central Tibet, the present-day Tibetan Autonomous Region (TAR). During the past millennium, Qinghai or Amdo has witnessed an ebb and flow of major and minor invasions by different Mongol, Chinese and Muslim forces, while local Tibetan tribes either affiliated with or fought against them. The eastern geopolitical margins of the Tibetan plateau were also an important trading zone for the exchange of Tibetan highland and Chinese lowland products, an exchange often mediated in recent centuries by the local Hui Muslim population. Until today, similar socio-economic structures continue to operate in Amdo. Local histories of warfare and alliances continuously inscribed themselves onto the landscape, culture and memories of the Tibetans living in Amdo. Thus, former Tibetan and Chinese warlords or generals became embodied as mountain gods who ritually protected Tibetan tribes settled in the area, maintaining their territory and the pre-modern political and social order.

After the largely nominal Qing political presence in the region had collapsed, and the Guomindang had come to power in the new republic, a ferocious Hui Muslim warlord family ruled over much of Qinghai between 1920 and 1950. Vividly remembered until today, its most infamous representative, Ma Bufeng, is still known to the Tibetans as the ›slaughterer‹. It is not hard to imagine that, following the initial Chinese Communist invasion into Tibetan areas of Qinghai in 1950, local Tibetans who had lived under Ma Bufeng's rule might have initially felt that they had indeed been ›liberated‹ by the Peoples' Liberation Army (PLA).

At the beginning of their encroachment, the Communists were friendly and helpful to local Tibetans, introducing and offering secular education and health services to ordinary people for the very first time. Thus in 1952, the first secular state school was founded in Tongren. Many of the pupils later became high-ranking communist cadres at various county and prefecture levels in Qinghai, among them were also public health and family planning personnel in Tongren, as will be further detailed in the next section. Most of them had to learn spoken Chinese from scratch, thus they now do not know how to read or write Tibetan, and some have lost their knowledge of local traditions, and never participate in religious festivals since cadres are generally discouraged from doing so. As graduates of this first modern Chinese school, they became responsible for implementing Chinese modernity in Tibetan territory. However, this image of the liberating Chinese state dramatically changed after 1955 during the period of so-called Democratic Reform. Chinese attempts to abolish the local social hierarchies and private land ownership were challenged by fierce, armed Tibetan resistance throughout Amdo between 1956 and 1958, after which the rebellions were quelled militarily. This was followed by a series of disastrous socialist campaigns. These included the Great Leap Forward (1958–1962), the Anti-Superstition Campaign (during which all religious activities were banned and monasteries began to be destroyed), and the infamous Cultural Revolution (1966–1976), all of which continued to cut through the social, political and ethnic fabric of Amdo Tibetan communities. Thus, 1958 became the landmark year for Amdo Tibetans' perception of ›before‹ and ›after‹, of an earlier time of their own ›tradition‹ versus a later period of alien and potentially hostile ›Chinese modernity‹ imposed upon them by outsiders.

This dramatic shift from local Tibetan communities leading relatively autonomous lives as farmers, nomads and traders, to having state-controls imposed upon them entailed their being defined collectively as a »nationality« (Chin. *minzu*), then as members of »communes« (Chin. *gongshe*) and then, after 1982, as official »families« (Chin. *jiating*, Tib. *khyim tshang*) in the Family Responsibility System (Chin. Jiating lianchan chengbao zerengzhi). Tibetans were left with a deep-seated and ongoing mistrust towards the Chinese state. Ethnically redefined and unified but administratively restructured and fragmented into various autonomous counties and prefectures that cut across former tribal borders and alliances, Tibetans were transformed into citizens of an alienating socialist motherland. Taken together, these transformations represented an ongoing homogenisation process that was being attempted by the state, with family planning campaigns being one of its more recent manifestations. Oakes concludes that, »modernity in China is thus characterized by shifting meanings that are contingent upon local histories and geographies, and the articulations of these with the state and global capitalism«.[40]

Agents and Targets

Among the first generations of Tibetan cadres from Tongren, who were educated in the 1950s or late 1970s, there are also those who are today responsible for local public health and family planning. Groups of such ›cadre‹ classmates have established new, modern social networks that now have a considerable local socio-economic and political impact in Tongren. As local Tibetans, they have become model citizens of China, rewarded with well-paid government posts but burdened with the task of locally implementing unpopular state policies. While being able to actively shape the way modernity develops in their social environment, they are also being held responsible for the success or failure of campaigns, something which can cause them to lose their positions. Caught between the local Tibetan population and Chinese state policies, they are nevertheless at the forefront of translating and implementing Chinese modernity in their local Tibetan area. Asked about the reasons for family planning, a high-ranking, male Tibetan health administrator stated, »Before we had many births, and also many deaths of children and mothers. Now we have fewer but safer births and healthier children. So the difference lies in the fact that less people die«. This is of course a somewhat blinkered but convenient view. Among those extended Tibetan families, whom I interviewed, there was an obvious decline in birth rates from 5–7 children per couple before 1980 down to just 2–3 children today. But how was this decline actually achieved? The following example of a woman who was forced to abort shows how families were coerced into limiting the number of their children:

A mother of five children in her sixties talks to me about her forced abortion with tears in her eyes. She is the wife of a high-ranking government official, and in the mid 1980s

---

40 Oakes, *Tourism and Modernity in China*, op. cit. (note 29), p. 20.

she fell pregnant for a sixth time, despite having taken contraceptive pills. Her fifth child was born just after the implementation of the two-child-policy in August 1980, but by officially putting back his date of birth to a couple of months earlier, she was able to keep him. But then, she and her husband were put under pressure for a sixth child was out of question and would have cost her husband his government job. She was even willing to divorce her husband, she said, just in order to keep their child. She was hoping for another boy to give her two sons and three daughters another brother but then they had to make this pragmatic decision. So they »took the baby« (Tib. *sha nye len*).

There are also mobile ›ambulances‹ in which family planning teams from the county level clinics visit – unannounced, of course – certain targeted villages and perform abortions[41] and sterilisations in their vehicle ›for free‹. They also collect women who have already had three children and perform sterilization operations on them. While it was extremely hard to find evidence for the secret mass mobilisation campaigns for family planning at the village level which have sometimes been reported, they clearly did take place at certain times and places. Information on them is hard to come by for several reasons. Only fertile women who would have become pregnant or wished to do so in the same year as a campaign in their village, would have experienced them. These campaigns were also secret enterprises, and were never publicly announced, a striking contrast to the wide coverage given public announcements of family planning policies in general with their slogans that function like advertisements for a better quality life and population. When asked directly, family planning personnel denied outright their involvement in control programs to achieve birth quotas per year and per village; they even denied the very existence of such things, in general. Thus, the existence of secret and mass family planning campaigns was only revealed through the personal accounts of the targeted women:

Once a village woman told me that she was ›lucky‹ in 1983 when she was pregnant with her second child – her first child was a girl and thus she was allowed to have a second chance – she was wishing for a boy that year, she explained. The authorities had targeted her village and had allowed only five births in that particular year. Other women of her village were not so fortuitous in 1983.[42] The same woman also stated that later on, and somewhat ironically, she had to apply for a special permit to get her IUD taken out since she did not need contraception anymore. Her husband had died the year before. Initially, the authorities refused her request, and she had to apply to the next (higher) level of administration in order to get permission to get rid of it, which was finally accepted.

It is not only the targeted women but also village family planning personnel, all of whom are female, who are in a difficult position. They are the main agents, and at the same time targets, of family planning programs at the village level and

---

41 Since about five years, there is an abortion pill in place making operations unnecessary, it seems.
42 Thus, I guess, abortions or postponements of pregnancies must have been the consequence.

are regarded as local – and the only tangible – embodiments of state power over women's bodies, especially in the village where they themselves live. They have to become models of family planning by undergoing their own sterilisation and bear the frustrations and anger of targeted women and their families on a daily basis. Physically intruding into the houses of those families who transgress quotas, and equipped with the law as part of state power or accompanied by county medical or administrative personnel responsible for family planning, they can force women to go to clinics for procedures or to the local government offices in order to pay fines for their transgressions. In the beginning of the 1980s, their only job other than giving out free contraception (condoms and the ›pill‹ – both methods not preferred and little used by Tibetans), was to count and report pregnancies and births – a task now increasingly taken over by *xiang* and higher level clinics if women choose to, or need to, give birth at a clinic. Village family planning personnel are not medically trained, and are not trusted by their neighbours to give out ›medicine‹ (the pill is locally called »medicine«, Tib. *sman*) since they are regarded as ›spies‹. On top of this, they are lowly paid compared to all the higher-ranking family planning personnel at *xiang*, county and prefecture levels. Between 1985 and 1988, their salary was about 150 Yuan per annum. It doubled in the following years, and since 2003 they earn 1000 Yuan annually, which is about two-thirds of an average farmer's annual cash income.

In addition, these village family planning women are looked down upon because their job is one intimately connected with what are considered to be very private matters of sex and reproduction. Also, everyone knows that they have to report excess births in their village and thus ensure that fines are collected by the *xiang* government, or that abortions of illegitimate (unregistered) children are performed. Nowadays, the salaries of female village family planning personnel depend upon the amount of fines collected. Most of these women come from a communist party background, and belonged to, or continue to belong to, the party's Women's Federation collective from where they were recruited, many of them in the 1970s. Often they are of low socio-economic background, have no husbands and were more or less coerced to take on this unpopular job. Their first task as models of ideal birth control practice was to be sterilised after having had two or more children themselves – if those children were born before 1980.

In contrast to such village family planning personnel, family planning cadres at the *xiang* (village cluster) administrative level are actually official government employees who are not only better paid, but are further removed from the implementation process at the village level. They are often not local inhabitants, which makes less likely corruption or favouritism for those in local social networks or those with whom one has family ties. This is because they usually do not stay very long in a particular position – least in family planning jobs – at any given place. Subsequent transfers to a different administrative unit are common, but depend upon cadres being able to meet set targets per district for birth limits. A good performance might mean a quicker rise to higher and better positions in another department of their preference. Even though being a family planning cadre is a much-despised job, it can also in many cases be a stepping-stone towards a better government career.

Like village family planning women, village leaders are directly involved in ensuring proper implementation of government policies at the village level, which includes family planning policies. However, they are – in contrast to the former– neither appointed by the government nor socially stigmatised, but are voted into their office by the village members every three years. What follows is a personal experience with family planning related by a village leader:

The village leader, 61 years old, welcomes me to his house. After we drink tea and chat about his job and responsibilities in the village, I ask him what he thinks about family planning and how – if at all – he has had to take on any responsibilities in terms of policy implementation in his village. All of a sudden he gets very upset, talking about a recent incident caused by the local family planning woman in his village – whom he pejoratively calls a ›government spy‹. The year before (2005), this woman forced 18 village women who already had given birth to two children to go together to be sterilised. If they did not comply (meaning that the family planning woman and the village were to be punished for not fulfilling the set quota of sterilisations), they were threatened with harsh punishments, such as loss of their husbands' government jobs or high fines of several thousand Yuan for non-government workers and farmers. I asked him what exactly had made him so angry about it. He replied that this family planning woman – in contrast to himself as an elected leader of the community – didn't do her job properly, since the local government had given orders to collect 18 women not just from his village (Tib. *sde ba*) but from the much larger area of several villages which together make up the smallest administrative unit, a *xiang*. He bemoaned her unprofessional and ignorant behaviour in neither consulting him nor complying properly with the orders – which would have targeted women in a locally less focused way. He did not complain about the general fact that she had done it at all, since that was her job. Although they are supposed to work together, the family planning woman had not informed him about her manoeuvre at all. Afterwards, upset families from his village complained to him about this even though he had not been personally involved. He pointed out that he even went to complain to the local government, trying to stop this unjustly targeted campaign. Yet, his efforts were in vain.

Only later did I hear that my village leader informant was himself a victim. The village leader's own daughter-in-law, living with him in the same household, was among the women targeted, and since she had previously given birth to only two girls, her sterilisation meant a terrible personal loss for him and his son – it meant that the patrilineal family lineage (Tib. *pha rgyud*) would be ›cut‹, i.e. not continue to the next generation.

In addition to family planning personnel and village leaders, the so-called barefoot doctors (Tib. *rkang rjen sman pa*) employed by the government at *xiang* level must also become involved in family planning. They must confirm statistics on the numbers of children per household when doing home visits for immunising young children. In fact, all doctors employed by the government are supposed to report the number of children their patients have, something many do not follow up on properly or strictly comply with. Whereas in the 1960s and 70s, barefoot doctors seem to have worked mainly at township (Chin. *xian*) level, from the 1980s onwards they only worked at the *xiang* level. It did not seem to matter what kind of medical training – whether in Tibetan or ›Western‹ medicine – they previously had. Their tasks included keeping records of the number of women using IUDs or being sterilised. Until the 1990s, they also helped women giving birth when requested. This task was then taken over by both maternal and child health care centres and family planning doctors at the county level. This clearly shows how the responsibility for dealing with birthing has been shifted to more centralised family planning, maternal and child health care centres and bureaucratic structures, eliminating the (more personal) involvement of *xiang* doctors from the birth process.

The Economics of Reproduction or the Costs of and for Life

In contrast to traditional views on having children (and especially sons, as illustrated in the example given above), the state's perspective is one of rational calculation of costs and of efficient administrative implementation. State family planning must be seen as part of larger institutions and projects, such as the public health sector, and of revised policies since the 1980s to do with education and economic development. In China as well as in Tibetan minority areas, family planning has become closely linked with the delivery of general public health services and with population statistics offices. For example, home visits by local barefoot doctors who immunise officially registered children under three years of age free of charge, also involve these health workers in reporting back the number of children per household to local statistics and family planning offices. On the other hand, a recently promoted ›biomedicalisation‹ of birth practices through their representation as ›safe delivery‹ and client-oriented quality health services has facilitated and legitimised family planning and birth control measures since about the mid 1990s, making them more popular. Yet, prices for reliable contraception – better quality IUDs and contraceptives with fewer health risks – as well as the costs of birthing in hospitals have increased and have widened the gap between rich and poor, making it increasingly difficult for poor women to control their fertility and have a safe childbirth.

Poorer families are under heavier pressure than richer ones concerning the number and maintenance of their children, unless they find other strategies, such as giving surplus children to relatives. Richer families are able to pay the state-imposed fines for excess children as well as cover the costs for a quality birth in a safe (but more expensive) prefectural or provincial hospital.[43] If necessary, they will be able to afford the transport to the hospital, in contrast to their poorer neighbours whose delivery might be hindered by not being able to afford these facilities with possible fatal consequences. A minimum of about 300 Yuan has to be paid to a local village clinic for a birth. Once in a public doctor's hands, a Tibetan family might be advised to go to a larger hospital with better equipment, but which will also be more expensive and further away. A minimum of about 800 Yuan must be handed over before being admitted into such hospitals; if not, admission will be refused. While Chertow highlights the pragmatic choices made by women concerning childbirth when it comes to the use of either biomedicine or traditional Tibetan medicine,[44] this is not my concern here, since many rural women do not have these choices. Most of the rural Tibetan women I questioned preferred to have children at home if the pregnancy and the previous birth were normal. It seemed to be primarily a matter of whom to trust – one's own health and strength, a local doctor or a hospital – and of money as well as access to health facilities, rather than it being a conscious choice of a modern versus a traditional way of going about childbirth.[45]

I summarise below the fines and approximate expenses for health care and education versus the financial awards or advantages if one has less children. Such figures also depend upon fluctuations in prices over time, upon personal relations that a family may have with officials, the medical standard of clinics and hospitals, and the strictness with which fines are levied and collected. One can usefully compare the costs below with the average annual cash income of farmers in Huangnan Prefecture, which is around 1.700 Yuan:[46]

---

43 Village clinics and county hospitals have fewer facilities and would refer a mother in childbirth to higher level hospitals if complications that make a cesarian necessary occur. The costs for the latter can amount to about 3–4000 Yuan, a horrendous sum of money that can financially ruin a family. Some children are even named after the costs the parents had to pay as fines. Thus, one child that I heard about was called the ›golden son‹ (Tib. *gser bu*).
44 See Chertow, »Gender, Medicine and Modernity«, op. cit. (note 21).
45 Also, it is common that Tibetans will wait quite long until they go and search for a doctor which means that a complication in pregnancy or childbirth (or other life-threatening ailments in general) are then already quite serious and more difficult to be helped with. Sometimes, hospitals can't help much then, and so it happens that still some women die in childbed. This does not add to the reputation of hospitals.
46 This does not take into account the biggest cash generator in the region through the collection

a) high fees or punishments in cases of excess children (more than two children among farmers, more than three for nomads), between 1.000 – 4.000 Yuan[47]
b) rising costs for education since 1989[48]
c) rising costs for IUDs, while sterilisation and oral contraception remain free[49]
d) rising costs for births and general health care in hospitals[50]
e) awards of money and food stuffs for voluntary early sterilisation after the first child
f) awards for couples without any children: annual old-age pension of between 1.000–1.500 Yuan

According to my interviews with maternal health personnel, in Tongren County about 50 per cent of Tibetan village women go to a county or prefecture clinic to give birth. Yet, only rarely do they visit the doctors at the county Maternal Health and Child Care centre who are able to ensure safe pregnancies and deliveries, as well as child healthcare including immunisation. The Maternal Health and Child Care centre's connection with family planning and statistics offices (and thus potential to impose fines and punishments for transgressors) makes women's contact with them a hazardous affair. In summary, the costs for safe contraception, for giving birth under medical supervision, of fines for having additional children, as well as the costs of higher education for children have all risen dramatically since the end of the 1980s, making having children

---

of the Caterpillar Fungus (*Cordyceps Sinensis* or »Jatsa Gumbu«, tib. *dbyar rtswa dgun 'bu*, »(in) summer (it is) grass, (in) winter (it is an) insect / caterpillar«) that can amount – if lucky – to several thousand, sometimes several ten thousands of Yuan.

47 It seems that it depends on the local family planning personnel how and whether the fines are negotiable. The highest fees that I recorded were until 2000 for 3rd child 1000 Yuan (more than half of an average annual cash income), and since then 3–4000 Yuan, so only affordable for rich persons.

48 According to my informants in Rebgong, primary school remained for free. However, between 1989 and ca. 2004, for the middle school until 9th grade, around 40 Yuan per year had to be paid; for high school, 500 – 600 Yuan have to be paid per year, including fees for books, computer usage, heating. The government helps with students' food allowance. College fees, however, remain very high, they amount to 5–7000 Yuan per year and are a pre-condition to get a much sought-after government job. Only since 2004 are primary and middle school until grade 9 free of charge. Loans at local banks for paying the educational fees are difficult to get, especially if one is a farmer or nomad without guaranteed annual cash income.

49 Whereas at the *xiang* level, the cost for IUD remain rather low (around 15 to 40 Yuan), many women prefer to go to county or even prefecture hospitals for ›safety‹ reasons (since those are better equipped) but where they need to pay much more. Since 1993, private doctors are allowed to open up clinics, so they, too, insert and take out IUDs.

50 To give birth at a (presumably better equipped) prefecture level peoples' hospital, it would cost a minimum of 800–1500 Yuan for a normal birth, approx. half an annual income. For a cesarian or a complicated birth, 3000 to 4000 Yuan would be necessary to be paid. In a *xiang* clinic, however, the cost for a normal birth are around 50 to 200 Yuan – still a lot of money for poorer people and nomads, coming from remote places, even more so.

an extremely expensive affair compared to the recent past. Additionally, and in contrast to the 1980s and 1990s, investment in expensive secondary education for children no longer ensures a secure government job, and the unemployment level among well-educated Tibetans has risen in recent years. As stated by many of my informants, this is one of the reasons why the governments' ›less is more‹ formula regarding family size and the quality of life is not just taken for granted anymore.

Childbirth and Birth Control

Birth control is closely connected with matters of childbirth wherein both state and public health services work hand-in-hand, implementing modern biotechnologies for limiting the number of births. Next to birth control, childbirth is the second major area where the gap between Tibetan traditional beliefs or practices and modern technologies of biomedicine and state health institutions puts Tibetan women into a very vulnerable position. As mentioned above, the relationship of inside to outside is crucial when it comes to matters of the body, family and state (or outsiders in general). The following sketch from my 2006 visit to an Amdo Tibetan farming household may illustrate this point:

I enter the family house through a big wooden gate adorned with a juniper branch, a sign that a woman in this house has just given birth and is staying at home to rest. High sand-brown adobe walls protect the inside of the courtyard and the inside of the house from any outsider's eyes. This construction is similar to that of most of the houses in the Tibetan farming villages of the rather fertile Rebgong, valley in Qinghai Province. Before entering the house, however, I have to jump over a coal-fire next to the gate to purify myself; the young mother needs special protection from any outsiders who could – unintentionally and unknowingly – introduce malevolent spirits into the house, spirits that Tibetans believe might be sitting upon their backs. They could threaten the health of both the mother and the newborn. My assistant, a young local Tibetan woman from the same village, also jumps over the fire and introduces me to the family. I automatically feel like an intruder and imagine how it must be, as a family planning official, to knock upon such a door in order to tell the family that they need to pay a fine for their excess child, or worse, to accompany them to the local government office or clinic for sterilisation.[51]

The potential ›danger‹ posed by outsiders to childbirth is so strong that already during pregnancy women avoid contact with them. Traditionally, and possibly for the same reason, there have been no professional midwives who have specialised in helping Tibetan women to give birth. Instead, knowledgeable moth-

---

51 Excerpt from my fieldnote book, 2006.

ers or older sisters, and sometimes an experienced and trusted female neighbour would take care of the mother during childbirth. Doctors of Tibetan medicine do not seem to have been heavily involved in childbirth. Rather, lamas could be called upon in difficult cases and would roll their rosaries on the expectant mother's belly, pronounce mantras and offer prayers to facilitate the birthing process. Disquieted husbands would walk to the top of the local protector mountain to make a fumigation offering by burning juniper branches and flour for the mountain god. A woman in the bed in which she will give birth and her family must obey many rules if conditions permit. They must keep very warm, eat and drink only warm nourishing food, and avoid outsiders' visits for a certain length of time, etc. More often than not, Tibetan women – especially nomads – used to give birth all by themselves, often having to continue working immediately afterwards.[52]

Another aspect of traditional Tibetan reproductive practices, which stands in stark contrast with modern birth control policies, is the complete lack of birth control. According to Tibetan Buddhism (and Bon religion), preventing and taking a human life[53] runs completely contrary to the moral cosmology of karma and rebirth. To be born human – rather than an alternative birth as an animal, hungry ghost or demi-god – represents the best of the six possible rebirth states, and the only one through which enlightenment or ›liberation‹ from the inherent suffering of existence is possible. For the same reason, abortion is still commonly thought of as a ›sin‹ (Tib. *sdig pa*).[54] Also, from the point of view of traditional Tibetan medicine, sterilisation (locally called »*tshe*«) hinders the flow of bodily substances whose free circulation is crucial for general wellbeing.[55]

---

52 While blood, especially birth blood, is generally believed among Tibetan (and other societies) to be polluting (Tib. *sgrib*), i.e. dangerous for health and also morally contagious. I could not find evidence for this kind of belief among present-day Tibetan farming women. Instead, they pointed out to me that to give birth in a physically ›lower place‹, i.e. one that lies closer to the ground than the usual living area or the bed, would facilitate and fasten the birth process. Furthermore, to hold a newborn under an animal or name it for example ›dog‹ is believed to avert evil spirits (who like to attack vulnerable human beings) and thus protect the child.

53 Tibetans calculate human age from conception onwards, hence newborns are already one year old. Also, each Tibetan New Year (Tib. *lo gsar*) everybody gets one year older.

54 However, especially young unmarried women have no choice but to abort because of today's social and political stigma of illegitimate children – contrary to the former Tibetan society!

55 In Tibetan medicine, as expounded in the classical Tibetan medical book of the Four Tantras (*Rgyud bzhi*), the bodily substances are: starting with the nutritive essence of food and drink (chyle), that nourishes the blood, that nourishes flesh, building up fat, bone, marrow and finally sperm and ovum. Since birth control is not part of Tibetan medicine, yet Tibetan doctors have collected experiences with patients who were sterilised since more than 25 years, there seems to be a danger of attracting wind disorders, especially of the heart wind type (*snying rlung*) that can cause madness (conversation with a doctor of Tibetan medicine, April 23, 2007).

»I will not die from that« (Tib. *Da nga du gi shi thug ni ma red*)[56] was an oft-heard comment by Tibetan women speaking about their modern birth control experiences. Many of the older (40+) generation of women informants, however, reported temporary or long-term physical problems with contraception. This might have been for several reasons: the foreignness of newly imposed ideas and intrusive bodily practices of contraception in general in the 1980s; the fact that birth control was initially conducted by Chinese government officials and work units; the less well-developed contraception technology of the 1980s; and local sterilisation campaigns that these women may have been the targets of. Other younger female informants, mostly in their 20s and 30s, seemed to experience either no physical problems with contraception – usually IUDs or sterilisation – or, if they experienced them, they were reported as rather common or trivial issues. Yet, abortion always remained an extremely sensitive subject among my informants of all ages, and one that was only talked about indirectly. Its existence as part of the state's birth control regime was only rarely mentioned in interviews and sometimes denied, although certain accounts leave no doubt about its occurrence. More often nowadays, abortion appears to be the option for young unmarried women who have an unwanted pregnancy. During my fieldwork I heard of three cases during the past five years where young women died due to birth complications either because they could not afford medical treatment or could not be transported to clinics in time. Even though the issue of a ›safe delivery‹ is now a recognised part of maternal and child health care services, having a safe birth is not supported by health insurance and thus must be paid for privately, something that is not within the reach of a large proportion of the Tibetan population. Furthermore, Tibetan women expressed their concern or contempt for the often mechanical, insensitive and denigrating ways in which the state implements its birth control policy through its doctors, most of whom only speak Chinese. Tibetan women report being treated in disrespectful ways, such as being shouted at, or receiving no explanation about what was or will be happening to them, how they should care for their health following procedures, and so on. This is also reported of childbirth experiences in clinics or hospitals, where Chinese doctors usually outnumber Tibetans. Most informants are very aware that as women they are caught between strict state controls, unfriendly doctors, and male ignorance concerning contraception.[57] Additionally, at least in Tibetan farming areas, husbands, parents and parents-in-laws all wish for, and

---

56 Colloquial expression when people talk about past illnesses or health problems. Tibetans have a high tolerance for pain and look down on people who complain a lot about their ailments.
57 A so-called ›barefoot‹ doctor from a small village clinic told me that she as a Tibetan women's doctor was the most popular and sought-after doctor of the whole area because women trusted her much more, partly because they could communicate in Tibetan. According to my interviewees, condoms are rarely used on the countryside, while family planning women in the village,

expect to have, at least one son or grandson. This strong social expectation only adds additional pressure on women when it comes to the issue of childbirth, as will be shown below.

Depending upon their personal experiences with state-imposed (as opposed to voluntary) birth control, Tibetan women who had health problems expressed them through idioms of physical pain, such as backaches, and a general loss of physical power.[58] Many reported a weakness of their bodies, such as constantly feeling tired or not being able to carry heavy loads for a long time (often several years) following, or ever since, their sterilisation.[59] Apart from their own health problems, this confronts them with another dilemma; that of socially-mediated gender discrimination. It is crucial here to understand that in Amdo Tibetan communities, women's ability to work hard and carry heavy loads is an important gender marker for social status. A Tibetan woman who is considered »lazy« – because she can't or worse, doesn't want to work hard, does not get up early etc. – is regarded as the worst social disgrace imaginable for a family and in a community. This is especially true for the »naama«, the young wife who marries into and resides in her parents-in-law's household. Thus, physically weak and ›lazy‹ Tibetan women become socially stigmatised. They are teased with the name *rgya mo* meaning ›Chinese‹ or ›foreign‹ woman, who are believed not to work hard.

There are local examples of the testing of women's physical and moral strength. One is the annual village ritual of *chos skor*, literally »circling [with] the [religious] law/ *dharma*«. This a public rite enacted by mostly young and still unmarried women who have to carry extremely heavy loads of Buddhist

---

theoretically at least, hand condoms out for free. Nobody takes up their service, however, since they are regarded as ›government spies‹, and the whole issue of sex is a ›shameful‹ one.

58 Biomedical doctors whom I interviewed generally claimed that IUD and sterilisation are safe and unproblematic methods for birth control. However, several female doctors did admit that the quality of contraception has not been good until recently, many women getting pregnant anyway or having health problems after their use. Doctors of Tibetan medicine pointed to the many female patients that they try to treat who do have actual pain and physical problems caused by modern contraception. Many of them oppose these methods since they are seen to interrupt the natural flows in the body, or causing ›cold‹ disorders (IUDs are made from metal), a Tibetan medical illness category. In any case, the idea of cutting or loosing body strength, in particular through sterilization, seems to be a very common one among Tibetan as well as Chinese women. According to Yunxiang Yan, rural Chinese women explained this as a ›flowing out‹ of their life force or *qi*. This loss was then remedied by new gift rituals (Yunxiang Yan, *Private Life Under Socialism. Love, Intimacy, and Family Change in a Chinese Village 1949–1999* (Stanford: Stanford University Press, 2003), p. 194).

59 The report »Tears of Silence...« (see note 15) summarises women's health problems because of sterilisation and abortion in China as follows: »The symptoms described are remarkably consistent and include most commonly, backache, loss of appetite with attendant gastric problems, weakness and tiredness. Some report fever and headaches. There are even reports that some women have died or suffered chronic problems as a result of such operations«.

scriptures upon their backs while walking around a sacred mountain. On one occasion I accompanied them around the mountain and chatted with some of the female participants about gender relations. Two young girls reported their back pain from carrying the heavy, block-printed scriptures. However, they assured me that they would never complain about this in front of any Tibetan man, even when asked about it. Nor did they show any expression of pain when later on one of the accompanying young men tried to ›test‹ them by hitting them on their backs. Complaints about physical weakness between men and women is something that is a total taboo, and appeared to young Tibetan women as something which might narrow the chances of finding a good marriage partner.

The official limit of only two children per farming family puts additional pressure on rural couples who commonly also want to have at least one son. Especially among Tibetan farmers, sons are clearly more valued in terms of continuing the family lineage (i.e. »paternal lineage«, Tib. *pha rgyud*), and ensuring parental care in old age.[60] Also, several older Tibetan men and the parents of young couples, expressed their concerns about Tibetans as a ›nationality‹ going into demographic decline, especially vis-à-vis the Chinese population.[61] Village fertility rituals in which young boys are showcased as a kind of ›lucky charm‹ are now booming in the region. Tantrists (Tib. *sngags pa*) are busy producing specific charms for pregnant women to ensure the birth of a son, and visits to local fertility temples are also very popular for the same reason. Having many sons defined – and still defines – the strong Amdo Tibetan family; sons have always been highly valued for defending the family during disputes. Thus, a strong family, that is, one with many sons, had a high status in the community, and even today this is still the case. Sons are proudly put forward as members of the village community and are presented to the public in the manifold, annual community rituals celebrated in the farming areas of Rebgong, or in the horse riding festivals on the nomadic plains of Amdo. Families comprised of two or

---

60 Among Tibetan nomads, women can also inherit and continue the lineage. A young father in a farming area of a little three-year-old boy whose wife was pregnant again expressed his strong wish for a second boy, so that his son could have a real ›friend‹ to play with. Friendship seems culturally only sanctioned among same-sexed siblings since there are many tabus between sisters and brothers. Before this birth, he was eager to explain to me the signs that surely, this second child would be a son – explaining the shape of the belly of his wife, analysing his and her dreams and her eating habits, moods and so on. He was bitterly disappointed when the baby turned out to be a girl. He strongly believed that his second sons' sex was switched into that of a girl – a very common belief still today, and even among well-educated young Tibetans.

61 However, as Geoff Childs has now demonstrated, fertility decline among both exile Tibetans and those living in China is a complex issue. It depends not only upon political agendas, but also on social, economic and cultural changes, as well as re-emerging patterns of the past, such as low fertility through polyandrous marriages and the existence of a celibate clerical population. See Geoff Childs, *Tibetan Transitions. Historical and Contemporary Perspectives on Fertility, Family Planning, and Demographic Change* (Leiden: Brill Publishers, 2008).

Figure 5: A modern Tibetan two-child family on their way to a village festival.

three daughters, feel ›doomed‹ by contrast, and perceive that they are additionally punished by the state for being denied another chance to have a son. But beyond gender preference, children – whether boys or girls – are never viewed as a burden by Tibetans, who merely say, »Where there is a mouth, there is a portion« (Tib. *Kha zhig yod na, skal zhig yod*). Rather, not being able to have children, not wanting them or simply being in a state of ›not having‹ children carries a social stigma.

Conclusion

We have seen how family planning through childbirth and birth control is strictly controlled by the state through health care institutions and statistics offices, doctors, family planning personnel, and a system of fines and punishments. Caught between Tibetan socio-cultural issues and the amenities of Chinese modernity such as health services for a safe delivery and an education that might give them more independence, Tibetan women, as explicit family planning targets *and* as traditional ›culture holders‹, are in a precarious situation. As Tibetans, whether in a self-reflective manner or not, they are having to renegotiate Tibetan and Chinese modernities in various contexts and at different times, and, additionally, they have to juggle culturally implicit gender issues that circumscribe their mobility and choices between these two poles. Tibetan modernity, which is impinged upon by ethnic gender expectations, the local community and state institutions, scrutinises Tibetan women even more than other women in China in terms of their moral as well as sexual and reproductive behaviour and bodily functions.

The tension-filled gap in modern family planning between ›the system‹ and individual human action or agency; between official, publicly displayed written and individual oral ›invisible‹ representation; between state and community and personal goals or experience only becomes clearly defined when examined through the experiences of the various actors involved. The implementers, models and targets of family planning have different collective and individual subjectivities and agencies, while local history shapes the way in which modernity is played out more generally on a local level. From a more philosophical stance, whichever general understanding and different types or figuration of modernity we try to define or juxtapose as realities being negotiated in China, they are also culturally constructed representations that are closely entangled with identity issues. Figurations of modernity are thus fragmented, constructed and negotiated differently by different peoples' subjectivities. Therefore, it is important to take an actor-centred approach to figurations of modernity – one that is sensitive to power and gender relations, looking at specific space and time frames in which ›authentic‹ modernity is an issue to be negotiated in particularly intensified and conflicted ways.

In the final analysis, the advantages and disadvantages of family planning depend upon access to a state modernity and on having the financial means. This clearly disadvantages poor rural families and especially women who are dependent upon labour-intensive, traditional subsistence economies. Thus, the government's implementation of strict birth control regulations for poor rural Tibetan families may also result in the gradual extinction of a Tibetan way of life, making way for a Chinese modernity with fewer possibilities for negotiating multiple Tibetan modernities.

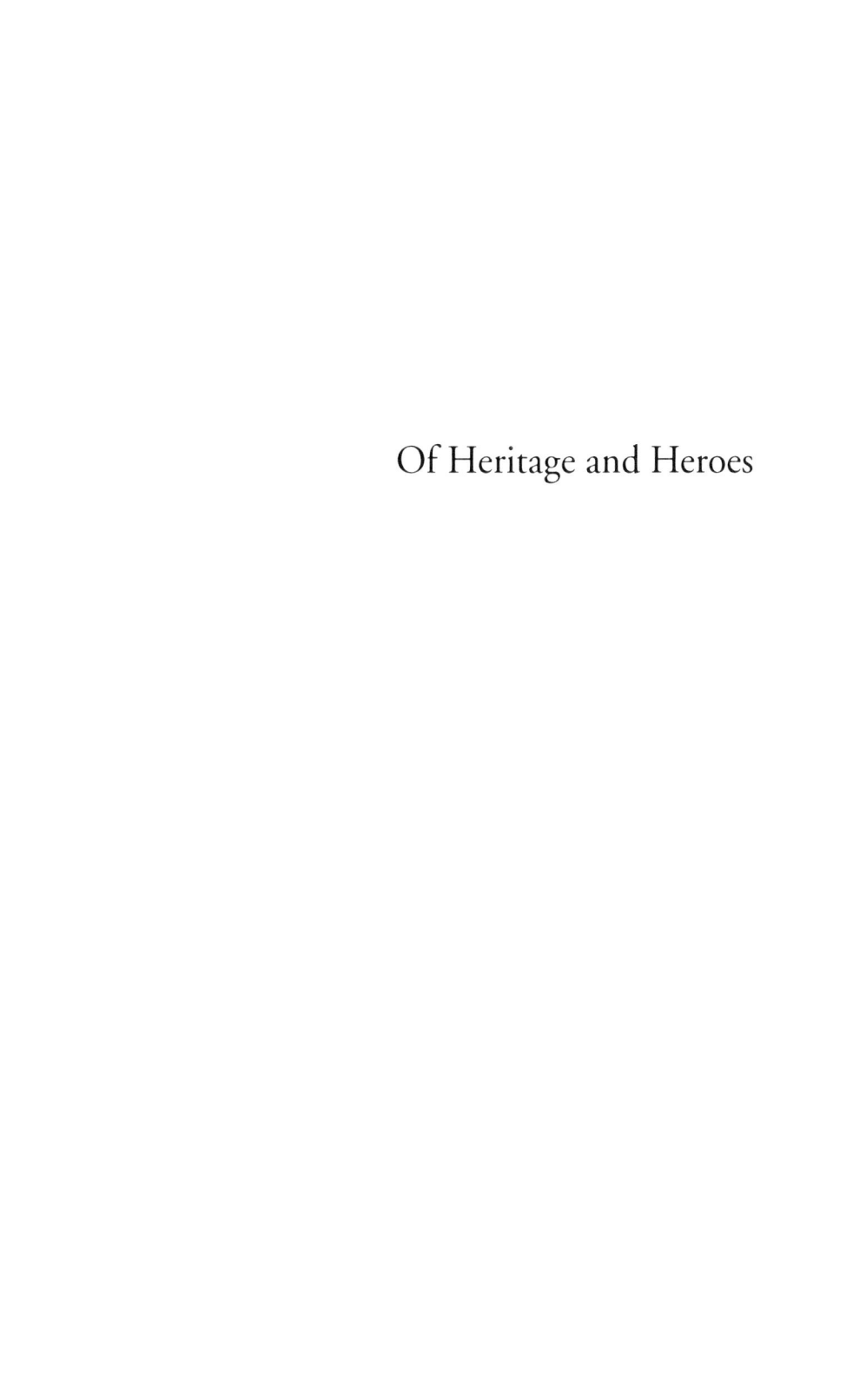

Of Heritage and Heroes

The Modernity of Heritage: Visualizing the Past in a Nigerian City Kingdom[1]

Peter Probst

Introduction

Some 10 years ago I was involved in organizing a lectures series on *African Modernities* which eventually appeared as a book under the same title in 2002.[2] Back in mid 1990s when we applied for funds to invite the speakers the debate was still very much focused on »multiple modernities«. The introduction to the book followed this figure of thought. Contrary to what we thought was an essentialist misunderstanding of modernity, we argued that modernity is not something given but primarily a metaphor used by members of a society to reflect upon themselves as a social and moral collective. Based upon a critical analysis of the history of the anthropological discourse on Africa, we distinguished between three different phases of this discourse which had produced three distinctly different variations or readings of modernity. The first reading, labelled *modernity as contagion*, was characterized by the colonial experience. The second reading conceived as *modernity as necessity*, was marked by the postcolonial achievement of independence. The third reading, dubbed modernity as c*ontingency*, was impregnated by the dynamics of globalization.

While I am still convinced in the usefulness of this approach, in the course of my own recent research in Nigeria I have lately come to realize its limitations. One of the reasons for this insight lies in the global success of museums. »We live in a world of museums«[3] James Clifford noted a few years ago and surely his diagnosis of late twentieth century culture has not changed since. In fact, the institution of the museum has become one of the most dominant signatures of our times. Limited not only to the West any longer where it was once established

---

1 Funding for research has come from the German Research Foundation (SFB 560-B4 & B7) and a 2006 FRAC research grant from Tufts University. I am grateful to the organizers and participants of the conference for their constructive critique and helpful comments.
2 Jan Georg Deutsch, Peter Probst & Heike Schmidt (eds.) *African Modernities. Entangled Meanings in Current Debate* (Oxford/New York: James Currey & Heineman, 2002).
3 James Clifford, *Routes. Travel and Translation in 20th Century* (Cambridge, Mass: Harvard University Press, 1997), p. 219.

as one of the pillars of the modern nation state,[4] the museum has transcended its territorial borders making its way to all corners of the globe. To cite Clifford again: »From new national capitals to Melanesian villages, from abandoned coal pits in Britain, to ethnic neighbourhoods in global cities, museums are proliferating at a remarkable rate«.[5] Truly, the sheer speed of its expansion is breathtaking. In an eerie way, it seems as if the moment of acceleration, one of modernity's often noted prime features, has swallowed even the cultural space of the museum, hitherto the epitome of slowness and tranquility.

Given the global scale of the heritage industry, it is hardly surprising to see that the most important player in his business is itself a global institution par excellence. Consisting of representatives from 21 states elected by the UN General Assembly on a rotating basis the UNESCO World Heritage Committee is an international body whose main responsibility is the implementation of the World Heritage Convention for which main instrument is the UNESCO World Heritage List. Over the past three decades, that is from the inception of the World Heritage Program in 1972, to the present the list has grown exponentially. While in 1972 it had only 12 entries it currently (2007) lists 830 so-called »properties«, consisting of 644 cultural, 162 natural and 24 mixed properties in 184 States Parties. In fact, for members of the various boards and subcommittees of the UNESCO World Heritage Center the world is literally a kind of meta museum in which the various nation states act as curators over UNESCO's ever expanding »properties«.

While it is easy to dismiss such figures as sheer institutional hubris, they do mark an important issue. Given UNESCO's self assumed omnipotence in matters of universal cultural value and collective memory, the question arises as to how and in what way UNESCO's politics world heritage network challenge the idea of »multiple«, »alternative« or »parallel modernities« as an academic counter model to the epistemological hegemony of the West? In other words: Is that what we are confronted with not still a modernity in the singular, that is to say, a distinct still ongoing historical epoch which started some three centuries ago in Europe as a result of a series of profound social and technological transformations whose peculiar implications we continue to grapple with up to the present?

Seen in this light, the »configuration of modernity« I am focusing on in this chapter is the modernity of heritage or, perhaps more precisely, the notion of heritage as a particular feature of modernity. Given this perspective, my interest lies in the effects of the spatial expansion of modernity in terms of a globaliza-

---

4 See Benedict Anderson, *Imagined Communities* (London: Verso, 1991); Carol Duncan, »Art Museums and the Ritual of Citizenship«, in: *Representing the Nation. A Reader. Histories, Heritage and Museums* ed. by David Boswell & Jessica Evans (London: Routledge, 2002), pp. 304–331.

5 Clifford, *Routes, Travel and Translation in 20th Century*, op.cit., p. 219.

tion of heritage as a spatial proliferation of heritage sites on a global scale. One of the most notable effects of this development is a marked increase in the production of images. As I argue, heritage serves as powerful motor for the visual depiction of the past. As such, the notion of heritage and the images it generates lies at the heart of what Benedict Anderson so famously dubbed an »imagined community«.[6] With the increasing globalization of heritage through institutions like UNESCO this visual production of local and/or national identities has not only increased. It has also led to numerous frictions and tensions within these social groupings. That is to say, global organisations like UNESCO ›reconfigure‹ national objects of memory into a universal global heritage. In doing so the idea of the nation state is at once dissolved and elevated. While the notion of world heritage works on the assumption that differences can be transcended, that there exist shared universal values, the actual policy to make this assumption work turns out to be a powerful machinery for the production of difference on the national and sub-national level. As James Clifford has put it:

> In a global context, where collective identity is increasingly represented by having a culture (a distinctive way of life, tradition, form of art, or craft) museums make sense. They presume an external audience (national and international connoisseurs, tourists, scholars, curators, ›sophisticated‹ travellers, journalists, and the like). These may not be the sole or even the primary audience for cultural display and performances, but they are never entirely absent. When a community displays itself through spectacular collections and ceremonies, it constitutes an ›inside‹ and an ›outside‹. The message of identity is directed differently to members and outsiders – the former invited to share in the symbolic wealth, the latter maintained as onlookers, or partially integrated (…) From their emergence as public institutions in nineteenth century Europe, museums have been useful for polities gathering and valuing an ›us‹. Thus articulation (…) collects, celebrates, memorializes, values and sells a way of life. In the process of maintaining an imagined community, it also confronts ›others‹ and excludes the ›inauthentic‹. This is the stuff of contemporary cultural politics.[7]

The present chapter aims to help to understand this process from a visual perspective. After a brief outline of the history of visual heritage politics in Europe the second part of the paper is focusing on a recently declared world heritage site in Southwest Nigeria. I plan to conclude by making some general remarks on heritage, style and the politics of appearance.

---

6 Anderson, *Imagined Communities,* op. cit. (note 3).
7 Clifford, *Routes, Travel and Translation in 20th Century,* op.cit., p. 218

Heritage, Modernity and the Visualization of the Past

As scholars from Hegel to Habermas have repeatedly pointed out, one of the basic features of modernity is the change of the consciousness of time.[8] Thus, from the late 18th century onwards people in Europe increasingly felt to be part of a *new* or *modern* age. The past was perceived as having lost its established role as a supplier of normativity and orientation. In was mainly in this sense that the very term »modern« established itself as a signification for a particular type of societal self-understanding. Deeply impregnated by the experience of historical acceleration, modern life was seen to be defined not only as standing in opposition to but rather as a constant break with the past. With the normative past being perceived as absent, however, the issue of memory emerged as one of the key concerns of modernity. On an institutional level, the result was to materialize memory in the shape of museums and monuments as a substitute for the absent normativity of the past.

The notion of heritage has its roots in these historical circumstances. Thus most scholars agree, that the origins of the current »heritage crusade«[9] needs to be located in the late 18th century generally considered to be the birth date of modernity. In fact, the very word heritage stems from the French *héritage*, a neologism first coined in 1795 by the Bishop of Blois, Henri Baptist Gregoire, in his critique of the excesses of the French revolution. What Gregoire was concerned about was looting of the Louvre, the former royal palace which had been transformed into a public art museum by the French revolutionary government. The very content of the Louvre, so Gregoire argued, not only belonged to the French nation as a whole. It also constituted the nation's collective memory and identity, something worth preserving as a *héritage*.

Seen in this light, heritage is defined in relation to history and memory for which it acts as a substitute. It appears as a conscious arrest and framing of the presence of a past, from which modernity constantly seeks to break away.[10] Urban life in late 19th and early 20th Europe and the US provided the prime context for this specific experience leading not only to a proliferation of monuments but also to a series of texts commenting on this development. The respective spectrum is broad ranging from Alois Riegl's classic study on *the Modern*

---

8   Jürgen Habermas, *Der philosophische Diskurs der Moderne* (Frankfurt/Main: Suhrkamp 1985).
9   David Lowenthal, *Possessed by the Past. The Heritage Crusade and the Spoils of History* (New York: Free Press, 1996).
10 See Habermas, *Der philosophische Diskurs*, op.cit.; Andreas Huyssen, *Twilight Memories. Marking Time in a Culture of Amnesia* (New York: Routledge, 1995).

Cult of Monuments[11], Georg Simmel's reflection on the aesthetics of ruins[12], and Robert Musil's ironic notes on monuments as billboards[13] to more recent works by David Lowenthal[14] and Pierre Nora.[15] In view of this tradition, Francois Hartog has reminded us to think of heritage

… less (as) a question of an obvious, assertive identity but (more as) a question of an uneasy identity that risks disappearing or is already forgotten, obliterated, or repressed: an identity in search of itself, to be exhumed, assembled, or even invented. In this way, heritage comes to define less that which one possesses, what one *has*, than circumscribing what one *is*, without having known, or even be capable of knowing. Heritage thus becomes an invitation for collective anamnesis. The ›ardent obligation‹ of heritage, with its requirement for conservation, renovation, and commemoration is added to the ›duty‹ of memory, with its recent public translation of repentance.[16]

Hartog's analysis can be read as an invitation to study the ›ardent obligation‹ of heritage from the perspective of the specific heritage practices aiming to secure this obligation. The particular heritage practice I am focusing on in this chapter is the practice of photography. As part of the same discourse on loss and absence, photography functioned to ›substitute‹ or ›refill‹ the absence of the past by producing or, in the sense of Roland Barthes, by »certifying« presence.[17] Photography was therefore not only part of heritage. As »objects of melancholy« as Susan Sontag[18] has aptly put it, photographs helped to create it. In 1853 for example, the French government began to document its patrimony by making photographs of its architectures.[19] In 1897 the National Photographic Record Society was founded in England with the purpose of documenting the quickly

---

11   Alois Riegl, *Der Moderne Denkmalkultus. Sein Wesen und seine Entstehung* (Wien & Leipzig: W. Braunmüller,1903).
12   Georg Simmel, »Die Ruine. Ein Ästhetischer Versuch«, in: *Philosophische Kultur*. Gesammelte Essays (Leipzig: Kröner 1919 [1907]).
13   Robert Musil, *Denkmale. Gesammelte Schriften*, Bd. 7 (Frankfurt: Fischer, 1978), pp. 506–509.
14   David Lowenthal, *The Past is a Foreign Country* (Cambridge: Cambridge University Press, 1986).
15   Pierre Nora, »Realms of Memory«, in: *Representations* Vol. 26, (1989), pp. 7–25.
16   Francois Hartog, »Time and Heritage«, in: *Museum International* No. 227 (2006), p. 12.
17   Barthes himself was quite aware of the relationship between photography and heritage. As he wrote: »By making the (mortal) Photograph into the general and somehow natural witness of ›what has been‹, modern society has renounced the Monument. A paradox: the same century invented History and Photography. Contemporary with the withdrawal of rites, photography may correspond to the intrusion, in our modern society, of an asymbolic Death, outside of religion, outside of ritual, a kind of abrupt dive into the literal Death« Roland Barthes, *Camera Lucida. Reflections on Photography* (New York: Hill and Wang, 1981), p. 93.
18   Susan Sontag, *On Photography* (New York: Penguin, 1977).
19   Christine Boyer, »La Mission Héliographique. Architectural Photography, Collective Memory and the Patrimony of France 1851«, in: *Picturing Place. Photography and the Geographical Imagination* ed. by Joan Schwartz & James Ryan (London: Tauris, 2005), pp. 21–54.

disappearing English customs.[20] Along the same line, photographic societies in North America started to make portraits of the vanishing cultures of American Indians.[21]

In view of these circumstances it can be argued that photography quite literally played a constitutive role in the imagination of national identities discussed so prominently by Benedict Anderson.[22] In fact, given the attention Anderson devoted to Walter Benjamin's ideas about technological reproducibility on the one side and the very title of Anderson's seminal work on the other, one could expect to see an interest in the role of photography. As we know, however, he focused on the role of printing instead. Except for a small footnote on the »museumizing of the Borobodur«[23], photography has remained curiously absent from his analysis. In a way, the same holds true for the subsequently evolving studies focusing on the role of photography in the »imperial imaginary«.[24] Since the early 1990s numerous works have shown how the colonial state used photography to imagine itself.[25] As we have learned, issues of surveillance reflected issues of orientalism and vice versa. The value of these insights stands without question. Yet, with few exceptions[26], the interest has been to understand only the colonial state as such. The perspective was thus to look rather from the outside. Hardly any research has been devoted to the photographic imagination of communities *within* the colonial (and postcolonial) state.

Arguing that the increasing globalization of heritage through institutions like UNESCO provides a powerful framework for the visual production of local and/or national identities, the remainder of the paper aims to help to understand this process within the context about the local debate on a recently declared UNESCO world heritage site in Osogbo, Nigeria.

---

20 Jens Jäger, »Picturing Nations. Landscape Photography and National Identity in Britain and Germany in the Mid-Nineteenth Century«, in: *Picturing Place. Photography and the Geographical Imagination* ed. by Joan M. Schwartz & James Ryan (London: I.B. Tauris, 2005), pp. 117–140.
21 Brian Dippie, »Representing the Other. The North American Indian«, in: *Anthropology and Photography* ed. by Elizabeth Edwards (New Haven: Yale University Press, 1992), pp. 132–136; Fleming, Paula & Judith Luskey, *The North American Indians in Early Photographs* (New York: Harper and Row, 1986).
22 Anderson, *Imagined Communities*, op.cit.
23 ibid. p.179
24 Ella Shohat & Robert Stam, *Unthinking Eurocentrism* (New York: Routledge, 1994).
25 See Paul Landau & Deborah Kaspin (eds.) *Images and Empires. Visuality and Colonial and Postcolonial Africa* (Berkeley: University of California Press, 2002). Focusing mainly on issues of formal aesthetics, the same applies to works devoted to single African photographers as the other main strand of research on photography in Africa.
26 Christopher Pinney, »The Nation (Un)Pictured? Chromolithography and ›Popular‹ Politics in India 1887–1995«, in: *Critical Inquiry* Vol. 23, (1997), No. 4, pp. 834–867.

Figure 6: Palace sculptures associated with local deities in Osogbo. The turban is a visual reference to the local dominance of Islam.

New Images for Old Beliefs

In summer 2005 the Nigerian press was celebrating the UNESCO decision to add the grove of the Yoruba river goddess Osun in Osogbo to the UNESCO world heritage list. Over and over again it was stressed that the event would increase the nation's visibility at the international scene. Along the same line, Osogbo's traditional ruler, Ataoja Matanmi III equally declared: »There is need to recognize, honor, appreciate, and celebrate this evergreen achievement and epoch history making of Osun Grove's new status as the nation's cultural renaissance. This development has indeed further positively posted Osogbo on the World map.«[27]

Surely, to understand the listing of the Osun grove as a boost of Nigeria's and Osogbo's visibility in the global arena was hardly more than a phrase. Yet, in view of the fact that this boost of visual presence was actually prompted by a series of image works, the phrase was quite an appropriate one.[28] Spread around a forested area of 75 hectares, the grove houses more than 40 sculp-

---

27 *The Vanguard* (25.July 05)
28 A more detailed account of the events leading to the transformation of the Osun grove is given

Figure 7: Cement sculpture by Susanne Wenger and Adebisi Akanji in the Osun grove representing Obaluaye, late 1970s.

tures and architectures. Compared to the serenity and controlled expression of the works depicted in exhibition catalogues about Yoruba art, they mark a strong and provocative contrast. Instead of wood and mud, the primary media in Yoruba art and architecture, most structures in the Osun grove are made of cement. While Yoruba art has a clear sense of symmetry, the design of the sculptures in the Osun grove is bold and monumental showing seemingly no regard for formal order (Figures 6 & 7).

The story which has led to these works goes back to the year 1959 when a delegation of Osun officials visited the Austrian artist woman Susanne Wenger in the nearby town of Ilobu and persuaded her to move to Osogbo. By that time Wenger's work as an artist devoted to Yoruba religion was already known. In Ede as well as in Ilobu she had started to build shrines sculptures. Having heard about her activities, the Osun officials in Osogbo asked her for help in repairing the main Osun temple and stop the local farmers and businessman

in Peter Probst, »Keeping the Goddess Alive. Performing Culture and Remembering the Past«, in: *Social Analysis* Vol. 48, (2004), 1, pp. 33–54.

from encroaching into the grove thereby threatening the sanctity of the place. Herself an initiate and devotee to Obatala, one of the main Yoruba deities, the artist accepted and the repair began. However, what was initially intended to be just a kind of minor face lift, ended in nothing but an iconic riot. While, with the exception of some ephemeral mud sculptures and a modest temple, the Osun grove had been formerly devoid of any images works, it now became filled with new sculptures and architectures all of them radically departing from so-called classical Yoruba art. In fact, what had started was an artistic project which aimed to revitalize traditional Yoruba religion by lending the various Yoruba deities believed to reside in the grove a new visual presence.

As it turned out, the project proved to be successful. Not only did the Osun grove become a prominent site within the memory and heritage-scapes of the members of the Yoruba diaspora. The prominence of the grove also gave a major boost to the annual Osun festival. Thus each year in August, the festival attracts thousands of visitors, many of them coming from as far as Europe and the Americas to attend the grand finale which consists of a public sacrifice made by the representatives of the king of Osogbo to the deity at the bank of the Osun river in the Osun grove.

Between Progress and Rescue

Entitled *Landmarks in the History of Osogbo*[29], *Sacred People, Sacred Places*[30] or simply *History of Osogbo*[31], one of the visible results of Osun's rise into the global public sphere is the series of locally produced and published heritage brochures. Though their primary audience are the foreign visitors coming to attend the festival, as historical texts, the brochures form a special genre of literary products in Yorubaland that precedes the emergence of the Osun grove as a popular heritage site.

Thus the origin of the brochures goes back to the 1930s when members of the new (Christian) literates were allowed to work in the local councils as mediators between the king and the colonial administration. Often organized as so-called »progressive unions«, its members formed a network of like minded people mostly devoted to individual career advancements. As Toyin Falola[32]

---

29 Jacob Aofolabi, *Landmarks in the History of Osogbo* (Ibadan: Landmark Publications, 1999).
30 Osogbo Heritage Council, *Sacred People, Sacred Places* (Osogbo: OHC, 2000).
31 Osogbo Heritage Council, *History of Osogbo* (Osogbo: OHC, 1994).
32 Toyin Falola, »Yoruba Town Histories«, in: *A Place in the World. New Local Historiographies from African and South Asia*, ed. by A. Harneit-Sievers (Leiden: Brill, 2002), pp. 65–86.

has noted, it was this very experience of change which provided the context not only for the embracing of progress but also for the embracing of the past. Thus, writers of Yoruba town histories understood their work quite explicitly as a »rescue mission«[33], a notion articulated already in 1897 in the Samuel Johnson's preface to his classic *The History of the Yoruba*: »What led to the production was not a burning desire of the author to appear in print ... but a purely patriotic motive, that the history of our fatherland might not be lost in oblivion, especially as our old sires are fast dying out«. [34]

The organizing concept for this experience of loss was *olaju*, a Yoruba word which can be rendered as enlightenment or modernity. Stemming from the two Yoruba words *la* (to open) and *oju* (eyes), in its literal meaning *olaju* is »to open the eyes«. As such *olaju* was deeply associated with the experience of the colonial world. Peel[35] has described it as a specific »syndrom« or »ideology« comprising bureaucratic and administrative as well as economic, educational, and religious ideas. Since printing belonged to that »syndrom« it is not surprising to see a connection between the two. As Falola noted in his analysis of Yoruba town histories: »All the texts, without exception, define what ›modern‹ is; either directly or implicitly by way of making demands for change.«[36] In other words, more than just associated with changes, *olaju* was the justification for the demand of change expressed in Yoruba town histories. Underlying these conceptions was an adoption of the aesthetic elements of modernity that combined the metaphorical features of light and darkness with a linear, goal orientated time perspective. Thus the slogan of the *West African Pilot*, the widest-circulating nationalist newspaper, read »Show the light, and people will find the way«. Similarly, local newspapers like the *West African Vanguard* carried articles which celebrated *olaju* with phrases like »The veil is removed and the fetters of darkness and ignorance are broken and must naturally give way to the rays of light and hope, the spirit of understanding and steady progress for all and sundry.«[37]

Given the specific resonance this Judeo-Christian trope had within the Yoruba colour symbolism, it is hardly surprising to see photography playing a prominent role in the *olaju* complex. In fact, with their mastery of the technology of light, the new profession of photographers became popular role models

---

33 Ibid., p. 75.
34 Samuel Johnson, *The History of the Yorubas* (London: CSS, 1921), p. vii. Applying Anderson's printing thesis to the Yoruba context, Peel has argued that writers like Johnson and missionary institutions like CMS helped to bring about the ethnic category of Yoruba into existence. See J.D.Y. Peel, »The Cultural Work of Ethnogenesis«, in: *History and Ethnicity* ed. by E. Tonkin, M. McDonald & M.Chapman (London: Routledge, 1989), pp. 198–216.
35 J.D.Y. Peel, »Olaju. A Yoruba Concept of Development«, in: *Journal of Development Studies* Vol. 14, (1978), No.2., pp. 139–165.
36 Falola, »Yoruba Town Histories«, op.cit., p. 81.
37 Peel, »Olaju. A Yoruba Concept of Development«, op.cit., p. 154–155.

for the *olaju* ideology. Waldwin Holmes, for example, born 1865 in Accra and reputedly the first black photographer, was enrolled as a member of the Royal Photographic Society of Great Britain in 1897, the same year Johnson wrote the preface for his book on Yoruba history. In 1910 Holmes went to England to study law. Seven years later he returned to Lagos to practice both as a barrister and as photographer. Examples of his work can be found in MacMillan's *Red Book of West Africa* which appeared in 1920.[38] Equally a contributor to this book was George Da Costa. Born in 1853 in Lagos, he was educated at the local CMS Training Institution. In 1895, after having worked as the manager of the CMS Bookshop in Lagos for 18 years, he resigned and turned to photography eventually becoming a respected photographer. For the colonial government he did the photographic recording of the construction of the Nigerian Railways, a project which was followed by the participation in MacMillan's *Red Book of West Africa*. As can be seen from Olu Oguibe's description of the photographs, not only the pictures, but also the subjects represented *olaju*.

Rather than a society of ›cannibals‹ and ›pagans‹, Da Costa's photographs of early-twentieth-century Africa led us to a cosmopolitanism steeped in the awareness of other cultures., a world of burgeoning elite and savvy literati, a society of international merchants, high-flying attorneys, widely travelled politicians, newspaper tycoons, and society ladies, the same images we find in contemporary portrait painting of the period.[39]

It was these representatives of the new elite which also formed the foundation of the Osogbo Progressive Union. Established in 1936, its main aims were the »social, moral and intellectual improvement of its members« and the »promotion of the spirit of unity and patriotism«. Like many unions of its kind, membership was organized in local branches with the Ibadan branch being the most influential one.[40] As a result, in Osogbo itself the union remained rather inactive. From the 1950s onwards, however, the situation changed. In 1944 *ataoja* Adenle had succeeded Latona II who himself had ascended the throne in 1933. For both of them, the past was not seen as a value in itself but rather as a tool to serve the dynamics of *olaju*. Both were the first Christian rulers of Osogbo; the letter head of Latona II, for example, carried the title *deo adjuvante*. Before his coming into office he had been a successful trader and during World War I he had served in the British army as a sergeant major. Committed to the ideals of *olaju*, he is praised in local history for having popularized the Osun festival by actively inviting the white colonial elite to the festival and thus turning it into a colonial spectacle, similar to the institution of the Northern Nigerian durbar. These

---

38 Allister MacMillan, *The Red Book of West Africa* (London: Cass, 1968 [1920]).
39 Olu Oguibe, *Culture Game* (Minneapolis: University of Minnesota Press, 2004), p. 76.
40 See Samuel A. Falade, *A Comprehensive History of Osogbo* (Ibadan: Tunji Owolabi Printers, 2000), p. 153ff

changes were assisted by the building of the first aerodrome in Osogbo in 1936 and the construction of a suspension bridge over the Osun river to the Osun grove in 1938. He also commissioned the erection of a new council house, demolished the old storey house palace built back in 1910 und substituted it with a new, more imposing one. Upon his death in 1943, his successor Adenle, a former school teacher and successful trader in *adire* cloth, continued to »open up« Osogbo and make it fit for modern times.[41] Thus new schools were established, the road network was improved, and electricity and street naming introduced. In addition he ensured that Osogbo would be adequately represented in the new administrative set up. By 1952 the Osun Division was created and Osogbo had been made the Divisional Headquarters.

Given these developments, it is hardly surprising to see that the publication of the first Osogbo town history by a member of the Osogbo Progressive Union fell in the very same year as the beginning of the artistic transformation of the Osun grove by Wenger and her collaborators.[42] From the perspective of the palace that had sanctioned the projects, both were primarily political enterprises deemed to underline the importance of the historical and cultural heritage of Osogbo as a major force in the new independent Nigeria. In the sense given by Toyin Falola, both projects were truly »rescue missions«. That is, both sought to save and preserve the past from the perspective of the experiences of change. But whereas the town history project was written in view of a bright future, the grove project was carried out under the impression of a past glory. As I am going to show below, the conflicting approaches or *styles*, as I would prefer to call them, how to construct and represent heritage form the basis of the reluctance and subtle criticism with which people see how the palace is instrumentalizing the grove and the festival for his own political ends. A good deal of this reluctance concerns the history presented in today's publications of the Osogbo Heritage Council to which I would now like to turn.

From Legendary to Traditional History

While the documentation of the past as heritage is understood as part of *olaju* in the sense of »opening up the eyes«, the very representation of the past does not

---

41 On Adenle as a writer and inventor, see the Karin Barber, »Writing, Genre and a Schoolmaster's Invention in the Yoruba Provinces«, in: *African Hidden Histories. Everyday Literacy and Making the Self*, ed. by Karin Barber (Bloomington: Indiana University Press, 2006), pp. 385–415.

42 Deji Olugonna, *Osogbo. The Origin, Growth and Problems* (Ibadan: Fads Printing Works, 1959). An account of the history of Osogbo was published already in 1911. It was, however, part of the history of Ibadan written by Oba I.B. Akinyele, then the ruler of Ibandan.

follow *olaju's* linear temporality but follows local traditions of narrating what had happened in the past. The Yoruba word indicating such narrations is *itan*. Though ubiquitously translated into English as »history«, the Yoruba understanding of *itan* is much broader entailing a different approach and attitude towards the past than in modern European discourse.[43] Operating on two different levels, Yoruba town histories represent a clear proximity to these traditions. After a short introductory section, explaining the location and geographical background of the town, what is presented first as »legendary« or »mythical history« is then followed by »traditional history«. While the former deals with issues of creation, the latter focuses on aspects of migration. The reference to Oduduwa constitutes a crucial element in this context. For Yoruba, the possession of power is derived from the capacity to prove a link with Oduduwa, the Yoruba culture hero who is said to have founded the Yoruba race by descending from heaven and establishing civilization on earth with Ile Ife as its centre.[44] Respective accounts vary as to the very process of this foundation. The marked political dimension of these stories have been interpreted as a mythologization of different phases in history wherein different waves of immigration led to different processes of subjugation of earlier populations with a subsequent deification of the prime figures involved. While such a differentiation between ›myth‹ and ›history‹ makes sense on an analytical level, in everyday life these levels are constantly blurred. In actual political practice, deities function as role models for secular political allegiances, just as political allegiances function as models for the understanding of deities.

Accordingly, the ›official‹ history of Osogbo as narrated in the publications of the Osogbo Heritage Council, regularly begin with the life and deeds of Osun. The actual time is not specified except that it was »as early as the Oduduwa period«[45]. Depicted as a queen and endowed with magical powers, she is said to have lived along the Osun river in a palace of her own assisted by her own »cabinet«. Everybody had his or her task. People were engaged in dyeing and fishing, protecting the grove from outside attack or maintaining internal security. As time passed by, the queen and her people gradually »disappeared into the spirit world«.[46] The question how this happened is seen as irrelevant just as the question

---

43 See Karin Barber, *I Could Speak Until Tomorrow, Oriki, Women and the Past in A Yoruba Town* (Edinburgh: International African Library, 1991); Olabiyi Yai, »In Praise of Metonymy. The Concepts of ›Tradition‹ and ›Creativity‹ in the translation of Yoruba artistry over time and space«, in: *Research in African Literature* Vol. 24, (1993), No. 4, pp. 29–37.
44 Cornelius Adepegba, »The Descent from Oduduwa: Claims of Superiority among Some Yoruba Traditional Rulers and the Arts of Ancient Ife«, in: *International Journal of African Historical Studies* Vol. 19, (1986), No. 1, pp. 77–92.
45 Osogbo Heritage Council, *History of Osogbo*, (Osogbo: Local Council, 1994), p. 12.
46 Aofolabi, op. cit.

... whether these spirits and fairies were aborigines (real human beings with super-natural powers) or whether they were only imaginary beings is (considered to be) not important. What is important is that their period provided the basis of our history. This period should not be seen just as a myth of the origin of Osogbo but rather as an end of one era (the mythical Oso-igbo) and the beginning of another period. (of traditional history of Osogbo).[47]

The »traditional history« usually starts off then with the narration of the migration from Ile Ife to Ipole via Ibokun. It was in Ipole the forefathers of the Osogbo people experienced a water shortage. As a result, a delegation was sent to find a new settlement. After experiencing a number of obstacles, they eventually discovered the Osun river where Laroye, the leader of the delegation, made a pact of mutual protection with the deity residing in the river. Just as Osun promised to provide peace and prosperity, Laroye promised to respect and honour the goddess by making annual offerings to her at the river bank. At first, Laroye and his people enjoyed the new environment. But the activities of the immigrants disturbed the deity and her people and the settlers had to move to the upper terrace of the plain. The new place turned out to be a good one. Soon a flourishing market developed. As the population increased, however, the need to move arose once more. Again the ifa oracle was consulted and its advice resulted in the third palace opposite today's market place. It was here that Laroye finally passed way.

Picturing the Past

The history texts I have summarized above are profusely illustrated with photographs. In fact the latest production is called *Osun in Colors. A Pictorial History of the River Goddess Osun*.[48] (Figure 8) They are not unique in this respect. The introduction of visual material goes back to the first publication of a festival brochure in 1984. Subsequently photography was incorporated in the strictly historical brochures as well. Falling into two categories, people and places, they represent a kind of royal family album, in the way alluding to the Yoruba word for heritage, *oguntihi*, literally meaning, »something we possess or inherit«. In other words, the photographs represent elements of a collective memory that in turn is represented by the figure of the monarch and his subjects.

---

47 Osogbo Heritage Council, *History of Osogbo* (Osogbo: Local Council, 1994), p. 13.
48 Afolabi Kayode, *Osun in Colors. A Pictorial History of the River Goddess Osun*, (North Charleston: BookSurge, 2006)

Figure 8: Afolabi Kayode, Osun In Colours, 2006.

In the *History of Osogbo*,⁴⁹ the oldest photograph depicts Matanmi II. A date is missing but given the time of his reign (from 1903 to 1917) the picture obviously stems from the early 20th century. In the brochures and local praise songs (*oriki*) Matanmi II is praised as having witnessed the transformation of Osogbo »into a modern town«. In practice, this meant the establishment of a district office and a customary court, the building of schools, the founding of colonial business enterprises, the construction of roads, the arrival of the railway; motor vehicles *and*, though it is not explicitly mentioned, photography as well. In fact, the linkage between the arrival of the railway and that of photography was no coincidence. The Yoruba word for photograph *aworan yiya*, literally meaning »circulating image« points to the common denominator. Photography and railways were both prime agents of social spatialization and in this way deeply embedded in the projects of modern governance and nation-building.⁵⁰ Though we neither know the name of the photographer of Matanmi's picture nor the exact date when it was taken, probably sometime in the 1910s, it is safe to say

---

49 Ibid.
50 As mentioned above, the construction of the Nigerian railway was accompanied by its photographic recording, a job given to George Da Costa as one of the first Nigerian photographers in the country.

that when photography did reach Osogbo, it was already part and parcel of the »modern times«. As such its establishment not only included the learning of the cultural conventions towards the new medium but also its local appropriation.[51] In the case of the black and white photograph of Matanmi II, its mise en scène coupled with the label »Oba Atanda Olugbena Matanmi II« clearly indicates its representational function or style.[52] Just as Matanmi II used the new colonial architecture to change the old palace into Osogbo's first »storey« building, he used the new technology of photography to magnify his status. The age of the photograph allows only a schematic recognition. Still the picture gives a clear impression of age and respect. Wearing a plain cap and dressed in what looks like a white embroidered robe, Matanmi II sits on a chair, slightly bent forward, his hands in his lap, his eyes looking straight into eyes of the beholder. His face has a serene, withdrawn and composed expression conforming to the aesthetics of Yoruba sculpture.[53] With Matanmi placed in the very center of the photograph, the sides and top of the picture are framed in faded white causing a stark contrast to the dark features of the idealized portrait. Partially blending with the figure they convey a kind of double perspective, giving an impression of not only a spatial but also a temporal depth as if the portrayed is looking at the beholder from a distant past. In other words, the appearance of the image is conveyed as a kind of revelation, an abrupt jump from the dark past into the light of the present.

The same holds true of the photographs of the successors of Matanmi II. Sitting before a plain white backdrop or a mountain scene like in the case of Latona I and Latona II, they all allude to the relationship of presence and absence characteristic of photography. Its hidden cipher or code is of course the moment of death as the primal scene of memory and the very birthplace of signs and images. As Wendl[54], following Debray[55] has reminded us, the root of the word sign is the Greek word for tomb, *sema*. Similarly, the Latin word *imago* from which the English image is derived originally meant the wax print of the face of a deceased person, thus a death mask, which was carried during the burial ceremony and

---

51 Unfortunately, it was not possible to trace the exact time when the first photo studio opened up in Osogbo.
52 See also Westermann's observation from Ibadan: »The Oba was constrained to relax his patronage of the artists' works: very much like other African chiefs he thought he could hand on his image to posterity more beautifully by means of an enlarged photograph than by a wooden statue.« Dietrich Westerman, *The African Today* (London: Oxford University Press, 1934), p. 102.
53 Cf. Farris Thompson, *African Art in Motion* (Berkeley: University of California Press, 1974); Stephen Sprague, »How Yoruba see themselves«, in: *African Arts* Vol. 12, (1978), No. 1, pp. 52–69, in particular p.110.
54 Tobias Wendl, »Tod und Erinnerung«, in: *Snap me One. Studiophotographen in Afrika*, ed. by Tobias Wendl & Heike Behrend (München: Prestel, 1999), pp. 40–49.
55 Regis Debray, *Le Vie et Mort de l'Image. Une Histoire de Regard en Occident* (Paris : Gallimard).

later stored in the Atrium. In the same vain, the word portrait has its origin in the process of taking the facial traits of the deceased (*portrahere*) to create a death mask. Surely, Margaret Drewal is right when she writes about Yoruba portraiture: »The power of portraits is the ability to construct a reality.«[56] Yet we need to be aware that reality is a misleading concept in this context. Presence is probably a better word, at least, if we accept that the notion of representation necessarily implies the act of substituting something absent by evoking it as something being present.[57] Along this line then, it seems only too plausible that the heritage brochures not only present photographs of the deceased rulers but also photographs of the tombs of Ajobogon and Adebuyisoro, the ancestors of Laroye, the founder of Osogbo, in the town of Ibokun. The reproduction is poor. Hardly anything can be seen. But the bad quality of the picture only enhances the idea that the photograph can be seen and understood as a medium which is able to produce presence by visualizing absence.[58]

Just as the technical quality of the photographs of the former monarchs gradually improves, the photographs of the historically important places change as well. The events which happened in the grove are depicted by photographs of Wenger's shrines and architectures. The visual narration follows the series of palaces built by Laroye and his successors that is, from the very foundation of Osogbo up to the present. All together seven palaces are represented. Photographs of the architecture reshaped by Wenger document the first three. The first one shows Osun ojubo at the river side. The second depicts Iledi Ohuntoto. The third one represents the market shrine. The remaining four show the changes of the palace architecture from Oba Kolawola up to Matanmi III in what is now the present palace compound. Quite strikingly it shows a development which first went into the height and then, since Matanmi III, into width. The very last pages usually depict the prime icon of rulership in Osogbo, the fish as Osun's messenger or medium, *iko*. It is either shown by a fountain in the shape of a large fish or a bust showing Laroye holding the fish that jumped out the river as a sign of acceptance of the sacrifice to Osun.

We should note that the photographs published by the Heritage Council are not just mere »illustrations«. Rather they express a particular ›style‹ of imagination which in itself is part of a wider ›national‹ narrative about the emergence of Osogbo and its way from the past into the present and a glorious future.[59]

---

56 Margret Drewal, »Portraiture and the Construction of Reality in Yorubaland and beyond«, in: *African Arts* Vol. 23, (1990), No.3, pp. 40–49, in particular p. 49.
57 See Wendl, »Tod und Erinnerung«, op. cit.; See also Gerhard Plumpe, »Tote Blicke. Fotografie als Präsenzmedium«, in: *Medien der Präsenz. Museum, Bildung du Wissenschaft im 19. Jahrhundert* ed. by Jürgen Fohrmann et al (Köln: Dumont, 2001), pp. 70–86.
58 Martin Schulz, »Spur des Lebens und Anblick des Todes. Die Photographie als Medium des abwesenden Koerpers«, in: *Zeitschrift für Kunstgeschichte* Vol. 3, (2001), pp. 381–396.
59 I am grateful to Birgit Meyer for having drawn my attention to the importance of the concept

The emptiness of the cenotaph, stressed by Anderson[60] as one of the primary emblems of the emergence of nationalism in 18th and 19th century Europe, correlates with the play of presence and absence in the photograph of the tombs of Osogbo's ancestors in Ibokun. Framed in this way, photography is not only an element in local process of nation-building. It has also remained to be an element of *olaju* in the sense of ›opening up‹ Osogbo for change, for progress, and modernization. The use of English as the language in which the heritage publications are written, indicate the nature of the being addressed. The target group is not primarily the local population, but e people inhabiting the ›modern world‹, the world of *olaju*. The palace' interests thus meet with that of the Ministry of Culture and Tourism which is eager to »develop« the Osun grove and Osun Osogbo festival by turning them into profitable assets of a growing heritage industry. The same goes for UNESCO which is selling its world heritage program on the premise that it is possible to convert cultural into economic capital. As a technique to visualize the absence, either the past or the future) photography quite literally creates dream worlds. It is no coincidence then that the Heritage Council likens the Osun grove with »Hollywood« as a dream factory. As such, however, the photographs published and circulated by the palace based Heritage Council stand in a double conflict with Wenger's image works erected in the Osun grove. That is to say, in contrast to the future oriented photographs, the image works in the grove do not only point to the past, the past is also different.

As mentioned above, Wenger began her project to lend a new visible presence to the withering influence of Yoruba deities. For this she collected information on the history of Osogbo and the various deities believed to reside in the grove. Other than the narrative presented in the heritage brochures, however, the traditions that instructed Wenger's work do not focus on Laroye but on Timehin, a courageous hunter, devotee of Ogun and ›brother‹ of Laroye.[61] According to these versions, the different places referred to in the brochure as Laroye's palaces are not traces of Laroye's deeds but rather signs that mark the events that happened in the course of Timehin's exploration of the area. Laroye is said to have come only after Timehin had prepared the ground, and hence much later. In this way, the numerous sculptures and architectures standing in the grove act as

---

of style. For Meyer's inspiring discussion of the relevance of style for the study of contemporary religion and politics see Birgit Meyer, Modern Mass Media, Religion, and the Dynamics of Distraction and Concentration. Lecture given at the conference on Modern Mass Media, Religion and the Question of Community, University of Amsterdam, June 30, 2006.

60 Anderson, *Imagined Communities,* op. cit., pp. 9.

61 In a series of publications, not surprisingly unavailable in Osogbo itself, Wenger has explained her work in some detail. See Susanne Wenger, *The Timeless Mind of the Sacred. Its Manifestation in the Osun Grove* (Ibadan: Institute of African Studies, 1977); *The Sacred Groves of Osogbo* (Wien: Kontrapunkt, 1991); Susanne Wenger & Gerd Chesi, *A Life with the Gods* (Woergl: Perlinger, 1983).

Figure 9: Group of four cement figures by Adebisi Akanji in the Osun grove alleged to represent the founders of Osogbo.

visual references, or as I would prefer to call it, as visual *gestures* of the enduring importance of these events.

A prominent example for the difference between the two styles in the visual representation of the past is a group of four small figures, which stand unobtrusively in the bush along the way to the main Osun shrine (Figure 9). The figures represent two important pairs in the history of Osogbo: Laroye and Timehin and Ogidan and Ohuntoto. Oral traditions held by Wenger and her collaborators understand Ohuntoto and Ogidan as the ›mothers‹ of Laroye and Timehin respectively. In the heritage brochures of the palace, this interpretation is missing. However, the site the heritage brochures refer to as the »second palace« can be see as an indirect confirmation of that reading.

Named *iledi ohuntoto*, the site houses an architectural ensemble erected in the late 1970s by Wenger and her collaborators (Figure 10). The protruding zoomorphic forms at the front allude to the building's use as a meeting house for *ogboni*, a ritual institution that in the past, and to some extent still up to now, acted as an element of control over the power of the palace. Art historical research has interpreted the brass emblems of *ogboni* as a possible reference to incidents of subjugation and the subsequent introduction of a gendered system of ritual dualism in early Yoruba history.[62] Translated into the history of Osogbo, it is possible to conclude that the relationship between Laroye and Timehin versus

---

62 Suzanne Blier, »Kings, Crowns and Rights of Succession. Obalufon Arts and Ile-Ife and other Yoruba Centers«, in: *Arts Bulletin* Vol. 68, (1985), No. 3, pp. 383–401; Babatunde Lawal, »A YA GBO, A YA TO. New Perspectives on Edan Ogboni«, in: *African Arts* Vol. 28/1, (1995), No.4, pp. 37–49, 98–100.

Figure 10: Part of the Ohuntoto Ogboni Shrine Complex, built by Wenger, Gbadamosi, Saka and Akangbe in the mid 1970s.

Ohuntoto and Ogidan functions as a variation of the well known ritual system whereby institutions like *ogboni* stand for the (aboriginal) power of the land whereas the king – representing the late comers – embodies the public power. Indeed, a correlation also exists on the level of the relationship between Osun and Ogun. Thus, the superhuman beings inhabiting the area under the leadership of Osun complement the human invaders arriving under Ogun's devotee Timehin. While Osun is female and associated with brass, Ogun is male and associated with iron.[63]

Surely, a straightforward translation of the classical case of the Northern Ghanaian Tallensi[64] into the context of Southern Nigerian Yoruba does not

---

63 It is interesting to note that there exists an avoidance relationship between the king and Ohuntoto and Ogidan. During the Osun festival the king must make sure that he is not present when the chief priest of *oro*, the executive arm of *ogboni*, makes a sacrifice to them in the Osun grove. Further, Ohuntoto and Ogidan seem to have been condensed into one single complex. The two have the same drum rhythm. They make an acoustic appearance only during the funeral ceremonies of a deceased kind.

64 Meyer Fortes, *The Dynamics of Clanship among the Tallensi* (Oxford: Oxford University Press, 1945).

work. Due to the multitude of migration waves and the constant interplay between *eniyan* and *irunmole*, the humans and the superhumans, a clear distinction between immigrants and an autochthonous population does not exist. Yet, resentments have remained. Thus, one of Wenger's closest collaborators, Kasali Akangbe, stems from the Gbonmi compound whose history clearly predates the arrival of the Ipole immigrants. Others, like Adebisi Akanji, are members of *ogboni* or stem from the lineages that go back to Timehin. For all of them, the reshaped ritual landscape of the grove represents a kind of Foucauldian heterotopia. As such it conflicts with the way how the palace has captured the message of the sculptures and architectures by putting them in a photographic frame more suitable to his its interests. Murmurs of a counter memory can be heard but public criticism is not only dangerous but pointless for among her many characters and appearances Osun is known and praised as »the one who dances to take the crown without asking.«[65]

Conclusion

The configuration of modernity I have chosen to discuss in this paper is the notion of heritage. As I have shown, the development of the Osun Osogbo grove into a UNESCO world heritage site ought to be seen in the context of an understanding of heritage as being itself a heritage of modernity. Thus, rather than arguing for a pluralization of modernity, I stress its singularity in terms of its understanding as a distinct historical epoch. As such, the distinct practices that shape and impregnate modernity, also shape and impregnate the notion of heritage. A case in point is the process of visualization. Seen from this perspective, it might be argued that the rise of the Osun grove into a UNESCO world heritage site and the heritage practices that accompanied this process confirm Agamben's[66] and Debord's[67] analysis of the »spectacular phase« of modernity and capitalism. Written roughly around the same time Beier and Wenger started to create a forum for the production of »new images« in Osogbo, Debord had argued that in order to ensure continued economic growth, capitalism has created »pseudo-needs« to increase consumption. In his view, modern capitalist society had to be conceived as only a huge spectacle, a society of plain surface with social relations held together by the fetishistic consumption of commodities consisting

---

65 Pierre Verger, *Notes sur le Culte de Orisa et Vodun* (Dakar: L'Institut Francais d'Afrique Noire, 1959), p. 426.
66 Giorgio Agamben, *Means without Ends* (Minneapolis: University of Minnesota Press, 2000).
67 Guy Debord, *The Society of Spectacle* (New York: Zone Books, 1994).

of a series of endless images each copying the other making society devoid of both meaning and history.

As we have seen, the Osogbo situation paints a different picture. What it draws our attention to is not the death of meaning but rather the contest over it, not the issue of spectacle but the issue of style. In other words, what the finding urges us to do is to shift the debate on heritage and spectacle from the nostalgic lamento about the loss of unity and identity to that of the politics of recognition and appearance. In fact, the two notions of recognition and appearance are crucial for any understanding of style.[68] That is to say, in order to be recognized, style has to appear and in order to appear it has to be appropriated / animated/embodied by people who identify with it. Framed in such a triangular constellation, style is then always a public style. It is tied to the public domain, outside of which it cannot exist. Conceived in this way, the study of style is not its result in terms of the end product of a historical process which is kept, analysed, and preserved in a museum, but the study of its social realization as a »forming form«.[69] As such, it is necessarily both framed and contested. For not only is the public domain in which style materializes itself fragmented by the existence of multiple actors all claiming for recognition. Also, the way how this realization proceeds is always embedded in a temporal frame which entails the very experience of time itself.

The material I have presented in this chapter both confirms and differentiates this argument. Thus, in terms of institutionalisation of the concept of heritage the style of Wenger's »new images«, explicitly created by the desire to re-enchant Yoruba society, did indeed give rise to new social forms that produced ever more images.[70] As I have noted above, the image works in the Osun grove did lead to a heritage industry whose characteristic feature is the production of images representing heritage. The use of photography in the publications of the Osogbo Heritage Council illustrates this feature. However, as we have equally seen, just as Wenger's »new images« were able to revitalize religion by shifting old religious practices into the new context of an international roots tourism these new social forms have also helped to prompt a series of conflicts between Wenger and the palace. Both groups operate under the banner of heritage. Yet while the former sees the shrines and architectures as an effort to enhance or at least sustain the

---

68 See Andrew Benjamin's illuminating treatise on "sites of style", Andrew Benjamin, *Style and Time. Essays on the Politics of Appearance* (Evanston: Northwestern University Press, 2006). I would like to acknowledge my gratitude to Birgit Meyer for having drawn my attention to the question of style in the study of contemporary African religion and politics.

69 Serge Maffesoli, *The Contemplation of the World. Figures of Community Style* (Minneapolis: University of Minnesota Press, 1996), p. 97.

70 Yoruba language does acknowledge the relationship between style and religion as *religio*. Thus the semantic spectrum of the Yoruba word for religion (*isin*) ranges from worship, service to that of *bondage*.

religious aura of the grove, the latter is using the works to boost its own political hegemony by substituting religion through remembrance.

Heroes in the Museum: Soviet Hero Constructions and Multiple Meanings of Modernity on the Soviet Periphery

Olaf Guenther

Introduction

Norbert Elias has stated that social movements and all historical processes are a result of certain figurations to which several dozens of individuals actively contribute. Such movements are so multifaceted and complex that they cannot be the outcome of any single person's endeavours. History and historical change are, therefore, the results of a complex web of actors. Instead of falling into the trap of »man makes history«, according to Elias, it is only possible to describe these figurations as an attempt to understand historical processes.[1] By contrast, what I aim to demonstrate in this essay is how modernity is constructed out of moves and movements that are often individualistic and unspecific in their circumstance. This essay will focus upon two personalities who, during the Sovietisation period in Central Asia, stood at the center of public opinion in a little town famous for being the former capital of the mighty khanate of Kokand (1760 – 1876). By presenting the life stories of two of Kokand's citizens and examining the posthumous creation of their heroic personalities, I will show how various people inscribed their ideas of modernity upon them. The people who constructed these modern heroes were members of various Soviet institutions, including the museum, local newspaper and party or Komsomol.[2] Their common task was to translate and transmit political ideas into the public sphere by way of exhibitions and festivities. Analysing their reflections on modernity, I will reveal the complexity of constructions of heroes and of modernity, which were anything but straightforward even in a top-down regime like the Soviet Union.

Modernity or modern thought came to Islamic Central Asia by way of colonisation, just as it did in most other Islamic (or non-European) countries. Following Russian colonisation of the entire area to the north of the Amu Darya region and the consolidation of its colonial rule there in 1863, a modern discourse fos-

---
1 Norbert Elias & Eric Dunning, *Sport und Spannung im Prozeß der Zivilisation* (Frankfurt/M.: Suhrkamp, 2003), pp. 341 – 343.
2 The Komsomol was the youth organisation of the Communist Party in USSR.

tered by a group of reformers called the Jadids slowly came into being in Islamic Central Asia. These reformers argued that the impact of modern technology and of modern political communication through the institutions of the colonial system called for a renewal of their own strategies of adaptation and for a new religious and philosophical understanding of nature, society and the individual. For them, the reinvention of school curricula and the adaptation to a modern lifestyle were the main needs of their time.[3] In their propagation of modernism, religion and education were regarded as their first priorities.

With the Soviet revolution and accompanying civil war, the Soviets came to power in what was then Turkistan, being the region which presently includes Uzbekistan, Tajikistan and Kyrgyzstan. Modernisation accompanied the Sovietisation of the entire region.[4] Sovietisation itself was a long-term process, one that began in 1917 and was almost completed by the time of Stalin's death and the emergence of the Khrushchev thaw in 1956. By the middle of the twentieth century, most parts of the Soviet Union had undergone Soviet-style modernisation. As part of the takeover of power, the Soviets also maintained hegemony over the writing of national history. Eric Hobsbawm once argued that the most important impact of socialist politics lay in its achievement of making libraries and museums accessible to all.[5] Bypassing industrialisation, improvements in transportation and other forms of modernity, the goal of Soviet modernisation in terms of cultural politics had already been achieved during the 1930s and 1940s when Soviet schools, museums and libraries were established in all parts of the Soviet Union. Highlighting another dimension of modernisation, Benedict Anderson argued that censuses, maps and museums were part of the establishment of colonial hegemony everywhere in the world, while at the same time they were tools for creating a sense of community.[6] Both are true for the Soviet Union, because Sovietisation was a project in which questions of hegemony were clearly combined with secular education, creating memory and resulting in the making of a socialist community. Museums were an important tool for achieving these aims. Through the Soviet enlightenment project, museums created a new space for imagining history, identity and community. This political program was initially strongly influenced by the Kraevedenie campaign. During this campaign, local teachers, academics from several history faculties and journalists

---

3 Regarding social politics and early modernism in Islamic Central Asia see Adeeb Khalid, *The Politics of Muslim Cultural Reform. Jadidism in Central Asia* (Berkeley, Los Angeles, London: Univ. of California Press, 1998).
4 Alexei Yurchak, *Everything Was Forever, Until It Was No More: The Last Soviet Generation* (Princeton, NY [et.al.]: Princeton University Press, 2006), pp. 10 – 18.
5 Eric J. Hobsbawm, *The Age of Empire, 1875–1914* (New York: Vintage, 1989), p.7.
6 Benedict Anderson, *Imagined Communities* (London, New York: Verso, 1999), pp.163 – 186.

highlighted the importance of local history, thereby establishing numerous museums and restoring noteworthy edifices and sites.[7]

In contrast to western publications, which view the Jadid Islamic reformist movement as the first modernisation movement,[8] Soviet history describes the history of modernisation as beginning with the October Revolution in 1917. From Russian urban centres, it expanded to peripheral regions some months later, albeit at first hindered by the civil war in the years following 1918. Eventually, modernisation became consolidated and stabilised through Soviet institutions, including the Communist Party, communist youth organisations, various trade unions, deputies congresses, and so on. The Soviet history of modernisation is a history of the institutionalisation of state power.

Investigators of the modernisation processes in the Soviet Union observe contradictions (namely, double talk or double standards) [9] within several spheres of Soviet society. Even though many contributions to the making of Soviet society were based on a common motive, that is, modernisation, the making of modernity had various outcomes, which were not in contradiction, but rather existed alongside each other. I would like to illustrate this by referring to one important modern institution that was established in Soviet Central Asia in the 1920s: the museum as a site for the creation of heroes. Unlike in the west, where the museum has often been a site for the display of various items of culture, social history and art compiled by way of various private collectors, regional museums in Soviet Central Asia were mostly aimed at educating the visitor. In the Marxist sense, the display of history is understood as a linear process from Stone Age to communism, depicting evolution in stages from feudalism to capitalism and so on. Alongside such Soviet displays, one invariably encounters sections with local items, such as animal species from the region, stones found in mines, items of everyday life or knowledge about various crafts, thus connecting Soviet with local history.

In this essay, I would like to illustrate certain attempts to make modernity visible through the construction of heroes during Soviet times. Whenever I mention Soviet or official history, I am referring to the stories printed in official newspapers or books. These written historical accounts where sanctioned by a collective of censors in the form of editorial staff. In her investigation of Soviet literature, Katerina Clark has argued that most of this literature was constructed

---

7   During the Kraevedenie campaign cultural politicians called upon the local intelligentsia to explore local history; see Ingeborg Baldauf, *'Kraevedenie' and Uzbek National Consciousness* (Bloomington: Indiana Univ. Press, 1992) (Papers on Inner Asia, 20: Central Asia).
8   See for example Hélène Carrère d'Encausse, *Réforme et Révolution chez les Musulmans de l'Empire Russe* (Paris: Colin, 1966).
9   See Anna Shternshis, *Soviet and Kosher. Soviet Popular Culture in the Soviet Union, 1923–1939* (Bloomington, Ind. [et.al.]: Indiana University Press, 2006).

and compiled according to an officially accepted codex of rules in which specific items had to be discussed and various formulas had to be transferred into the production of the text.[10] My discussion of this local history is supported by documents that I collected in museums in the Ferghana Valley between 2005 and 2007. These documents were originally collected by academic staff in the museum, who created several files (*papki*) about certain persons and wrote their biographies on the basis of personal interviews and scientific research. Some of these documents were brought to the museum by the people themselves, mostly honoured citizens who wished to leave their personal memorabilia in the regional museums.[11] In the following, I will present two cases of the construction of heroes in the regional museum of Kokand during the Soviet era.

Becoming a Founder of the Local Komsomol

On 1 November 1978, a crowd assembled in the main square in Kokand, a district city in the Ferghana Valley of Uzbekistan. They were waiting for the unveiling of a monument, a statue which was dedicated to Abdulla Nabiev, a local citizen of the city and a young communist, who died in November 1925 during an attack by counter-revolutionary forces. But what had made him so famous that people chose him as a symbolic representation of the city's revolutionary past?

During the beginnings of the Soviet Empire, Abdulla Nabiev was a very young parvenu from a lower middle-class family in Kokand. His father and mother died when he was still a child, so responsibility for his education and socialisation fell to his uncle who sent Abdulla Nabiev to a reformist school. At that time, reformist schools attempted to combine traditional Muslim education with modern curricula, although they still insisted on education in an Islamic manner, especially because they were still under the eyes of suspicious *ulema*.[12] In Abdulla Nabiev's class, there were children of middle-class craftsmen who founded an organisation for social support in 1920. They called it the »Komsomol Cell«. The exact meaning of Komsomol was most likely unclear to them

---

10 Katerina Clark, *The Soviet Novel. History as Ritual* (Chicago: University of Chicago Press, 1985).
11 The material used was stored in the Kokand city Regional Museum which is mainly devoted to displaying local history. Kokand, as a former capital of the khanate of Kokand, has since 1925 had its museum located in the former palace of the last Khan of Kokand and thus has nearly a century of well-documented local history.
12 *Ulema* means literally »the wise believers« referring to orthodox religious specialists such as mullas, teachers, leaders of mosques, madrasas and holy places.

all, because at the time it was a new term for a reformist understanding of social support and did not match that of a youth organisation of the Communist Party (Bolshevik) in the strict sense. Due to their education in the reformist movement, the founders of Komsomol Cell were enthusiastic about modern ideas, which included ideas about social activities. It is possible that Abdulla Nabiev sympathised with the idea of social support because he himself had become an orphan in 1916. After the foundation of the Komsomol Cell in Kokand, and following several years of work within local institutions, Abdulla Nabiev made his way up to the regional level due to his membership in several communist youth organisation cells. At that time, it was common Soviet practice to move cadres away from home and place them outside of their native districts. On foreign ground, people were less embedded in local power relations and could thus implement reforms much more strictly than they would have been able to on their own home soil. For this reason, Abdulla Nabiev was sent to different districts. In one of them, Surchandaryo, he was killed in 1925 when he was only 21 years old.

By the time of his death, Abdulla had never founded a school, had never written an article, nor did he leave any visible traces of his life behind. He was a young boy closely connected to one particular political organisation who died too young at the hands of the enemies of the Soviet system. Abdulla Nabiev was the ideal template, the *tabula rasa,* upon which various local and non-local actors could inscribe their own visions of a heroic nature. Like his numerous comrades who also worked in the Komsomol Cell in Kokand, nothing that he did was outstanding or in any way heroic. He merely attended a school where an organisation for social support had been founded in 1920. In reformist circles, such foundations had been a common practice and a widely accepted concept for many years. Throughout the country since 1910, reformists or so-called Jadids had founded charitable trusts to help local people and to educate them.[13] After 1918, the very same idea was appropriated by the Communists and such organisations became Komsomol. It was a time when the Communist Party, the Red Cross and other institutions served as instruments for elite interests in order to gain more power on the ground. Though Abdulla Nabiev was enlisted together with many other combatants in this first Komsomol organisation, he was later made out to have been the very first. In their understanding of history the Soviets needed founders. Because of their agenda to establish a new society, everything in their version of history was accordingly new. Not only were they

---

13 For details regarding *Turon* in Tashkent, refer for example: Begali Qosimov, »Oq tonglarni orzulagan shoir«, in: *Tanlangan asarlar,* ed. by Abdulla Avloniy (Taschkent: Manaviyat, 1998), pp. 10 – 11.

the first who created Soviet culture, they were also the ones who created its founders.[14]

Already in the initial hours following his shooting by anti-Soviet rebels, Nabiev's burial ceremony served as an occasion and a space used by fellow communists, combatants and close friends to make a hero of him. The burial ceremony was eternalised by a series of photographs. These pictures show some interesting details. First of all his body was on display to the public which is extremely unusual in the local Muslim burial tradition. Normally, a dead body is wrapped in cotton material (*kafan*) and as soon as possible – often on the same day – it is brought to the cemetery and buried by family members. Contrary to this tradition, fellow communists exhibited Nabiev's body in public. The wooden casket was decorated with the Russian slogan: »In eternal remembrance of the young Komsomol com. Nabiev«. The photographs show comrades displaying a flag by which the organisers of the burial ceremony identified the communist party at large and the local party cell as the sponsors of the ceremony. Surrounded by his comrades, Abdulla was buried in the wooden casket while some people held a red banner onto which photographs of him had been attached. The photographs present the burial as an event which incorporated the dead Abdulla into a scene fully dominated by party slogans and the symbols of the revolutionaries. In this way, the photographs construct a new space in which the burial ceremony is perpetuated with each viewing of the images. The underlying message in the images can be read in several ways, but must surely include the idea that Nabiev was deeply involved in the communist fight against the rebels. Furthermore, he was the communist with whom his friends shared his last moments on earth. If we take into consideration that, during the 1920s, most of the peoples in Central Asia were unable to speak any Russian, this could have meant several things: the message on textile was either addressed to Russians and a Sovietised Russian-speaking elite of locals, or it was a symbol of Soviet hegemony over Central Asia and its citizens. In this way, the burial ceremony 'Sovietised' Abdulla Nabiev as a hero.[15]

By using photography as a form of memory recording, the death of Abdulla Nabiev could be incorporated into Soviet history making and also into the rituals through which a community could solidify its communist identity. Public celebration of the anniversaries related to revolution and state building were also suited for this. Opportunities to commemorate individuals in Islamic Central Asia prior to the revolution could only be found in private occasions, such as memorial days for deceased family members (*hatm-e qur'on*, *yil*) and during

---

14 For example, Hamza as the founder of the Uzbek Drama. See: Mamadjan Raxmanov, *Xamza i uzbeksij teatr* (Tashkent, 1960).
15 Kokand Regional Museum Archive: Shk2,P.3,No.1b, (21–23).

meetings of institutionalised circles of close friendship (*gap*).[16] These circles where exclusively limited to family members, close relatives and friends. People participated by invitation only. After the revolution, such traditional rituals of commemoration were paralleled by new observances and rituals in the public sphere. One such public site was the museum, which provided an extraordinary space for public relations and celebrations of the new Soviet system. However, the photographs by themselves did not enable the life story of Abdulla Nabiev to be memorialised. Photographs were merely an instrument for the imagining and solidifying of identity.[17] And in the peripheral regions of Uzbekistan during the 1920s, photographs were still uncommon in everyday life. Thus, photography was a way of demonstrating the potential power of a modern communist community. Abdulla Nabiev's burial was one element in this demonstration of power, one offering the community a common communist identity.

With the help of the series of photographs the corpse of Abdulla Nabiev was integrated into the new community rituals. However, a story still had to be added to memorialise his life. Some years later, a suitable event for this purpose seems to have taken place. This was revealed in the first story that I discovered about Abdulla Nabiev. In 1958, the academic staff at the Regional Museum of Kokand prepared one of the first exhibitions to portray the life, work and the circumstances of the death of Abdulla Nabiev.[18] Photographs of his birthplace and of the room where the Komsomol Cell had been founded were taken and then displayed. Photographs of Abdulla Nabiev's funeral ceremony were also reproduced and added. One detail of the 1958 exhibition material is striking. In one of the photographs a prominent tree can be seen in the courtyard of his birthplace. We learn from the caption that this is thought to be the tree where Abdulla Nabiev was hiding when enemies of the Soviets attacked the city. Subsequently, this tree became associated with Abdulla Nabiev as a sacred symbol. In local hagiographies, trees are a common feature associated with saints. Trees are believed to connect people to a holy sphere to which they send their prayers, and such prayers are then memorialised or symbolised by a small piece of cloth. In order to construct an illustrative picture of a hero at the museum in 1958,

---

16 Arnaud Ruffier, *To'y, gap, ziyofat et bayram, espaces de construction des identiés et des solidarités en Ouzbékista.* (Unpublished Manuscript of a Ph.D.-thesis at the EHESS Paris, 2003).
17 For detailed discussion on images see Eleanor M. Hight & Gary Sampson, Gary (eds.), *Colonialist Photography. Imag(in)ing Race and Place* (London: Routledge, 2002). For the soviet context, see Margarita Tupitsyn, *The Soviet photograph, 1924–1937* (New Haven, Conn.: Yale University Press, 1996) and Margaret Dikovitskaya, »Central Asia in Early Photographs. Russian Colonial Attitudes and Visual Culture«, in: *Empire, Islam and Politics in Central Eurasia*, ed. by Tomohiko Uyama (Sapporo: Slavic Research Center, 2007), pp. 99–121.
18 The documents concerning this exhibition were the first documents that were filed under the name of Abdulla Nabiev. The museum's academic staff were not able to confirm if this had really been the first exhibition.

people assigned local hagiographic motifs to Abdulla Nabiev's life in order to show his extraordinariness.[19]

Ten years later, in 1968, a memorial day was organised by the Komsomol of the Surchandarya district where Abdulla Nabiev had died. Komsomols brought flowers to the memorial stone which had been erected by the local communist party in 1925, shortly after the shooting of Abdulla Nabiev. During the memorial meeting, the members of the Komsomol remembered his life along the following lines: In 1920, after they had received news about the Komsomol Cell in Kokand, counter-revolutionaries sent an ultimatum, demanding that the Komsomol should be abolished. Not surprisingly, most of the Komsomol Cell founders went into hiding for a while. Nabiev, however, remained in the open and connected his own Komsomol Cell to the Komsomol of the old city, of which he had become the leader. Because of this act of unification, people were saved.[20] During Abdulla Nabiev's leadership of the Komsomol Cell, musical and drama circles were organised and orphanages were founded throughout the town. Alphabetisation movements all over the city helped to eradicate illiteracy, and Nabiev took part in these as well. Furthermore, he collected money from the citizens to support the Red Army in their fight against the counter-revolutionaries. He then went to fight the enemies of the Soviet empire in various campaigns in the Ferghana Valley. Finally, after being sent to a district in the south of Uzbekistan, he lost his life while visiting Komsomol branches in local villages.[21]

Thus, Abdulla Nabiev's life story became associated with the whole spectrum of modernist ideas of the period: social support, cultural politics and alphabetisation. His biography can be read as the idealised representation of a Sovietised modern hero of his time. At the end of the memorial meeting, people enjoyed a motocross race which was conducted by some two dozen drivers of the region in honour of Abdulla Nabiev.[22] The motocross race was clearly a modern version of *Buzkashi*, a traditional game on horseback resembling polo, and one that is always organised at big festivals.[23]

Another decade later, in 1978, Abdulla Nabiev's image was cast as a huge – 5.8 meters high – bronze statue which was erected in the city centre. For the inauguration of this new memorial, a document was issued in which Abdulla Nabiev was now declared to be the one who had founded the Komsomol in

---

19 Kokand Regional Museum Archive: Shk2, P.3, No.1b.
20 Though it is more likely, that some powerful men in the old city gave shelter to the cell, so that they would not be attacked by counter-revolutionaries.
21 Kokand Regional Museum Archive: Shk2,P.3,No.1b, pp. 8–12.
22 Kokand Regional Museum Archive: Shk2,P.3,No.1b, pp. 28–32.
23 For further reading see G. Whitney Azoy, *Buzkashi; Game and power in Afghanistan* (Philadelphia: University of Pennsylvania Press, 1982).

Kokand. Yet, a statue almost six meters high obviously required additional justification for its placement at the very heart of the urban space. Therefore, he was also credited as being the founder of a school in the old city, a school that was built much later but that stood in the same place as the original school which he had attended from 1917 to 1920.[24]

Thus, step-by-step, on various occasions, different social actors from the museum, Komsomol organisation and city administration inscribed their own ideas about heroism and modernity upon the life of young Abdulla Nabiev. Furthermore, it was impossible for his biography to be contaminated by the turmoil of the Stalinist terror in the late 1930s. He could not be unmasked as a nationalist since, along with most other »founders« and heroes of the Soviet empire, he had already died during his youth.

The local Muqimi

In 1939, when Germany declared war on Poland and attacked Czechoslovakia, the Soviet Union commenced its propaganda in favour of war. For numerous nationalities in the Soviet Union, this meant a return to a national heritage, which had long been denied during the anti-nationalist campaigns in the 1930s. It also meant the rehabilitation of numerous poets of the nineteenth century, in whose work the communists saw some traces of progressive ideas. Among them was Muqimi, who had already been reviewed for potential eligibility as a national poet in 1938, when the capital of Uzbekistan honoured the thirty-fifth anniversary of his death.

An activist group in Kokand, which consisted of some teachers, staff from the Regional Museum of Kokand and local poets, nominated a former *madrasa* — or Islamic high school — called the *Madrasa-i Xazrat Miyon*, as the birthplace of Muqimi. In fact, his actual birthplace was situated some 100 metres down the road, but the house in question on this site was already owned by someone else. Consequently, local inhabitants of Kokand built a new house right next to the *Madrasa-i Xazrat Miyon*, just as if this had been the home of its gatekeeper. Although the new birthplace was completely imaginary, it served its purpose well, as we will see below. Charkhiy, a renowned poet at the time who was unfit to serve in the army, became the director of this new museum. It was he who prepared the first exhibition on Muqimi's life.

The official biography of Muqimi as a historical person consisted of the following elements: Muhammad Amin Hojja alias Muqimi was born in Kokand

---
24 Rafiq Otajonov »Shon Sharaf Haykali«, in: *Mehnat Bayroghi* (1.10.1978), p. 1.

in 1851. He became a local poet who studied and taught in a renowned Islamic high school, the *Madrasa-i Myon Hazrat*. His name Muqimi was derived from Arabic and meant »the settled [one]«. During the period of war propaganda from 1939 to 1945, this meaning was often emphasised. It was said that Muqimi had chosen this name for himself (*tahalus*) because he appreciated his roots in the Ferghana Valley, that is, in his »home country«. He was also praised because his poetry was adapted by ordinary people who used it in popular street songs. Muqimi travelled around in his home region and wrote several travel accounts in which empathic verses were combined with satirical vignettes of the people living in the Ferghana Valley. Muqimi was against the colonisation of his homeland by the Russian Empire, and he wrote some harsh and satirical poems concerning the Russian takeover. Contrary to the common interpretation of his songs as a mystical approach to God, it was held that most of his poetry consisted of love songs, which during the 1930s were interpreted as coming from a man who loved his people.[25]

During the early years of the Stalinist Period (1927 – 1937), a person like Muqimi would not have stood the slightest chance of any recognition. From the mid-1930s until World War II, anti-nationalist purges were undertaken throughout the Soviet Union. Everyone who had been connected or associated with national poets who had been active in the 1920s and 1930s was suspected of being an enemy of the Soviets. But Muqimi had already died long before the revolution, so he could not be regarded as someone suspected of working against the Soviet regime. In fact, the anti-Russian sentiments attributed to him at the end of the 1930s were framed instead as having been anti-feudal, anti-bourgeois and anti-colonialist in character. Thus, Muqimi was converted into an anti-feudal, progressive intellectual.

Soon after the recognition of Muqimi in 1938, the local elite of Kokand took all possible measures to advance this figure. The director of the Regional Museum of Kokand, who had himself been educated in the *Madrasa-i Hazrat Miyon*, found both the money and the necessary political will within the city administration to build the new birthplace house-cum-museum (referred to above) next to the *Madrasa-i Hazrat Miyon*. It was declared as the »House of Muqimi« as if the poet himself had been the gatekeeper of the high school. The director also found an acceptable person to lead the museum. Charkhiy had been a renowned poet prior to the revolution, and had also been educated at the *Madrasa-i Hazrat Miyon*. Right after 1919, he devoted his poetry to communist ideas and became a famous local poet in the 1920s and 1930s, and was thus officially fit for the job of leading the new museum. In 1941, Charkhiy staged an exhibition on Muqimi's life, which presented his life quite different from the official textbook

---

25 L. Klimovich, *Lirika i satira Mukimi* (Moskva: Gos. Izd. Xudozh. Lit., 1957), pp. 3 – 14.

version. Muqimi was supposed to have come from a poor background, and he was presented as a man of the Ferghana Valley who had devoted his life to knowledge. His imaginary birthplace was decorated with exhibits which typified the life of a mainstream intellectual of that time. A desk for reading holy books served as a symbol of his intellectual capacity, but could also be interpreted by the local population as a symbol of his faith and devotion to Islam. A *doira*, a musical instrument, showed his affiliation with the arts, a common icon of progressive men since musical education and service were unusual in a *madrasa*. The »birthplace of Muqimi« thus served in an exemplary way to depict everyday life before the revolution. The progressive aspects of Muqimi's life, as well as emphasis on his humble roots, was symbolised in the *doira*. Further progressive ideas were demonstrated by the display of his oeuvre in the form of books. In fact, the exhibition fell well short of being able to show why Muqimi was supposed to be so modern. He was commemorated only as a local historical person, lacking elements demonstrating the official emphasis on his progressiveness, i.e. modernity.

In any case, the whole Muqimi birthplace project was not intended to foster official modernity. Rather, it was a move to preserve the *madrasa*, since it had a greater importance as an educational centre for the local elite of teachers, poets and museum staff. That it only succeeded in preserving half of the actual *madrasa* premises (the other half of the building was already being used as a factory) indicates much about the urgency of the museum project in the eyes of these local agents. Most of the premises would have fallen into the hands of the factory staff not versed in, or ignorant of, the symbolic importance of the *madrasa*. By recasting it as the poet's birthplace, the remembrance of the oeuvre of Muqimi gave people a chance to conserve the *Madrasa-i Xazrat Miyon*. The newly created anti-feudal hero thus served to give shelter to an important, local Islamic intellectual tradition.

Nowadays, the *madrasa* also exhibits the life-stories of other personalities such as Zavqi, a renowned poet and reformist from the early 20th century who was shot dead by the Bolsheviks in 1921. Zavqi had been accused of being an enemy of the Soviets and an anti-communist politician during Kokand's short experiment with autonomy.[26] In the political climate of the 1940s, it was impossible to inform the public about such personalities. In summary, a few men managed to restore the place where many local intellectuals had been educated and where they can now be remembered by the public. The figure of Muqimi served as a *pars pro toto*, giving local people the possibility to create their own meaning by making a local hero.

---

26 Kokand' autonomy lasted from the winter of 1817 to 22 February when it was brutally terminated by the Bolshevists. See P. Alekseenkov, *Kokandskaja Avtonomija* (Taschkent: Uzgiz, 1931).

Hero Constructions and their Varieties: Layers of Meaning

This chapter concerns both Soviet and local constructions of modernity, but here we can only refer to a very small piece in the historical mosaic. Even if the »museumizing« and institutionalising of the commemoration of heroes was a part of Soviet modernity, the constructions of individual heroes are also replete with other meanings. If we read the official versions, as printed in history textbooks, the stories of heroes are heavily modernist because these hero constructions speak about individuals who were progressive and extraordinary when compared with their social milieu; their ideas were the ideas of the future. The outstanding subtext of modern hero constructions is of lone fighters in a »backward world«. By contrast, some of the hero constructions provided by local elites in the Kokand museum were much more traditional.

Constructions of heroes incorporate various meanings. Such conceptions of a heroic nature are primarily a mirror of the modern thoughts of their local academic or ideological architects. Thus, the hero himself serves as a container or a bricolage into which fit whatever meanings seem appropriate. The hero can simultaneously bear contradicting conceptions, those that not only emerge through differing local or regional contexts, but which also emerge through different individual understandings and *raisons d'être*.

If we consider Abdulla Nabiev, the contemporary hero construction is a result of more than four decades of ongoing production. The historical Abdulla himself contributed only a very small part to what was eventually made of him. Immediately following his death, his body and the burial ceremony already served as a space for demonstrating power, unity and strength. During the decades that followed this space continued to play an important role. The place where he was shot was marked by a memorial stone that made it possible to commemorate Abdulla and at the same time could serve as space for celebrating Soviet modernity.

From a modern perspective, Muqimi is constructed as a man with a nationalist love of his home country, a notion clearly unknown during Muqimi's lifetime, when nationalism in Central Asia was yet to be born.[27] At the time of the Socialist Internationale, strong local attachment did not stand the slightest chance of recognition. However, during the Second World II war period this aspect actually became a feature of progressiveness and modernity. If we only interpret Muqimi at the level of his official biography, we will miss out on seeing the local interpretation of his life. Modern official narratives appear to virtually overlay and mask local ones, which are not about progressiveness but rather rep-

---

27 Ingeborg Baldauf, »Jadidism in Central Asia within Reformism and Modernism in the Muslim World«, in: *Die Welt des Islams*, New Ser., 41 (2001), 1, pp. 72–88.

resent Muqimi as a man of his time. This demonstrates the strong embedding of ideas in their specific contexts, which can change from decade to decade or from region to region, but which are all still modern. From Muqimi, we can learn another lesson. Obviously, all these meanings can coexist at one time without contradicting or even interfering with each other.

Of modernity, Ibrahim Kaya states: »There is no single agreed idea of modernity, but there is a space which provides opportunities to interpret ›imaginary significations of modernity‹ in multiple ways.«[28] Through the making of the hero, a space for modernity is constructed, one in which interpretation in new and multiple ways and for various reasons becomes possible.

In both the Nabiev and Muqimi cases, heroic historical figures have been constructed bearing very similar characteristics. The ›museumised‹ Soviet hero is a product of the dialogue between state power and the individual who serves it. The various layers of local or regional meaning are re-constructed according to the needs of the period in which actors operate, and not according to the demands of the time in which the hero lived. The architects of modernity had to fulfil its requirements, but they did so by employing their own circumstances. The motocross race dedicated to Abdulla Nabiev is just one very evocative example of the variety of translational processes that operate while remembering and memorializing historical personalities. The actors in these translational processes need to choose the right features for exhibition. In the example of the creation of Muqimi's birthplace, they had to understand how they could use a hero's background to preserve local sites of commemoration, which in their view were extraordinarily important. Heroes, thus, are not only the symbols, but the founding representations, of an imagined modernity, one which has to be constructed and is not a given or a ›static‹ historical fact.

In the case of Abdulla Nabiev, a process of multilayered embellishment occurred in which more and more characteristics were ascribed to quite an ordinary man, thereby transforming him into one of the avant-garde of his time. This was a translational process, which can be traced back over several decades during the Soviet era.[29] The features of Nabiev's progressiveness in terms of Soviet ideals were a continually updated vision, inscribed step-by-step into an image of a hero. Modernity, thus, reinvents itself over a long period of time. As temporal distance extends between the historical personality and its current hero construction, the hero is pushed more and more into the foreground, while the local embeddedness of the person is gradually lost.

In the case of the construction of Muqimi's birthplace, we can see how an

---

28 Ibrahim Kaya, »Modernity, openness, interpretation: a perspective on multiple modernities«, in: *Social Science. Information sur les sciences sociale* 43 (2004), 1, pp. 36 – 57.
29 For a similar case of constructing history see Douglas Northrop, *The Veiled Empire. Politics of women's liberation in Central Asia* (Ithaca, NY [et.al.]: Cornell Univ. Press, 2006).

officially depicted hero can serve as a representation for a whole group of local intellectuals who were attached to, and grew up in, the *Madrasa-i Hazrat Miyon*. Whereas Abdulla Nabiev had to be filled with a sense of modernity, the local Muqimi construction was less interested in his person. His life was expounded without much evidence that he had ever been a hero of modernity. But the site itself was a symbol for a generation of reformist teachers and politicians who utilised it to find their place in the academic world of the Soviet Union. With the ›museumising‹ of the *madrasa* as ›Muqimi's birthplace‹, we can also observe how ordinary people took part in the construction of modern meanings. Thus, the demand for heroes was not only coming from elites and implemented in a top down manner, but it also came from within a society oriented towards the outside world. Initiative came from locals, who directed their demands for preservation and memorializing towards the governing powers, in order to find a niche for an identity – and a modernity – of their own.

In her investigation of literature in the Soviet Union, Katarina Clark interpreted Soviet history production as a ritual in which certain elements, such as a background of poverty for the active fighter against Soviet enemies, always had to be performed.[30] The layers of meaning within official interpretations of history were indeed constructed according to several ritual necessities. Modern Soviet men had to come from poor backgrounds if they were born before the revolution. Modern men were founders of Komsomols, of collective farms, of the regional branches of the Communist Party, of polyclinics or schools, of theatres and operas, and they were involved in the writing of drama and prose. Modern men were socially engaged. Modern men were anti-colonial, anti-capitalist and patriotic. Yet an alternative narrative can always be found as well, one in which men were more embedded in local values or in the modes of local history production. In the case of Muqimi's birthplace, we can even find a kind of virtual hero who was used by the locals to save the symbolic meaning of a locality and who was represented in both a local and an official way. The official version provided the guidelines serving as a handbook detailing the rituals to which attention had to be paid. But in the material contents of the rituals of commemoration we also discover the second and even unrecorded third voices of the recipients who, construct their own modern heroes and who contribute several different layers of meaning to their personalities. Muqimi's story is one that fits the argument made by Katherina Clark, yet it also demonstrates a new perspective. It was necessary to know the official guidelines, the rules that constructed the historical ritual of commemoration, or rather to know the grammar of the system, and use

---

30 Katerina Clark, *The Soviet novel. History as ritual* (Chicago [et.al.]: University of Chicago Press, 1985). A more recent but similar publication on the same topic is: Yurchak, *Everything was forever, until it was no more*, op. cit. (note 4).

it for one's own purposes. Thus, the Soviet system was also a space for modern representations that could be used by various actors to achieve different aims.

The representation of the modern socialist hero thus provides a space for polyphonic reflection on modernity. It becomes a product of a dialogue between official institutions, individuals and also spectators who learn about the modern heroes in the museum. They themselves reinterpret the hero due to their personal understandings, preferences and convictions. The wooden desk at the Muqimi exhibition, upon which holy books where placed to be read, could be interpreted in three ways: as a symbol of an intellectual; as a piece of pre-revolutionary local culture; and as a symbol of faith and devotion, clearly reactionary in Soviet times. It is the viewer of the wooden exhibit who interpret its meaning.

List of Figures

1. Wissmann meets chief Lukengo on his first travel through Africa. Hermann von Wissmann, *Unter deutscher Flagge quer durch Afrika von West nach Ost : von 1880 bis 1883 : Ausgeführt von Paul Pogge und Hermann von Wissmann* (Berlin: Walther & Apolant, 1890).. 54

2. The members of the Kassai expedition of 1883 photographed before their travel to Africa. Hermann von Wissmann, *Im Innern Afrikas. Die Erforschung des Kassai während der Jahre 1883, 1884 und 1885* (Leipzig: Brockhaus, 1888) 59

3. A drawing of the members of the Kassai expedition together with Tschingenge and a certain Sagula. Hermann von Wissmann, *Im Innern Afrikas. Die Erforschung des Kassai während der Jahre 1883, 1884 und 1885* (Leipzig: Brockhaus, 1888) . 60

4. »To control population growth is to increase the quality of the population.« (Tib. *Mi 'bor 'phel tshad tshod 'dzin dang/ Mi 'bor spus ka je legs su gtong dgos.* Chin. *Kongzhi renkou zengzhang tigao renkou suzhi*). Government slogan on road signs in Tongren, Tibetan Autonomous Prefecture of Huangnan. Photo: M. Schrempf, 2005 123

5. A modern Tibetan two-child family on their way to a village festival. Photo: M. Schrempf, 2005 150

6. Palace sculptures associated with local deities in Osogbo. The turban is a visual reference to the local dominance of Islam. Photo: Peter Probst, 2003. 161

7. Cement sculpture by Susanne Wenger and Adebisi Akanji in the Osun grove representing Obaluaye, late 1970s. Photo: Peter Probst 2002. 162

8. Afolabi Kayode, Osun In Colours, 2006. 169

9   Group of four cement figures by Adebisi Akanji in the Osun
    grove alleged to represent the founders of Osogbo.
    Photo: Peter Probst 2002. 173

10 Part of the Ohuntoto Ogboni Shrine Complex, built by Wenger,
    Gbadamosi, Saka and Akangbe in the mid 1970s.
    Photo: Peter Probst 2002 174

Notes on the Contributors

Vincanne Adams is a professor in the Department of Anthropology, History and Social Medicine, where she is director of the Program in Medical Anthropology, at the University of California, San Francisco. Her publications are based on research in the Nepal Himalayas and the Tibetan Autonomous Region exploring Tibetan experiences of medicine, modernization and social change with an emphasis on women and religious sensibilities.

Olaf Guenther has studied Islamic Central Asia, South Asia and History at Humboldt University Berlin. His doctoral research concerned acrobats in the Ferghana Valley. He is interested in cultural sciences and social history of the Silk Route region (19th – 20th centuries) and is presently writing a book on Turkestan in the Soviet Era.

Vincent J.H. Houben is professor of Southeast Asian History and Society at Humboldt University, Berlin. He studied history and Southeast Asian languages at Leiden University, the Netherlands. He has written extensively on various aspects of Indonesian and Southeast Asian history, politics and culture.

Verónica Oelsner is research fellow at the collaborative research centre »Changing Representations of Social Orders« and doctoral student based at the Centre of Comparative Education at Humboldt-University Berlin. Her research focuses on the historical and semantic foundations of the configuration of vocational education and training in modern Argentina.

Michael Pesek studied performance theory and African studies as well as sociology. His doctoral thesis concerned the establishment of German colonial rule in Eastern Africa. Currently he is a research fellow at the collaborative research centre »Changing Representations of Social Orders« at Humboldt University, Berlin.

Peter Probst is associate professor of African art and visual culture at the Art History Department at Tufts University, USA. His current research interests include heritage and the globalisation of memory, the aesthetics of place, and the history of African art.

Mona Schrempf is an anthropologist and research fellow at the Central Asian Seminar, Institute for Asian and African Studies at Humboldt University Berlin. Her research involves cultural revival and social change among Tibetans in exile and in China, with a more recent focus on Tibetan medicine and public health issues, family planning and modernity.

Eugenia Roldán Vera is research fellow at the collaborative research centre »Changing Representations of Social Order« and at the Centre of Comparative Education at Humboldt University, Berlin. She specialises in the comparative history of education (19th and 20th century) and in processes of knowledge transfer with a focus on Latin America.

History

Steffi Richter (Hg.)
**Contested Views
of a Common Past**
Revisions of History
in Contemporary East Asia

2008, 422 Seiten
ISBN 978-3-593-38548-8

Sylvia Paletschek, Sylvia Schraut (Hg.)
The Gender of Memory
Cultures of Remembrance in Nineteenth- and Twentieth-
Century Europe
2008, 287 Seiten, ISBN 978-3-593-38549-5

Martina Heßler, Clemens Zimmermann (Hg.)
Creative Urban Milieus
Historical Perspectives on Culture, Economy, and the City
2008, 435 Seiten, ISBN 978-3-593-38547-1

Waltraud Maierhofer, Gertrud M. Rösch, Caroline Bland (Hg.)
Women Against Napoleon
Historical and Fictional Responses to his Rise and Legacy
2007, 304 Seiten, ISBN 978-3-593-38414-6

Mehr Informationen unter
www.campus.de

campus
Frankfurt · New York

Social Science

Felix Kolb
Protest and Opportunities
The Political Outcomes of Social Movements
2007, 341 p., ISBN 978-3-593-38413-9

Karolina Karr
Democracy and Lobbying in the European Union
2007, 209 p., ISBN 978-3-593-38412-2

Stefani Scherer, Reinhard Pollak,
Gunnar Otte, Markus Gangl (Hg.)
From Origin to Destination
Trends and Mechanisms in Social Stratification
Research
2007, 323 p., ISBN 978-3-593-38411-5

Johannes Harnischfeger
Democratization and Islamic Law
The Sharia Conflict in Nigeria
2008, 283 p., ISBN 978-3-593-38256-2

Helmut Willke
Smart Governance
Governing the Global Knowledge Society
2007, 206 p., ISBN 978-3-593-38253-1

Michael Dauderstädt, Arne Schildberg (Hg.)
Dead Ends of Transition
Rentier Economies and Protectorates
2006, 249 p., ISBN 978-3-593-38154-1

Mehr Informationen unter
www.campus.de

campus
Frankfurt · New York